A THEORY OF HEDGE INVESTMENT

How to protect your wealth against natural disaster is the central theme of *A Theory of Hedge Investment*. The investor must acknowledge the albeit small chance of catastrophe occurring, whether in the form of world war, hyperinflation in the USA, world food shortage, energy shutdown, vanishing of investment opportunity, slump, international banking crisis or major earthquake. In a defensive strategy the investor builds a hedge portfolio consisting of assets that would yield especially high income if a catastrophe were to occur.

Those assets which possess defensive properties – 'bad news goods' – have in common certain characteristics and their price behaviour is distinctive. In this book Brendan Brown derives propositions about hedge assets relating to their price behaviour and the proportion which they should represent in the investor's total portfolio.

The appetite for particular hedge assets varies between different types of investor. The rentier who is utterly dependent on income from capital is particularly anxious to safeguard his wealth against both a fall in the rate of profit and social revolution. The small saver, caught in a liquidity trap, where his home and human capital are his principal assets, has more limited – yet important – scope for hedge investment. The investor in a country which issues a hedge money (e.g., Switzerland or Britain) will see investment opportunities differently from the investor in a country which is very exposed to natural risks.

Real estate, gold, Swiss francs, oil equities and collectables are some of the hedge assets examined, and the 'practice of hedge investment' is described. The reader will discover many new insights in the critical analysis of the roles of real-estate investment, and its appropriate valuation relative to other assets. Rare books, oriental carpets, stamps and works of art are cited as examples of a general proposition about the hedge function of collectables.

Failure to index the taxation of savings has aggravated the investor's anxiety about inflation. In the final part of his book Dr Brown shows how the full-scale indexation of taxation, by reducing the present distortion of relative asset values caused by penal tax rates on real income from money and bonds, would encourage economic growth and break the oligopolistic power of investment institutions.

Brendan Brown is a currency consultant and economist. He is a graduate of Trinity College, Cambridge, and of the University of Chicago, and was awarded a PhD by the University of London. He has had wide experience of using and developing investment analysis, first with the Bank of England and then with the American Express Bank, Phillips and Drew and London Business School. The author of many articles in academic and financial journals, his previous books are listed below.

Also by Brendan Brown

MONEY, HARD AND SOFT
THE DOLLAR–MARK AXIS

A THEORY OF HEDGE INVESTMENT

Brendan Brown

First published 1982 by
THE MACMILLAN PRESS LTD
London and Basingstoke
Companies and representatives throughout the world

ISBN 0 333 31992 3

Printed in Great Britain by
Pitman Press Ltd, Bath

To Irene Brown

Contents

*These sections may be omitted by the general reader – see p. xiv.

List of Tables and Figures

Tables

Figures

List of Abbreviations

CD	Certificate of deposit
Comecon	Council for Mutual Economic Aid
CPI	Consumer price index
DM	Deutsche mark
EEC	European Economic Community
EMS	European Monetary System
FRN	Floating-rate note
GNP	Gross national product
LDC	Less-developed country
MLR	Minimum Lending Rate
OECD	Organisation for Economic Co-operation and Development
OPEC	Organisation of Petroleum Exporting Countries
PSBR	Public Sector Borrowing Requirement
SDR	Special drawing rights

Preface

Fortunately, the probability of major disasters occurring is small. Man does not walk in continuous dread of world war, a cut-off of energy supplies, and of hyperinflation in the USA. Indeed, if he did, we would describe society as gripped by mass hysteria. Yet nobody can ignore the albeit small risk of disasters without diminishing his potential for human freedom. Yes, most individuals are pawns, whose welfare can be influenced seriously by events which they are powerless to control. But by providing himself with reserves on which he can draw in times of catastrophe, the individual can reduce the risk of his enslavement. The subject of *A Theory of Hedge Investment* is intimately connected with the individual's search for insurance against global disasters. A central question is how the individual can maximise his use of what little scope he has to prevent his life's direction being thwarted by economic or social events beyond his control.

The quest for reserves against disaster should be distinguished from compulsive gambling on the long chance of disaster occurring with the hope of making huge gains. The person who takes a considerable long position in gold and a short position in other assets stands to make a great gain in the unlikely event of disaster happening. Like Dostoyevsky's gambler who stakes all his wealth on the unlikely numbers at the roulette table, the speculator on gloom stakes all on the low chance of a catastrophe. Far from having relieved his anxiety about catastrophe, the speculator on gloom has heightened his concern about the changing risks of its occurrence, in which he has a macabre interest. The hedge investor, unlike the gambler described, tries to reduce the welfare-loss which he would suffer in the event of a disaster, rather than to turn it into a gain at the expense of misery in other possible scenarios.

In *A Theory of Hedge Investment*, the question of how the individual should balance his portfolio between investments which pay off especially highly at times of general prosperity – *good news goods* – and investments which pay off especially highly at times of disaster – *bad news goods* – is discussed in Chapter 1. Various types of bad states of the world, against which hedges are commonly sought, are distinguished in detail. These include war, hyperinflation, revolution, vanishing of investment opportunity, food shortage, energy catastrophe, confiscatory taxation, space shortage, slump, banking crisis, and earthquake. Principles of hedge investment are developed in Chapter 2. This chapter particularly describes how hedge investments (also termed bad news goods) are priced. The very small probability of the disasters occurring, contingent on which hedge investments would produce large income, is shown to make them highly volatile in price.

In Chapter 3, specific hedge strategies for the rentier are discussed. Even though Keynes's prediction that the rentier would suffer euthanasia as the rate of profit diminished has proved false to date, the rentier should be keen to include in his portfolio those few assets that would gain in value from a redistribution of income from capital to labour. In Chapter 4 the problems of hedge investment for the small saver are considered. The small saver is shown to have an especially great need for hedge investments. For him, the breaking of a link between the major currencies and gold has been a special blow, since no longer is gold – the most powerful of hedge assets – of low price-risk in normal times. Yet the construction of a diversified portfolio of hedge investments, towards constraining price risk, is particularly expensive for the small saver.

In Part II, the subject is hedge investment in practice. In reality we cannot go out into the market place and buy, amid the plethora of security packages on offer, distinct assets which provide pure insurance against identifiable macro-disasters. There is no asset, for example, which pays a large return in a state of world war and nowhere else. The investor, when constructing his hedge portfolio, selects assets whose income he expects (but cannot know with certainty) to be relatively high in one of the disaster scenarios considered explicitly.

These impure hedge assets, which have expected, but uncertain, defensive power, can take various forms, including real estate, some types of equities, bonds, certain currencies, gold and collectables. Each of these forms is analysed chapter by chapter in Part II. Issues raised include the suitability of different types of property as inflation-hedges; the role of oil, armament, and bank shares; fixed-rate bonds as a hedge against slump; Swiss francs as a hedge against

US inflation; British pounds as a hedge against energy crisis; the suitability of different types of collectable as hedge assets.

One potential disaster which has preoccupied investors increasingly is a further marked acceleration of inflation in any of the countries issuing a major reserve money – especially in the USA. Ever-growing fears of inflation have contributed to the notable popularity of inflation-hedges. The potential losses inflicted on the investor by high inflation have been aggravated by tax regimes remaining essentially non-indexed.

In Part III, the combination of fiscal privileges for institutional savers, non-indexed taxation of personal savings, and heightened inflation risk, is shown to have a harmful influence on the pattern of productive investment. The book concludes with a description of the benefits of an indexed regime and a look at a possible method of application.

Inevitably, in writing about a theory of hedge investment, I have had to make use of a theoretical framework. I have drawn on the literature in which the 'state-preference' theory is developed (see Notes and References following Chapter 2). However, the reader who is most interested in the applications of the theory developed in the book can simply omit the two sections starred in the contents list – in Chapters 2 and 4 respectively. The ideas developed in each of these are summarised for the general reader in the preceding sections.

Essential to the completion of the volume was the help, both in provoking ideas and preparing the manuscript, of my mother, Irene Brown.

B.B.

Part I

The Theory of Hedge Investment

1 Defensive Investment

A fundamental motive for saving is self-defence against nature. Just as Man builds shelter against the elements, he saves to provide himself with means of survival during periods of economic hardship caused, for example, by famine, sickness or war. The accumulation of personal capital makes life less nasty, less brutish, and hopefully less short. In more advanced societies, another motive for saving increases in importance – to raise one's living standards. By sacrificing present consumption and investing in so-called 'growth assets', the saver hopes to 'become rich'.

In this book, the primary purpose is to analyse saving motivated by the first concern of self-defence. A theory of rational behaviour under uncertainty is described, and is applied to the study of a class of assets – hedge investments – which feature largely in defensive strategies. In Part 2, the properties of certain popular hedge investments – real estate, defensive equities, petro-monies, fixed-rate bonds, gold and collectables – are examined critically. In Part 3, the wider issue of reforming social institutions to reduce the hazards of saving is explored. In particular, could inflation risk be reduced by official sponsorship of indexation?

Choice under Conditions of Uncertainty

Extending the method of Arrow[1] and Hirshleifer,[2] reality may be described as a vector $x=(x_1, x_2, \ldots, x_n)$ where the components x_i are state-variables, which vary between a bad extreme (set equal to zero) and a good extreme (set equal to one). Examples of state-variables are belligerency, world economic activity and US inflation. Taking the state-variable belligerency, x_j, this varies between full-scale war ($x_j = 0$) and universal peace ($x_j = 1$). Any particular value of a state-variable is described as a 'state of the world', which is given by nature – the individual has no control over the probability of its occurrence.

Each individual assigns a subjective probability distribution to each state-variable, and the distributions are likely to be interdependent (for example, a low value for the state-variable of belligerency is likely to be accompanied by a high rate of US inflation). From the individual state-variable distributions, probability distributions may be derived for each possible reality.

The individual is uncertain about which combination of states of the world will hold at each date in the future: but beyond that, all is certain. He is assumed to have complete knowledge of his income and the returns available from all securities in each combination.[3] Securities may be constructed in two elementary forms. An *elementary state-prospect* offers income at a given interval of time contingent on the current value of one state-variable only (for example, a security promising $1 in state of war, $0 in state of peace, and 50¢ in cold war, irrespective of what other states war is combined with, whether boom or slump, famine or plenty, etc.). An *elementary combination-prospect* offers specified income, at a given interval of time, contingent on one possible reality $(x_1, x_2, \ldots, x_n)$.[4]

A *multi-period* elementary state-prospect is a combination of elementary state-prospects for different dates of the same state-variable. A *multi-period* elementary combination-prospect is a combination of elementary combination-prospects for different dates but otherwise identical. *Complex* prospects are combinations of elementary prospects.[5] Most securities found in practice are complex multi-period combination-prospects, offering specified income contingent on each possible reality in every future interval.

Incomes contingent on each possible reality (i.e. combination of states of the world) in turn are assumed to be the ultimate object of economic choice concerning the future. The individual is concerned with his level of income in each possible future reality. This so-called state-preference framework for decision-making, used throughout this book, should be distinguished from the 'two-parameter' model popularised for security analysis in the late 1970s.[6] In this model, the mean and standard deviation of the probability distributions of income that are obtained from holding alternative portfolios of securities are regarded as the underlying objects of choice.

In the two-parameter model, the individual regards all securities as lotteries: their incomes are like successive chips from a roulette wheel. He does not map the future into well-defined states and check painstakingly that he has attained, via market exchange or direct investment, an optimum distribution of income contingent on each possible reality. The two-parameter model is too primal for distinguishing a hazard from a lottery;[7] a hazard promises a definite contingent income for each possible reality, whereas a lottery is a mere gamble, whose outcome is not dependent on which state of the world occurs. Someone who buys a season ticket to a casino to play roulette, staking the same amount of money each night, will face the same probability distribution of returns regardless of which state of the world occurs.

The defender of the two-parameter model may question the idealisation of the state-preference theory – that the individual knows with certainty the income and lotteries to which he will be entitled, in each possible combination of states of the world. He would argue that at best the individual can ascribe statistical parameters to this distribution of income in the future, but he cannot begin to map out different states of the world with their contingent incomes. However, the criticism flounders on the realisation that investors do search for hedges, or insurance, against certain bad states of the world occurring – war, hyperinflation, energy crisis, and many others. It would be unsatisfactory to analyse defensive saving, using a model of analysis which failed to acknowledge the individual's concern with his welfare in fairly well-defined future scenarios.

Bad and Good States of the World – the Concept

States of the world may be divided into good and bad categories from both a general and a particular viewpoint. A bad general state of the world x_0 (one value of state-variable x) is one for which income contingent on its occurrence sells for more than its actuarial value. More precisely, if an elementary x-prospect which yielded \$1 whenever state of the world x_0 occurred but zero elsewhere, where state x_0 had probability p_x of occurrence, sold at more than p_x dollars, then state x_0 would be labelled a bad general state. A good general state X (one value of state-variable x) is one for which contingent income sells for less than its actuarial value. A good particular state for an individual is one where given his present endowment he would enjoy relatively plentiful contingent income; a bad particular state – for example, ill-health – is one for which contingent income would be relatively scarce.

Note that the definition of general states as good and bad presupposes a market in elementary state-prospects which promise income contingent on only one value (or small range of values) of state-variable x. This is, of course, an idealisation; in practice, incomplete markets may be identified. For example, an investor who sells a 10-year US Treasury Bond in exchange for a share in IBM is implicitly selling income contingent on state of the world 'slump' in exchange for income in state of the world 'boom'. That expected real yields on the Treasury Bond are lower than on the IBM share would suggest that income contingent on state of the world slump is relatively expensive – evidence that slump is a bad general state of the world.

As in any market, prices in the state-prospect (state-contingent income) market are determined by the interplay of supply and demand, given the constraints of initial endowments, tastes, and existing technology of production. The tastes of those with large marketable wealth are more important than the tastes of those with small marketable wealth in the determination of prices.

Thus, if Marx were correct, and war were good for the capitalist class, we would find that income contingent on the state of war would be priced relatively cheaply – traditional war-hedges, such as gold, would have a high expected yield. Although Marxists may contend equally that war is bad for the labouring class, which would lose more than the capitalist class would gain therefrom, labour has less influence than capitalists in the securities markets where state-contingent income is priced implicitly. Equally, labour-capitalists – labourers who possess a large quantity of embodied human capital through education or in the form of innate ability – have only small influence on the price of state-contingent incomes. Human capital is not negotiable, and its returns contingent on the state of peace cannot be exchanged, in the market-place, for returns contingent on the state of war.

Hence the definitions of bad and good general states do not in any way imply that a good state is one which the majority of the population concerned would consider good. Further, for some market participants, a good general state will represent a bad particular state. For example, an oil producer would consider the good general state of energy plenty as a bad particular state for himself.

Although empirical identification of bad states of the world requires a comparison of prices of state-contingent incomes (either directly or indirectly) with their respective actuarial values, *a priori* considerations suggest certain states which may fall into the category 'bad'. These are outlined below.

Energy Crisis

In an energy crisis, caused most likely by a reduction of supplies from a major producing area, the price of oil and oil-substitutes shoots upwards, oil revenues of OPEC surge, whilst the real disposable income of the oil-consumer countries is reduced. At 1980 prices, a further doubling of the oil price would, on impact, cause oil-importing countries in the OECD to pay a further 4–5 per cent of their national products to OPEC.

An energy crisis is clearly a bad particular state for energy-importing countries, and a good particular state for energy-exporting countries, but is it a bad general state? Four considerations suggest that indeed income contingent on the state of the world 'energy crisis' will be valued highly or equivalently; will be scarce in the supposed market for state-contingent claims.

First, OPEC is unlikely to be a willing seller of large quantities of income contingent on the state of 'energy crisis'. Its principal method of selling such income would be to issue bonds indexed to the price of oil. But buyers of such bonds would require a large political risk premium – given the shakiness of many of the political regimes in OPEC. Large political risk premiums would, in turn, deter borrowing by OPEC.

Second, although energy crisis brings in its wake high revenues for oil-exporting countries, many wealthy private investors (including royal families) who reside there may suffer large losses. Energy crisis is likely to be ignited by political and social revolution in a major OPEC country: many a wealthy investor in OPEC can associate, with the general state of energy crisis, particular states where his wealth would be reduced and he may become an exile. Given the very unequal distribution of income across the possible realities in which energy crisis features, the wealthy OPEC investor should be keen to buy certain income contingent on energy crisis, and so he contributes to its scarcity.

Third, real output in oil-consuming countries in the OECD is likely to fall in the aftermath of an oil crisis. An increased oil-tax levy by OPEC deflates aggregate demand in the OECD, which is replaced only in the longer term by increased OPEC spending and by stimulatory effects from falling real interest rates. In the longer term, income is likely to remain depressed below the path it would have followed without the oil cut-back, because labour and capital must be substituted in part for energy in the production process. In both the short and the long run, an oil crisis followed by a lower level of oil production leads to an income loss in the world economy, not simply a transfer from oil-importing to oil-exporting countries.

OPEC investors themselves have a large vested interest in the welfare of oil-consuming economies, from which the bulk of their investment income is derived. The greater is the value of their present portfolio, and the more shaky are their ownership rights to future oil revenues, the less attractive to them is the prospect of an energy crisis, albeit with its promise of enlarged revenues thereafter. OPEC countries ruled by a royal family of uncertain future tenure and with vast accumulated wealth are unlikely to view the state of energy crisis with enthusiasm.

Fourth, an oil-tax levy is likely to leave the distribution of income between labour and capital in oil-importing economies unchanged or alter it in labour's favour. In a neoclassical model, labour is paid at a rate equal to its marginal product. An oil price rise, on impact, depresses the value of the marginal product in terms of oil, and so in real terms; profit falls by the same proportion in real terms and the distribution of income is unchanged. In the longer term, if capital were a closer substitute than labour for energy, energy-saving demands may cause a scarcity of capital and a transitory rise in profit; but in the long run in the neoclassical model, the income-shares of labour and capital are fixed.[8] In other models, where labour is assumed to have the power to resist real wage cuts, the share of profit falls following an energy crisis. Thus the capitalists in oil-importing countries are anxious to buy income contingent on the state of energy crisis – and their tastes are most important in the determination of prices in the contingent-income market.

War and Reparations

According to the Marxists, capitalist society has a tendency to develop an increasing propensity to wage war.[9] Capitalist enterprise in building up profit by 'exploiting' the labouring class becomes faced with lack of demand for its products. Hence capitalists, as a class, have an interest in the conquest of foreign markets, or foreign sources of raw materials.

It is doubtless possible to find examples of wars that have brought benefits to the capitalist class in certain countries. Kindleberger quotes the Boer War and the Belgian conquest of the Congo as wars that were waged directly in the interest of capitalist enterprise.[10] Such wars were, however, limited and colonial in nature. Generalised war, as we know it in the twentieth century, imposes huge net costs in terms of loss of disposable income and destruction of capital. Both labour and capital must pay heavy taxes towards a war effort, and suffer physical restrictions (in particular, rationing) on their expenditure.

War brings in its aftermath the payment of reparations by the vanquished to the victor. Modern examples of reparation payments include France to Germany after the Franco-Prussian War of 1870-71, Germany to the Allied Powers after World War I, and Finland to the USSR after World War II.[11] Both labour and capitalists in a country which enters a state of conventional war run the risk of facing heavy tax obligations thereafter to meet reparations – should their nation be defeated.

The burden of reparations is generally greater than apparent on impact. Thus, suppose the victor dictates that the vanquished pay reparations at the rate of $\$x$ million per year for 10 years, where x is indexed to the dollar price of internationally traded manufactures. The vanquished must switch resources into industries producing internationally traded goods from those producing non-traded goods; similarly, consumer demand must be deflected in part from traded to non-traded goods. Both switches are essential to the generation of a trade surplus out of which reparations are paid. The switches are induced by the relative price of non-traded in terms of traded goods falling; reparation obligations expressed in terms of a given volume of traded goods rise as a proportion of national income as the relative price shifts. The increased proportion reflects the burden of reallocating domestic resources at the margin from where they satisfy most efficiently domestic tastes (given individuals' budget constraints) in the reparations-free society to where they satisfy most efficiently both the victor's demand for reparations – in effect, demand for traded goods – and domestic consumer demand, shrunk to fit a post-reparations budget constraint.[12]

In addition to the burden of reparations, the defeated power has territory and assets sequestered by the victor. Owners of tangible property in the defeated country can realise large losses in the state of the world 'defeat'. For example, after the Franco-Prussian War,[13] the Alsatian Railways (owned by a joint-stock corporation) were transferred to Prussia without compensation. After World War I, some great properties owned by Prussian Junkers were broken up by the partition of Upper Silesia between Germany and the new Polish state.

The treaty of Versailles required the liquidation of all property belonging to Germany in Alsace-Lorraine; further, iron, steel, and coal works held by German firms in the Saar and Luxembourg had to be sold to French buyers.[14] The forced nature of these sales resulted in knock-down prices being obtained. After World War II, the USSR annexed from Finland, without compensation, Karelia – the richest province of pre-war Finland.

Sometimes the government in the defeated country will compensate its citizens directly affected, and the losses will be distributed widely according to some principle of equity. After World War I, the German Government paid large sums to businesses, forced to liquidate their establishments in Lorraine, towards reconstructing their plant in Germany.[15] After World War II, Finns were compensated by their government for loss of property in Karelia.[16]

A particular war may, of course, bring benefits to certain groups, even in the defeated country. Industries producing armaments, iron and steel, and chemicals could make a large war profit.[17] In the victorious country, spoils are divided unevenly. For example residents of Alsace-Lorraine, re-united to France in 1918, were entitled to sell stipulated amounts of mark balances to the French Government at a fixed rate of exchange. The actual exchange was to be effected in 1922. Windfall profits were made from immediate disposal of marks for francs in 1918 and their re-purchase at a tiny fraction of the price in 1922 for delivery to the French Government.[18]

However, the heavy running costs of war, and the risk of confiscation and reparations obligation if unsuccessful, must surely make the income contingent on the state of war – equivalently, assets which produce relatively high income in times of war – expensive. Indeed it is with reason that war is supposed to be a bad general state.

Hyperinflation

All states of the world with high inflation are not bad general states. We must subdivide inflation into different types – hyperinflation, ordinary inflation of monetary source, and inflation of non-monetary source.

Hyperinflation – defined somewhat arbitrarily as when inflation exceeds 50 per cent per month[19] – can be expected to be associated with breakdown of social and political institutions and with falling aggregate real incomes. Bresciani-Turroni[20] gives details of how average living standards surged in the months following the stabilisation of the mark at the end of 1923.

Yet great fortunes are likely to be made at times of hyperinflation. Those with foresight, and liquid wealth (not in domestic money), can obtain real assets at bargain prices from less fortunate investors often trapped in illiquidity crises. Speculative opportunities abound as relative prices of goods or assets to each other depart far from traditional norms. Financial frauds flourish. In the immediate aftermath of the German hyperinflation, luxury expenditures fell sharply[21] – an indication of a return to a more equal income distribution.

Although fortunes can be made in hyperinflation, it is likely that income contingent on the state of hyperinflation would be highly priced in the hypothetical exchange market for state-contingent incomes. Aggregate real income of both labour and capital can be assumed to be low in the state of hyperinflation. Further, for each individual, the distribution of income, between the many particular states which may be combined with the general state of hyperinflation, is very unequal: there is a wide range of possible real values for his labour services and non-labour assets. Riskiness of income, together with its shortage, makes the marginal utility of certain income, contingent on the state of hyperinflation, particularly high.[22]

Inflation – of Non-monetary Source

A rise in the price level is of non-monetary source if it would be sustained without any monetary expansion: equivalently, any occurrence which reduces the amount of real money balances per capita held in equilibrium is a non-monetary source of inflation. For example, if the productivity of labour and capital falls, the output of an economy falls; with the fall in real incomes is associated a fall in the demand for real money balances. Hence, for a given stock of money, a fall in productivity leads to a rise in the price level. The state of the world in which productivity falls is, of course, a bad general state.

Other examples of non-monetary sources of inflation include an adverse movement in the terms of trade, food shortage, housing shortage, rising charges for public services and income redistribution towards profits from wages. All these states of the world, with the exception of the last-mentioned, where inflation of non-monetary sources occurs, may be described as bad general states, as is demonstrated below. They should be identified separately rather than under the general heading of inflation.

An adverse terms-of-trade change describes the rise of a country's import prices in terms of its export prices. The change reduces the real incomes of both labour and capital, and so describes a bad general state. Labour's marginal product falls in terms of a shopping basket including imported goods, and so the real value of wages falls. Profits in domestic enterprise fall also in real terms – the share of labour and capital remaining unchanged in a neoclassical model. Aggregate demand for real money balances is reduced by the fall in real incomes, and so the adverse change in the terms of trade represents both a non-monetary source of inflation and a bad general state.

A temporary food shortage or famine is a special instance of falling productivity: output from the soil falls for the same aggregate supply of labour and capital. In general, the aggregate real income of labour falls, albeit with a lucky few employed on still fertile farms making transitory gains; real profits fall also in commercial and industrial enterprise as the relative price of agricultural output in terms of other commodities rises. Owners of agricultural land which remains fertile make huge rental income from current output.

To some extent, agricultural capitalists are willing to sell income contingent on the state of temporary shortage or famine. However, there is some chance that famine may represent a bad particular state for any farmer – his land may be in the centre of the famine area, becoming completely unproductive, and so making no gain but a loss from the rise in food prices. This uncertainty as to which particular states will be found in combination under the general heading of 'state of food shortage' restricts severely the supply of famine-contingent income in the market for state-claims. Such income would thus be highly priced – evidence of famine being a bad general state.

A state of Malthus-type food shortage – due to population growth outstripping that of agricultural output – has less unpredictable consequences than has temporary famine for the agricultural capitalists. In the Malthusian world they are sure to enjoy relatively high incomes, whilst those of labour and industrial capitalists would be depressed – in aggregate by more than the agriculturalists' gains. Agricultural capitalists should be more willing to sell Malthus-type than famine-contingent income in the market for state-claims.

Indeed, it is possible that Malthus-contingent income may be relatively cheap if the bulk of labour does not have the means to buy contingent income, and so effective demand comes from only the few rich. On *a priori* grounds, famine, but not Malthus-type food shortage, is necessarily a bad general state. Both types of food shortage represent a non-monetary source of inflation; for both are associated with a fall in aggregate real income and hence in demand for real money balances.

In the state of the world labelled 'housing shortage', house rents are very high due to pressure of demand on limited land space. Although the construction of high-rise buildings can alleviate land shortage, the marginal cost of adding each additional floor becomes successively larger. Where land space becomes very scarce, in aggregate the population must adjust to a smaller living space per person – which represents a decline in real living standards. Hence demand for real money balances falls, demonstrating land-space shortage as a non-monetary source of inflation.

The state of the world 'land-space shortage' is likely to be in combination with 'rapid population growth' or 'rapid productivity growth'. In the first combination of states, aggregate real income of labour is well depressed although large landowners enjoy high real income. Large landowners would be sellers of 'rapid population growth-cum-land shortage' contingent income. Such income need not necessarily be highly priced, for neither the new (yet to be born) population nor labour without capital endowment is a source of effective demand in today's market for state-claims. *A priori*, this first combination including land shortage may be generally bad or good.

In the second combination of states – 'rapid productivity growth-cum-land shortage' aggregate real income of labour and capital is relatively high, albeit depressed by high house-rents. Income contingent on this combined state should not, therefore, be highly priced – and the state combination should not be described as generally bad.

A rise in prices charged for public services and goods can be either a spurious or a non-monetary source of inflation. As an example of a spurious source, suppose a government reduced direct taxation and subsidies to public industries by equal amounts, so that prices of public goods rose. Aggregate real income would be unaffected: instead of some public goods being paid for by taxes they would be charged for directly. The purchasing power of money in terms of both private and public goods would be substantially unchanged. The apparent rise in the consumer price index would be a misleading indicator of changes in the purchasing power of the money, due to its exclusion of public goods bought against tax payments.

Suppose, instead, that the government raises the charges for public goods and uses the proceeds to reduce its borrowing requirement. Assuming that tax payers do not fully discount future tax liabilities arising, for example, out of servicing the public debt, their perceived real incomes and so their demand for real money balances would be reduced by the change. Thus, for a given money stock, the purchasing power of money would be reduced. Increases in direct taxation or indirect taxation can similarly be non-monetary sources of depreciation in the purchasing power of money.

Income contingent on the state of the world 'reduction in government deficit-cum-increase in public sector charges and in taxation' should be relatively highly priced – given the reduced real incomes of both labour and capital in that state. The state of the world described is a bad general state.

A rise in the share of profit in GNP is both a non-monetary source of inflation and a good general state. For a transfer of income from wage-earners to capitalists reduces the aggregate demand for real money balances, on the normal assumption that low income-earners have a higher propensity than high income-earners to invest marginal income in money.[23] A rise in the profit share may, in the short-run, be due to factors such as devaluation of the national currency or a wages policy. Yet income contingent on states of the world, where national income is redistributed in favour or profits, will sell cheaply in the state-claims market; those with high purchasing power in the market – the wealthy – would be sellers, not buyers, of such income.

Inflation – of Monetary Source

Inflation of monetary source is that which can be attributed to growth of money supply per capita; equivalently it is the rate of inflation that would occur if the equilibrium demand for real money balances per capita remained unchanged. Many different rates of monetary inflation are of course possible, and for simplicity of exposition, they are grouped into three possible states of the world – hyperinflation (already discussed), high monetary inflation (where the rate of inflation can vary between 5 and 20 per cent, the actual rate being the outcome of a lottery), and low monetary inflation (where inflation can vary between 0 and 5 per cent, the actual rate again being the outcome of a lottery).

Aggregate real income of capital is lower in the state of high monetary inflation than in the state of low monetary inflation. First, investors in aggregate are net holders of assets denominated in nominal terms, corresponding to net outstanding government debt.[24] If the state of high inflation occurred, securities with their nominal interest rate fixed now (in an assumed state of low inflation) or in previous periods of low inflation would show a very low or negative real income.

Second, in the transition to the state of high inflation, the services of money deteriorate in value. Real returns on nominal assets and liabilities become highly uncertain.[25] Long-term contracting in nominal terms becomes hazardous (for example, in lease or assurance contracts) and clauses for revision of value are expensive in terms of transaction costs. Tax-rates, expressed in nominal terms, become highly uncertain in real terms. The medium of exchange – sight deposits and currency – is taxed at a high and unpredictable rate.[26]

The large reductions that occur in the real value of outside wealth, in the form of government bonds, could bring benefit to the labour income-earner, if tax revenues used to service the bonds were drawn disproportionately from labour. Even so, income contingent on the state of high inflation should sell at a premium in the state-prospect market, as those with large marketable wealth would, in aggregate, be badly off there.

The designation of states of the world as ones of high or low monetary inflation requires some care. Inflation is measured typically by the movement of a price index which is a combination of three types of prices – spot, forward and series. *Spot prices* are set in markets for immediate delivery of a commodity. For example, the spot price of sugar is what must be paid for a standard quantity to be delivered almost immediately. *Forward prices* are set in markets for delivering a commodity at a stated date in the future – typically several months ahead. For some commodities, the costs of determining spot and forward prices for each transaction would be very high. Instead, the supplier sets a price for his commodity for an interval of time; it is re-set only periodically. Such a price is defined here as a *'series price'*. Examples include rents on property, most wage agreements, and prices of many public services.

Both series and forward prices are influenced heavily by expectations of future movements of the price level. A landlord and tenant agreeing on a rent for the next year, or an employer and union agreeing on a wage-rate, form a view about the progression of spot prices and other series prices during that period. A general index of spot prices is less dependent than one of series prices on expectations of future prices (and hence, degree of monetary inflation in future intervals) and is more influenced by monetary conditions in the present. Series prices are pulled not only by expectations of the future but adjust also to mistaken expectations in the past. Thus, if a supplier under-anticipated monetary expansion during the last interval in re-fixing the price for the next interval, a catch-up would occur. The catch-up is not symptomatic of present monetary inflation but a correction of previous error.

High reported inflation due either to a catch-up of series prices following past under-estimation of spot-price inflation or to over-estimation of future spot-price inflation should not strictly be categorised as a state of high monetary inflation. Only if the rate of monetary expansion accelerates to validate inflation expectations, or to allow a catch-up of series prices without downward pressure being exerted on spot prices, would a state of high monetary inflation emerge.

Opaqueness of Future States of the World

It is assumed generally in the theory of finance that investors are risk-averse – that they must expect to earn a 'risk premium' on high-risk compared to low-risk assets. From the assumption of risk-aversion it follows that investors prefer, *ceteris paribus*, a limpid state of the world – where the future states of the world have objectively known probabilities attached and where there is little doubt as to which state will occur in each future time period – to an opaque state of the world – where probabilities attached to each future state of the world are objectively unknown (they can be estimated only subjectively) and where there is a wide range of states of the world with a significant chance of occurrence in each future time interval.

The distinction made between limpid and opaque states is, in effect, two-dimensional. First, are the probabilities attached to future states of the world discernible objectively or only subjectively (these are two extreme alternatives)? This distinction corresponds to that made by F. H. Knight between risk and uncertainty respectively.[27] Second, what is the shape of the probability distribution for future states of the world? The less wide is the distribution or the less skewed towards bad states, the lower is the degree of opaqueness.

Opaqueness about the future is a bad general state of the world. Growing opaqueness increases the riskiness of investment and so reduces the present certain income equivalent of total income contingent on future possible realities. Real incomes are influenced negatively by an increase in the degree of 'opaqueness concerning the future'.

Many contracts, which were entered into during periods of limpidity about the future, can, if still effective in a subsequent period of great opaqueness about the future, inflict large uncertainty on both parties. Costs of re-contracting, in a form suitable to the new state of opaqueness about the future, may be high: they may be described as the costs of financial instrument obsolescence. Transaction costs incurred each period are greater in states of opaqueness than of limpidity, because of the general shortening of the period of contracting.

Banking Crisis

A banking crisis is where a significant proportion of deposits become inconvertible into base money (central bank deposits or currency).[28] A crisis is set off normally by an event which calls into question the quality of the loan portfolios of a major sector of the banking industry. That sector then finds that deposits are withdrawn rapidly and that it is forced to re-finance its loan portfolio by borrowing from other banks, at a very high rate. Two factors restrict even this source of borrowing. First, at the rate charged on marginal funds, operations of the borrowing bank may become unprofitable. Second, banks normally eschew high-risk lending: the costs of policing necessarily strict covenants would be high and their loan portfolios would deteriorate in quality.[29]

Collapse of a major bank in the troubled sector would send shock waves throughout the banking system. Scared depositors would rush to exchange their bank deposits into default-free assets – US Treasury bonds, gold, and currency. Interest rates in the market for bank liabilities (deposits, certificates of deposit) would shoot upwards as banks competed hectically to obtain a greater share of the monetary base, given their increased demand for liquidity. Wherever possible, loan commitments would be cut back on, and the crisis of liquidity would spread throughout commerce. In extreme conditions, conversion of deposits into currency may be halted temporarily industry-wide or a bank holiday for several days may be imposed, both of which would impose illiquidity even on the small depositor.[30]

Hopefully the risks of a banking crisis have been reduced by the advent of central banks and their recognised function of being lenders of last resort. In this latter role the central bank would stand ready to discount assets of the healthy sector of the banking industry, and so accommodate the public's increased demand for base money: loans would not be extended to the banks whose rotten loan portfolio had been the source of the crisis. In practice, in modern times central banks have stepped into a further role of lifeboat for the troubled sector.

Today, banks which are involved heavily in offshore lending to the less developed countries or to Comecon are the most likely point of ignition for a banking crisis.[31] A major re-scheduling or a worsening of East–West relations would be the powder keg. Investors must acknowledge as non-trivial the probability of the state of the world 'international banking crisis' occurring.

For some, an international banking crisis would be a good state of the world. In the example of an LDC rescheduling or defaulting, many of its citizens would gain from an alleviation of taxes to service foreign debts outstanding to the international banks. However, it should be expected that income contingent on a banking crisis should be relatively expensive in the market for state-claims. For although the gains of the defaulter and losses of the creditor would cancel each other out, there would be many potential third-party victims of a banking crisis.

Major Earthquake

The hearts of both Japanese industry, and of the West-Coast economy of the USA, lie in dangerous earthquake zones. A major disaster would have a significant impact on the aggregate income level in the industrialised world. Not only would residents of the areas suffer loss; so also would investors worldwide who owned (directly or indirectly) assets in the affected area.

The risk of earthquake is insurable. Equity holders in insurance companies sell income contingent on the occurrence of major earthquake. But the large net-income shortfall in that state means that such state-claims sell at a relatively high price, confirming earthquake as a bad general state. Specifically, if it could be estimated that there was a 1 in 50 chance of an earthquake in Tokyo in the next year, the pure insurance premium (netting out administration expenses) would be considerably above $2 per $100 insured.

The state of major earthquake would very likely occur in combination with other bad general states. For example, demand for liquid assets would be likely to increase sharply as insurance companies' and others' need for immediate means of payment surged. Further, banks lent heavily against assets in the disrupted zone would become of high default-risk and face problems in re-financing their assets. Therefore the state of major earthquake disaster would be likely to be accompanied by the state of banking crisis.

Slump and Social Revolution

Neither labour nor capital income earners are likely to look forward to conditions of slump, where an economy's output falls far below its productive potential. Aggregate real incomes would be low. During slump, profits are typically a lower proportion of national income than during boom; aggregate real wages are less cyclical than profits.

Although the average real wage would fall by less than aggregate profits, the individual labourer is faced with particularly uncertain income prospects in a slump. In that state of the world his endowment takes the form of a gamble of, say, a 90 per cent chance of earning an average real wage 5 per cent lower than in a state of boom, and a 10 per cent chance of earning zero (if he became part of the army of unemployed). In a state of boom, in contrast, he may assume he has a 100 per cent chance of employment (other than for short periods). But for the capitalist the increased risk of income, during slump as against boom, should be less, because he can diversify his investment holdings. In summary, both labour and capital should be willing to pay high prices for income contingent on slump.

Changes in income can, of course, be due to political causes. A Socialist victory may entail tax reform aimed at (though not always resulting in) transferring fiscal burden from labour to capital. The state of the world in which tax is so changed would be one of comparative low income to those with large purchasing power in the state-prospect market, and so may be classified as a bad general state.

Political changes can result in mass exile from a country. A black revolution in South Africa, or a socialist revolution in Saudi Arabia, would result in an exodus of the wealthy class, who would be cut off from a main source of future income. If these particular groups have significant purchasing power in world markets, income contingent on the state of enforced exile from or expropriation of private fortunes in these countries would sell at a relatively dear price.[32]

Non-cyclical (Secular) Fall in Rate of Profit

States of the world in which the profit rate has a secular downward trend are poor compared to those where the rate of profit is set on a constant, or rising, trend – from the viewpoint of capitalists. Equivalently, general states of the world where the rate of profit is on a downward trend are bad. The Classical economists, and later the Marxian economists, believed that the rate of profit has an 'inherent tendency to fall'.[33] In the Classical system, the rate of profit was a residual determined by the difference between the amount of food produced on an acre of land at the margin of cultivation and the amount of labour employed there (labour was paid a fixed subsistence wage). As population grew, and the margin of cultivation was extended, the rate of profit would fall, given the assumption of falling marginal productivity of land.

In the Marxist system a falling rate of profit was due to excess accumulation. The tendency of variable capital to outpace the growth of the labour supply would bring upward pressure on real wages.[34] This would be resisted by investment in technological capital (that is, in labour-saving machinery). But the source of profit – exploitation gains from labour – would not expand with such investment: surplus value is earned only on variable capital, which tends to be a constant magnitude per labourer.[35] Thus excess accumulation leads to ever more investment in technological capital, a falling rate of profit, and the growth of monopoly capital (as only large enterprises can enjoy the economies of scale of technological capital).

The concern of both Marx and the Classical economists with the 'law of falling profits' was stimulated by observation that the rate of interest had fallen considerably from earlier centuries – although they did not consider how far the fall could be explained by reduced risk of lending rather than a changed rate of profitability. The second half of the nineteenth century, an age of unprecedented economic progress and wealth accumulation, belied their predictions.

Modern empirical study shows that the share of profit in national income has fallen significantly in the twentieth century. But the fall has not occurred continuously. It has been concentrated in three subperiods: during World War I, World War II, and the aftermath of the first OPEC oil crisis of 1973. Atkinson found that, in the USA, the wage and salary share in national income rose from 55 per cent in 1900–09 to 71 per cent in 1960–65, with no trend apparent in the period 1950–64.[36] According to Feinstein,[37] the share of wages and salaries in the UK's GDP rose from 45 per cent in 1860–69 to 66 per cent in 1950–59, with the main increases occurring during the two world wars. The OECD, in a 1978 study,[38] found that the share of wages in national income surged in the years 1973–76, rising by 5–8 percentage points in the West European economies: the share of labour declined subsequently but still leaving a net gain of around 2–3 points on average.[39]

The picture emerges of a rate of profit, or profit share in national income, that shows no secular trend for long periods of time, but over concentrated periods a secular shift downwards has occurred. In these latter periods, the state of the world may be described as 'a non-cyclical fall in the rate of profit'. Its occurrence is consistent with the view, often associated with the Marxist economists, that the rate of profit is not simply one component of a unique solution to a system of equations derived from the marginal analysis of neoclassical economics, but is dependent on the capitalist's power to exploit, or derive surplus value from, the product of labour. This power is limited by habit or social 'mores'.

During war-time, norms of acceptable rates of profit are shaken not least because of labour's use as human fodder in the war effort and the clamour of left-wing parties for greater social justice. Similarly, in the aftermath of an energy crisis, when oil-consuming economies are faced with an increased tax burden to oil producers, the rate of profit acceptable as normal by organised labour falls, as it is believed that capital should bear the lion's share of the new tax burden.

A non-cyclical fall in the rate of profit, like inflation of non-monetary source, should be regarded as a feature of several states of the world – in the main, bad general states – rather than itself a state-label. However, the investor in mapping out future possible realities should take careful note that he has identified those with the important feature of non-cyclical fall in the rate of profit and, for given prices, that he is holding an optimum number of contingent claims on each of them. One state of the world, in addition to those of war, energy crisis, and social revolution, deserving attention, is that of saving glut. In the state of the world 'saving glut', the rate of profit falls due to an increased degree of thrift (an increased propensity to save) or to diminishing opportunities for investment. This state of the world forms a large part of the subject-matter of Chapter 3.

Notes and References

1. See K.J. Arrow, 'The role of securities in the optimal allocation of risk bearing', *Review of Economics Studies*, vol. 31 (April 1964) pp. 91–6.
2. See J. Hirshleifer, 'Investment Decision Under Uncertainty: Choice Theoretic Approaches', *Quarterly Journal of Economics,* vol. 79 (November 1969) pp.509–36.
3. Excluded here are gambles, entered into deliberately, whose outcome is unrelated to any natural event or state of the world.
4. In each possible reality, each x must assume some value.
5. An elementary state-prospect is a special type of complex combination-prospect promising a certain income in each and every possible reality. Thus an elementary war-prospect yields certain income in war, with whatever other states it is combined, and elsewhere it yields zero.
6. See E.F. Fama, *Theory of Finance* (Holt, Rinehart & Winston, Inc., 1972).
7. See Hirshleifer, p. 217.
8. See H. Lydall, *A Theory of Income Distribution* (Clarendon Press, 1979), Chapter 4, for a summary of neoclassical distribution theory.
9. See P.M. Sweezy, *Theory of Capitalist Development; Principles of Marxian Political Economy* (Monthly Review Press, 1942).
10. See C. Kindleberger, *Power and Money* (Macmillan Student Editions, 1970) p. 75.
11. See F. Machlup, *International Monetary Economics* (Allen & Unwin, 1969), Chapter l5, for detailed statistics on the volume of reparations in each example.
12. In less-developed economies, elasticities of substitution both in production and consumption between traded and non-traded goods are especially low, and hence the effective burden of reparations is much more than on impact.
13. See 'Rapport fait au nom de la commission du budget de 1875 sur le payment de l'indemnité de guerre et sur les opérations de change qui ont été la consequence', reprinted in L. Say, *Les Finances de la France sous la Troisieme Republique*, Tome 1 (Paris, 1898).
14. See C. Bresciani-Turroni, *The Economics of Inflation* (Kelley, 1968) p. 205.
15. Bresciani-Turroni, *op. cit.*, p. 203.
16. See Lauri Levamaki, 'The Index Clause in Finnish Banking', *Monthly*

Bulletin of the Bank of Finland (Helsinki), March–April 1958.

17. See Bresciani-Turroni, *op. cit.*, for an account of the huge profits made in Germany of World War I under the so-called 'Hindenburg Programme'.
18. M. Wolfe, *The French Franc between the Wars 1919–1939* (Columbia Press, 1951).
19. This definition is found in P. Cagan, 'The monetary dynamics of hyperinflation', in M. Friedman (ed.) *Studies in the Quantity Theory of Money* (University of Chicago, 1973).
20. Bresciani-Turroni, *op. cit.*, p. 379.
21. Ibid., pp. 377–9.
22. In the market for contingent-income claims it is, of course, certain income for each general state of the world that is exchanged.
23. For the theoretical basis of this assumption, see K.J. Arrow, *Essays in the Theory of Risk-Bearing* (North Holland, 1974) pp.103–7.
24. Expressed in the terminology of monetary theory, investors hold outside wealth in nominal form, which is subject to inflation risk.
25. Even for a period of fairly low inflation in the USA, in the 1960s, Fama shows how the nominal yield on 1-month Treasury Bills explained only 30 per cent of the variance of the monthly inflation rate. See E.F. Fama, *Foundations of Finance* (Basic Books, 1976) pp. 169–203.
26. For discussion of the inflation tax on money, see for example M. Friedman, *The Optimum Quantity of Money* (Macmillan, 1969).
27. See F.H. Knight, *Risk Uncertainty and Profit* (University of Chicago, 1971).
28. Banking crisis and a smoothly working financial system are the opposite forms taken by the state of the world variable 'liquidity'.
29. For an anatomy of banking crisis, see pp. 160–4 of the present volume.
30. For details of US banking crises in the nineteenth century, when bank deposits became temporarily inconvertible into currency, see M. Friedman, *A Monetary History of the United States* (Princeton University Press, 1963) Chapter 4. In the same work, Chapter 7, details can be found of the extended bank holiday of 1933.
31. See C. P. Kindleberger, *Manias, Panics and Crashes* (Macmillan, 1978) Chapter 10.
32. In practice, the South African white, by buying gold (albeit illicitly) obtains some insurance against the state of exile; for revolution in South Africa would send the price of gold shooting upwards. This is analogous to the OPEC wealthy investor buying energy hedges, for example the petro-pound.
33. For a discussion, see J. Schumpeter, *History of Economics Analysis* (George Allen & Unwin, 1967) pp. 645–54.
34. Variable capital refers to the stock of consumer goods existing at any time – which is a wage fund, being consumed in advance of current production (viz. Schumpeter, *op. cit.*, pp. 632–3).
35. It is the inability of the labourer to finance his consumption in the period up to the eventual sale of the goods in whose production he is involved, that makes him a victim of capitalist exploitation.
36. See A.B. Atkinson, *The Economics of Inequality* (Oxford University Press, 1975).

37. C.H. Feinstein, 'Changes in the distribution of national income in the UK since 1860', in Marchal, J. and Ducros, B. (eds), *The Distribution of National Income* (Macmillan, 1968).
38. See *World Economic Outlook*, December 1978 (OECD, Paris).
39. The later period is covered in the June 1980 issue of *World Economic Outlook*.

2 Hedges: Concept and Pricing

Let us consider a world in which a market in claims contingent on each possible reality existed.[1] The rational saver would, by transacting in this market, ensure that the expected marginal utility from income in each possible reality (combination of states of the world) was equal to its price (in terms of current consumption). Thus, in a world described wholly by the state-variables of belligerency (varying between the extremes of war and peace), economic activity (varying between slump and boom), and liquidity (varying between banking crisis and perfect liquidity), a particular individual may find that he has very little natural endowment in the combination of war, boom, and banking crisis. He would go into the market place and buy income contingent on war-boom-banking crisis in exchange for either present consumption or income contingent on other combinations.

In practice, the number of state-variables, and the values (forms) each can take, are immense. No individual could map out every conceivable reality (combination of states), and securities in the form of elementary combination-prospects are rarely found. But the individual is aware of how changes in the value of certain crucial state-variables may affect qualitatively his future income, irrespective of how other state-variables change simultaneously. Thus, the owner of a group of retail stores realises that his natural income would be curtailed sharply in any combination of states of the world which included war (that is, where the state-variable of belligerency took the value (form) of war, rather than of peace). The businessman described would be keen to buy income contingent simply on the state of the world war occurring; equivalently, he would be a keen buyer of simple war-prospects.

Hedge Investments – Pure and Impure

Consider a bad general state of the world x_0 which is one extreme value of state-variable x. An elementary state-prospect, whose income is a function only of the value of x, and which rises the nearer is x to x_0, is defined here as a pure x_0 hedge. For example, a pure war-hedge is a security whose income depends only on the value of the state-variable of belligerency, of which it is a monotonically rising function. An example of a pure war-hedge would be an asset producing, say, zero in the state of peace, $500 in the state of cold war, and $1000 in the state of full-scale war.

In practice, it is difficult to imagine a natural security – a security whose income stream has as source a physical investment in the 'real' world – in the form of a pure x_0-hedge (or in the form of any elementary state-prospect). For example, although we may expect that gold yields its highest income in a state of total war, and its lowest income in absolute peace, its income is a function not only of the value of the state-variable belligerency, but also of the value of other state-variables that make up any particular reality. Thus gold yields a higher income in the combined states of war–hyperinflation–boom than in war–price stability–moderate economic activity.

Pure x_0-hedges can be constructed in the form of an insurance contract. Thus an enterprise may take out an insurance policy with Lloyds of London for war-risk: its payout will depend simply on whether the state-variable of belligerency assumes the form of war stipulated in the contract. Insurance companies (or syndicates) provide pure x_0-hedges only to a very limited extent. Insurance policies are backed ultimately by the funds supplied by shareholders (and bondholders) in the insurance company (or syndicate). If state of the world x_0 occurred, a large proportion of these equity funds would be written off. Yet in most possible realities in which state of the world x_0 features, the natural endowment of many shareholders, actual or potential, is low: an insurance company which intended to market x_0-hedges could draw equity capital from only a narrow clientele of shareholders – those who enjoyed relatively high natural endowment in state x_0. The company could of course combine x_0-hedge policies with conventional insurance business which involves insuring bad particular states of the world (for example, motor accident, ill-health, death) rather than bad general states.

However, the supply of equity capital to an insurance company which marketed seriously x_0-hedges would be high-cost and its policies of dubious quality unless very restricted in scope. Individuals do not obtain their natural endowment from policies or other elementary state-prospects but from securities which have an eventual counterpart in physical enterprise. Even those rare individuals with a high natural endowment in most state-combinations (realities) where state variable x takes value x_0, cannot be certain of high endowment in every such combination; indeed they cannot possibly envisage all combinations. Not only is the task of enumerating explicitly each combination mammoth and beyond ordinary human scope, but many state-variables are presumably as yet unknown to man. For example, the state-variable 'conditions in the world energy market' was not acknowledged widely, as a significant component of reality, before the early 1970s. Thus, not even the rare individual for whom the occurrence of state of the world x_0 was most likely associated with high income, would commit himself to the sale of large quantities of income contingent only on the occurrence of state x_0 (irrespective of what value other state-variables took). Moreover, the policyholder would not consider his cover as perfect, for he would realise that in some possible realities, albeit unknown, of which state of the world x_0 formed part, the insurance company would default due to insufficient funds being available from its investments.

An impure x_0-hedge takes the form of a complex combination-prospect rather than of a state-prospect. It promises high income in most, but not all, state-combinations in which x takes values near x_0. In practice, it is not possible to list all state-variables and consider explicitly all possible realities. Instead, the investor may select a subset of, say, three state-variables, to whose movement his income is particularly sensitive. These variables may include belligerency, economic activity, and rate of monetary inflation. The investor would calculate his likely endowment and the likely income from securities for each combination of states drawn from the subset. The calculation cannot be precise as income (and endowment) is influenced, albeit to a small extent, by state-variables outside the subset.

In the above simplified world, where only three state-variables are considered explicitly, an impure x_0-hedge is defined as a security whose expected (but uncertain) income, expressed as a function of $x,y,z,$ rises as x approaches x_0, for unchanged y,z. (Equivalently, the partial derivative with respect to x of $E(x,y,z)$ – the security's expected return – is a rising function of x.) If the expected return of the same security rises as y approaches y_0 – the extreme bad value of y – for unchanged x and z then the security would be described as an impure (x_0y_0)-hedge.

To take our war example again, gold would fit the definition of an impure (inflation, war)-hedge. In most state-combinations where the state-variable of belligerency (monetary inflation) takes the value of war (high monetary inflation) gold has a large payoff. But in some combinations the payoff may be low – for example, if the state of war (high monetary inflation) were in combination with the state of massive auctions by the US Treasury or the discovery of a large new gold-mining belt. Many state-variables that may affect the price of gold cannot be considered explicitly in each and every combination by the defensive investor; instead, he considers the return from gold as uncertain in the subset of possible combinations of states of the world drawn from three or four major state-variables; say, belligerency, monetary inflation, economic activity, out of a far greater set. The uncertainty is due to the unknown value of state-variables outside those specified. However, the expected return from an investment in gold rises as the value of the state-variable belligerency (monetary inflation) rises from peace to war (from low inflation to high inflation) – for given values of the other major state-variables given explicit consideration.

The less sensitive is the return from an impure x_0-hedge to the value of state-variables other than x, the more does it approximate a pure x_0-hedge. Further, even where an x_0-hedge is particularly sensitive also to other state-variables than x, it is preferable that these should be in the subset (x,y,z) from which the investor considers explicit possible combinations of states of the world. Otherwise the return from the x_0-hedge would be highly uncertain in explicit scenarios considered. By extension, a good (x_0y_0)-hedge is one whose expected return is particularly sensitive only to state-variables x and y.

Some (x_0y_0)-hedges approximate the simple addition of a pure x_0- and a pure y_0-hedge (a complex state-prospect) rather than a complex combination-prospect. Such an (x_0y_0)-hedge's expected return is markedly sensitive only to state-variables x and y. Further, its power as an x_0-hedge must be independent of the value of y and conversely. (Equivalently, if the partial derivative of the good (x_0y_0)-hedge's expected return with respect to state-variable x is not a function of y, and conversely, then it approximates an addition of a pure x_0 and pure y_0-hedge.) An (x_0y_0)-hedge with these properties is defined here as a good $(x_0 + y_0)$-hedge – a special type of good (x_0y_0)-hedge.

If there are N state-variables x_1 to x_N being considered explicitly, where each can take bad forms (described by lower-case letters) and there are N distinct good $(x_1 + x_2 + \ldots x_N)$-hedges, S_1 to S_N – where 'distinct' means that their expected returns are sensitive to $x_1, x_2, \ldots x_n$ in different degrees – then proxies to pure hedges can be found for x_1 to x_n. This follows from simple propositions in linear algebra.[2]

A simple example may be given of how pure hedges may be proxied by constructing a portfolio of good impure $(x_0 + y_0)$-hedges. Suppose there are two bad states – high inflation (x_0) and war (y_0) – and two good impure (war, high-inflation)-hedges, gold and Swiss francs respectively. If the expected return from 1 ounce of gold, $E(\text{gold})$, can be expressed as $E(\text{gold}) = 1.4(1-x) + 2(1-y)$, (where x and y are the state-variables of US inflation and belligerency respectively, $x=1$ is a state of zero inflation, $x=0$ a state of hyperinflation, $y=1$ is a state of peace, $y=0$ is state of total war) and if the expected return from 1000 Swiss francs can be expressed as $E(R_{\text{Sfr}}) = 1.2(1-x) + 1.1(1-y)$ then solution of these two simultaneous equations shows that a pure inflation-hedge would be proxied by a holding of 2333 Swiss francs, and a short position in 1.28 ounces of gold. As the state-variable of belligerency changes, the holding in gold and Swiss francs would change in value by equal and opposite amounts.

'Bad News' Goods and 'Good News' Goods

Hedge assets, whether in the form of pure x_0-hedges, impure x_0-hedges, impure (x_0y_0)-hedges or impure $(x_0 + y_0)$-hedges, may be brought under one general heading (invented here) of 'bad news' goods. The return from these is especially high when at least one state-variable takes a very bad value.

Good news goods are the mirror images of bad news goods. If in each of the definitions in the previous section x_0 and y_0 are replaced by X and Y which are good rather than bad general states of the world, we obtain the definitions for each corresponding type of good news good – described as pure X-fairweather, impure X-fairweather, impure (X,Y)-fairweather, and impure $(X + Y)$ fairweather goods respectively. For example, an elementary state-prospect, whose income is a function only of the value of x, and which rises the nearer x is to X – the good general state which is the opposite to the bad general state x_0 (for example, boom *v.* slump) – is defined as a pure X-fairweather good.

Examples of pure X-fairweather goods are few; like pure x_0-hedges, they must be contrived rather than found in 'natural form'. One illustration is a bond issued by the French Government in May 1956. The principal and interest on the bonds were regulated according to changes in the value of industrial production. Thus, if x is the state-variable of level of economic activity and X its top value representing economic boom, the bond was a pure X-fairweather good.

An example of an impure X-fairweather good is a share in a portfolio of industrial equities. For unchanged values of other state-variables, a rise in economic activity (state-variable x) raises the expected return from the share. A similar observation applies to many types of equities.

A security can be both an X-fairweather good and an impure y_0-hedge asset.[3] For example, the returns from real estate rise as the state-variable 'rate of monetary inflation' approaches the bad end of its range – real estate is an inflation-hedge. But it is also a boom-fairweather good. Such securities which are both bad news and good news goods are described here as convertible news goods. As we shall see in Part II, many collectables fall into this category.

An individual who is naturally endowed with bad news goods is richer than another naturally endowed with good news goods and the same expected income-stream in each interval ahead.[4] The advantages of endowment with bad news goods are analogous to those of endowment with atypical tastes: the person who derives above-average enjoyment (utility) from goods which are cheap (in the goods market) and below-average enjoyment from goods which are dear, has a higher standard of life than another with the same monetary income but more typical preferences. Included in goods which are cheap economically (but not in terms of human effort) are those belonging to the spiritual rather than to the material world.

The Pricing of Hedge Assets

Certain propositions can be developed about the price behaviour of hedge assets and of fairweather goods. Demonstration of their foundation, for the interested reader, is found in the subsequent section – which can, however, be omitted without loss of continuity in a more general reading.

First, a pure x_0-hedge – an asset whose income is dependent solely on the value of state-variable x, and which reaches its maximum when

x takes its worst form x_0 and its minimum when x takes its best form X – rises more in absolute price for an increase in probability of state x_0 than a pure X-fairweather good would rise for the same absolute increase in likelihood of state X.

Second, if the probability of the bad state x_0 occurring is less than that of the good state X occurring, then a given increase in the former has a larger proportionate effect on the price of a pure x_0-hedge than does the same absolute increase in the latter have on the price of a pure X-fairweather good. In a multi-period context, if the supply of x_0-hedges shows less or equal price elasticity than does the supply of X-fairweather goods, then greater volatility of the price of hedge assets than of fairweather goods would be typical even without making the assumption about x_0 being unlikely to occur.

Third, markets in hedge investments should tend to display a particularly great proportional increase in volume of speculative trading (where 'speculative trading' refers to that motivated by a change in an individual's opinion relative to the market's) in periods following release of important new information, when the dispersion of individuals' opinion about the market average is likely to increase.

Demonstration of Properties of Hedge Investment[5]

Let us turn to a simple two-period world in order to demonstrate an important proposition about the pricing of bad news and good news goods. The simple world in the future is described entirely by the state-variable x, which describes, say, the level of economic activity, and which may take the value of either x_0 (slump) or x (boom), with probability of occurrence of p_{x0} and p_x respectively. Suppose after market exchange and production an individual obtains C_0 of consumption goods in the present period, and C_{x0} and C_x contingent on states x_0 and X respectively. Then from the expected utility theorem,[6] the utility obtained, u, may be expressed as:

$$u = p_{x0}\, V(C_0, C_{x0}) + p_x V(C_0, C_x).$$

where $V(\quad)$ is a utility function, expressed in terms of present and future consumption, and u is a cardinal measure of utility.

Following Hirshleifer[7] it can be shown that in equilibrium:

$$S_{x0} = \frac{p_{x0} V'_{c_{x0}}}{V'_{c0}(1+N)} \text{ and } S_x = \frac{p_x V'_{c_x}}{V'_{c0}(1+N)},$$ [8]

where S_{x0}, S_x are the prices of consumption in state of the world X and x_0 respectively in terms of immediate consumption,[9] $V'_{c_{x0}}$ is the value of the derivative of the utility function V with respect to c, where c takes value c_{x0} – and similarly for V'_{c_x} and V'_{c0} and where it is assumed that:

$$V(C_0C_1) = V_{c0} + \frac{V_{c_1}}{(1+\mathrm{N})}, \text{ with } N \text{ fixed}^{10}.$$

From the equilibrium relations for S_{x0} and S_x, taking partial derivatives with respect to p_{x0}, we obtain:

$$(1)\ f'_{p_{x0}}(S_{x0}) = \frac{V'_{c_{x0}}}{\mathrm{V}'_{c0}(1+N)} \text{ and } (2)\ f'_{p_x}(S_x) = \frac{V'_{c_x}}{V'_{c0}(1+N)}$$

(where $f'_p(S)$ is the partial derivative of S with respect to p). But $V'_{c_{x0}}$ is greater than V'_{c_x} for the marginal utility of income in the bad state of the world x_0 at consumption level C_{x0} is greater than the marginal utility of income in the good state X at the higher consumption level C_x. The proposition follows that income in the bad state is more price-sensitive (in absolute terms) to a given absolute increase in its chance of occurrence than is income in the good state to the same absolute increase in its chance of occurrence.[11] *Equivalently, a pure* x0*-hedge (promising $1 contingent on state* x0*) rises more in absolute price for an increase in probability of state* x0*, than a pure* X-*fairweather good would rise for the same increase in likelihood of state* X.

The investor is likely to be interested in how a change in p_{x0} affects S_{x0} in percentage terms. From the equilibrium expressions (1) and (2) above, it follows that:

$$f'_{x0}(S_{x0})/S_{x0} = 1/p_{x0} \text{ and } f'_x(S_x)/S_x = 1/p_x.$$

Thus if p_{x0} is less than p_x – that is, the probability of state of the world x_0 occurring is less than that of state of the world X – then an increase in the former has a larger proportionate effect on the price of a pure x_0-hedge than does the same absolute increase in the latter have on the price of a pure X-fairweather good.

In practice for most state-variables, the chances of bad outcomes occurring are much less than of good. For example, the state-variables of belligerency (peace *v.* war), liquidity (well-functioning financial system *v.* banking crisis), agricultural output (plenty *v.* famine), economic activity (full-employment *v.* slump), monetary depreciation (stability *v.* hyperinflation), all display this characteristic of lower probability for the bad states of the world than for the good states.[12] Given this weighting of probabilities, it will usually be true – although not essentially so – that *'bad news' goods react proportionately more in price to bad news than 'good news' goods react in price to good news.*[13]

The amount by which an individual adjusts the proportion of hedge investments in his total portfolio in response to a given percentage disagreement with the market's assessment of the probability of the bad state can be shown to be particularly high. It follows that markets in hedge investment should tend to display a large proportional increase in the volume of speculative trading (where 'speculative trading' refers to that motivated by a change in an individual's opinion relative to the market's) in periods following release of important new information when the dispersion of individuals' opinion about the market average is likely to increase.

To demonstrate the above proposition, suppose an investor comes to believe that the probability of state x_0 occurring is not p_{x0} as believed by the market, but $p_{x0}(1+d)$. The elasticity of his (speculative) response is measured by how far he distorts his holding of income contingent on state of the world x_0 expressed as a proportion of his present endowment there, for a given proportion, d, disagreement with the market.

The investor described purchases extra income, e, contingent on state x_0 up to that point at which the ratio of marginal utility of income there to the marginal utility of present consumption equals its price, where:

$$p_{x0}\,(1+d)V'_{c_{x_0}+e} = V'_{c0}\,(1+N)S_{x0}.$$[14]

If his beliefs had been identical with those of the market, he would have purchased income contingent on state x_0 only up to C_{x0} rather than $C_{x0}+e$, where:

$$p_{x0}V'_{c_{x_0}} = V'_{c0}\,(1+N)S_{x0}.$$

Combining these two marginal equivalences, we obtain:

$$(1+d)V'_{c_{x_0}+e} = V'_{c_{x_0}}.$$

This can be re-expressed as:[15]

$$(1 + d)\ (V'_{c_{x0}} + eV''_{c_{x0}}) = V'_{c_{x0}},$$

ignoring second order of smallness, the above expression simplifies to:

$$d = \frac{e}{C_{x0}} \frac{(-V''_{c_{x0}}\ C_{x0})}{V'_{c_{x0}}}$$

Now the ratio in parentheses is a measure of relative risk-aversion which is an increasing function of C_{x0}.[16] Thus for given d, e/C_{x0} must be a decreasing function of C_{x0}, and so must be the elasticity of speculative response – measured as:

$$\frac{e/C_{x0}}{dp_{x0}/p_{x0}}$$

The discussion so far in this chapter about the pricing of hedges has been implicitly in a two-period world, divided into present and future. Consider, instead, a multi-period world, divided into sequential intervals of time, in each of which state-variable x can take the value of x_0 or X. Income contingent on x_0 or X for each period ahead can be bought and sold against present consumption in the market. Income contingent on x_0 in time interval t_i is termed an x_0t_i-hedge. Extending the method of Hirshleifer (see p. 31), in market equilibrium the price of an x_0t_i-hedge (offering unit income contingent on state x_0 occurring i intervals from now), $S_{x0}t_i$, must satisfy the equation:

$$p_{x0t_i} V'_{c_{x0t_i}} / V'_{c0}\ (1 + N)^i = S_{x0t_i}.$$

Equivalently, the expected marginal utility of income, discounted at the rate N, from the x_0t_i-hedge, must equal the marginal utility of present consumption forgone in acquiring it.

Now suppose the market re-assesses each p_{x0t_i} upwards to p'_{x0t_i}, where:

$$a + p_{x0t_i} = p'_{x0t_i}.$$

Suppose further that total income endowment is fixed for each x_0t_i, not being sensitive to S_{x0t_i}, and so C_{x0t_i} is fixed for the representative individual. Then for each i:

$$f'_{p_{x0t_i}}(S_{x_0t_i})/S_{x0t_i} = 1/p_{x0t_i}.$$

Assuming, as previously, that p_{x0t_i} is less than p_{xt_i}, then the price of time-state hedges for each interval ahead is more sensitive to a given increase in the chance of the bad state of the world x_0 than the price of time-state fairweather goods for each interval ahead to the same increased chance of the good state of the world X.

In practice, the amount of income endowed in time-state x_0t_i, and so C_{x0t_i}, for the representative individual, can be sensitive to S_{x0t_i}, the price of such income in terms of present consumption. For example, some types of physical investment may pay off especially highly in state x_0. A rise in S_{x0t_i} for future time-intervals would spur increased physical investment of this nature, whose returns would be expected after a gestation period. Thus C_{x0t_i} would become increasingly sensitive to changes in S_{x0t_i} the more distant is t_i from t_0.

An example of an investment providing income in bad states, and where the volume of such income in far-off intervals is sensitive to its price $S_{x0_{t_i}}$, (or equivalently to the rate of discount, $1/(1+C_{x0t_i})$), is an energy project. An increase in the perceived risk of energy crisis in every future interval would lead to an immediate increase in the price of oil equities, for these would produce especially large income when the oil price sky-rockets. The increased oil equity price, implying a reduced cost of capital for oil projects, would lead to a higher rate of investment in oil projects and so to a greater endowment of income in energy crisis if it occurs in the far-distant future.

The supply of energy-crisis hedges in the form of petro-money is also sensitive in far-off time intervals to changes in their price. An increased risk of energy crisis, x_o, and increased S_{x0t_i}, would be translated into an increased forward exchange value for delivery of the petro-currency in future intervals. But an up-valuation of the currency would be associated with a widening of current account deficits for the country of issue, whereby its residents would increase their borrowing (in domestic currency) from the rest of the world. The gradual increase in lending to the petro-economy (to finance its current account deficits) represents an increase of endowment of income, contingent on the state of the world energy crisis, for the rest of the world.

Given a significant supply-elasticity of x_0t_i-hedges with respect to changes in their price – an elasticity which increases with t_i – the change in S_{x0t_i} brought about by the market re-estimating the probabilities of $x0t_i$ to p'_{x0t_i} from p_{x0t_i} would be smaller for far-distant than for close t_i's. The equilibrium relation,

$$p'_{x0t_i} V'_{c_{x0t_i}} (1+d_i) = S'_{x0t_i},$$

holds for each i, where $d_i c_{x0t_i}$ is the increased endowment of state $x0t_i$-contingent income brought about by changes in S_{x0t_r} for $r = 0$ to i, and S'_{x0t_i} is the revised price for income contingent on time-state $x0t_i$. Now, by Taylor's expansion, we have approximately:

$$p'_{x0t_i} V'_{c_{x0t_i}} (1+d_i) = p'_{x0t_i} V'_{c_{x0t_i}} \left(1 - \frac{(-C_{x0t_i} V''_{c_{x0t_i}}) d_i}{V'_{c_{x0t_i}}}\right).$$

The expression $-C_{x0t_i} V''_{c_{x0t_i}}/V'_{c_{x0t_i}}$ is the measure of relative risk aversion which is an increasing function of C_{x0t_i}.[17] Thus, the lower is the level of endowment C_{x0t_i} the less is the percentage decrease in the price S'_{x0t_i} brought by a given proportional expansion d_i of the supply of $x0t_i$ hedges:[18] equivalently, the poorer is time-state $x0t_i$, the more price-elastic is the demand for income contingent on its occurrence.

The important result follows that a given percentage increase in each probability p_{x0t_i}[19] causes S_{x0t_i} to rise by a proportion which, for given price elasticity of supply of $x0t_i$-contingent income, is an increasing function of the degree to which $x0t_i$ is a bad state. Once we allow for the supply of contingent incomes being less than completely inelastic (with respect to price) and assume that they are not more elastic in the case of bad than of good states, demonstration of the potentially greater price-sensitivity of bad news goods to bad news than good news goods to good news need not depend on the assumption that the bad state is less likely to occur than the good state.

Elasticity of supply of $x0t_i$-contingent income is not synonymous with elasticity of supply of assets producing that income. For example, gold's quality of being a war-hedge is derived from the potential increase in demand for a non-political medium of exchange and store of value in time of war. But an increase in the world's gold stock from x to $2x$ million tons may not at all increase the supply of intermediation services or real consumption in other forms during war: the increase may merely reduce by half the contingent income of each ton of gold. If gold were the only war-hedge, then the price of income contingent on war would move simply in proportion to the probability of its occurrence. The forward price of gold for delivery at t_i would, in contrast to the price of income contingent on war at t_i, move to reflect expectations of the supply of newly mined gold responding to changes in its price. Equivalently, the increase in the price, $S_{x_0t_i}$, of war-contingent income has its counterpart not only in an immediate rise in the price of gold (the asset producing war-contingent income) but also in the expectation of a subsequent negative income, during periods when state-variable x does not take value x_0 (war) and the gold price reacts downwards to increased supplies: $S_{x_0t_i}$, however (in contrast to our petro-money example), may not react downwards and the expected returns on gold (unlike those on a petro-money) may not tend to rise as supply increases.[20]

Where the supply of x_0t_i-contingent income is price-elastic, the result emerges that an increase in the probability $p_{x_0t_i}$ of time-states x_0t_i occurring is associated with an increase in the expected rate of return on the holding of an x_0t_i-hedge. For the expected rate of return on the hedge may be expressed as $p_{x_0t_i}/S_{x_0t_i}$ and a given proportionate increase in $p_{x_0t_i}$ to $p'_{x_0t_i} = (1+a)p_{x_0t_i}$ leads to a less than proportionate increase in $S_{x_0t_i}$ given positive price elasticity of supply. The rise in the expected yield is due to its not being a function directly of the probability of state x_0 but to the marginal utility of income there;[21] the increase in the spot price $S_{x_0t_i}$ (which in contrast to the expected return, is a function of $p_{x_0t_i}$) leads to an increased supply of that income and hence to a reduction in its marginal utility.

The rise in the expected rate of return to an x_0t_i-hedge as the state x_0 increases in likelihood may be explained intuitively. The increased probability of state x_0 makes it more worthwhile to make physical investments that pay off especially highly there, and resources are diverted to this end from other projects. In consequence, poverty of income in state x_0 is reduced, should it occur, relative to that in other states – x_0 becomes less of a bad state – and so investors are prepared to pay a smaller premium for protection against its occurrence.

In practice, it is not possible to identify securities which are hedges against a particular state of the world x_0 in only one interval t_i. Instead, the security is likely to be a hedge against state x_0 whensoever it may occur and is described as a multi-period hedge-asset. The price of a multi-period hedge asset, providing \$1 in state x_0t_i for all i, from $i = 1$, is:

$$\underset{i=1}{E} \frac{S_{x_0t_i}}{(1+N)^i}$$

– the sum of the prices for each individual time-state x_0t_i discounted at the rate N which is the fixed rate of equivalence between the utility of income in two contingent periods.[22] From the construction of S^i_{x0} – the price of a multi-period x_0-hedge at t_i – the result follows that its sensitivity to a given proportional increase in p_{x0t_i} for all i is a decreasing function of the level of income in states x_0. For multi-period contingent claims, bad news goods are more price-sensitive than good news goods to a given proportional increase in the probability of state x(x_0 or x, as relevant) occurring – so long as the supply of x_0-contingent income is price-elastic, but not more so than the supply of X-contingent income.

A petro-money is an example of a multi-period hedge asset, which yields especially high income in time-states of energy crisis. These are where the real price of energy rises by an amount far in excess of normal expectations (due, for example, to revolution or war in the Middle East) – equivalently in any reality where the state-variable 'abundance of energy supplies' (x_e), moves sharply in the direction of E (energy shortage). A 'calm energy' fairweather good promises income contingent on time-states where x_e does not move significantly in an unfavourable direction. The probability of energy-crisis at t_i, p_{et_i}, is assumed to be much less than of energy calm.

Note that a petro-money is not a pure hedge asset, for it offers bonus income contingent on a period-to-period change in a state-variable, rather than on the actual value of that state-variable. The investor must evaluate the expected marginal utility of that bonus income at t_i for each possible time-sequence of realities at $t_i - 1$ and t_i where x jumps considerably in between the two. The exercise must be repeated for t_i, to $t_i + 1$, $t_i + 1$ to $t_i + 2$, etc. In practice, the investor is likely to attach a direct valuation to income contingent on a change in x, due to the impracticality of the above detailed calculation.

Note that p_{et_i} is distinct for each interval i. Further it is not necessary to assume that each p_{et_i} is independent of whether in the previous interval(s) energy glut or energy crisis occurred. If, for example, a state of energy crisis occurs at t_i, then the market may upgrade, at t_i, its estimates of $p_{et_{i+1}}, p_{et_{i+2}}$ etc. An increase in the probability of energy crisis from p_{et_i} to $p'_{et_i} = (1 + a)p_{et_i}$ in each future interval causes S_{et_i} to increase, but by less for far-distant than for short-distant dates: the elasticity of supply of the petro-money with respect to its price (real exchange rate) is greater over long periods than over short periods of time. The rise in each S_{et_i} is likely, though, to be large, due both to the high elasticity of demand for income in bad states (relevant for S_{et_i} where t_i is far-distant from the present) and the assumed low base-probabilities p_{et_i}.

The price, in terms of consumption at t_{i-1}, of a petro-money's promise of an income-bonus contingent on E at t_i, is made up of a shortfall of the t_{i-1} to t_i real interest rate (defined as the nominal interest rate minus the expected domestic inflation rate during the period t_{i-1} to t_i) below the average real interest rate on non-hedge monies plus a one-period premium of its real exchange rate at t_{i-1} over that if it offered no income contingent on E occurring at t_i (but continued to offer income bonuses contingent on E occurring at any other time). At time t_{i-1}, the total premium of the petro-money's real exchange rate over its level if it offered no hedge qualities for any t_i is the sum of the one-period premia for t_{i-1} to t_i, t_i to t_{i+1}, and so on, all discounted appropriately – where the premium for t_{i+s} to t_{i+s+1} is discounted by the factor $(1+N)^s$.

The increase in p_{et_i}, to p'_{et_i}, causes the total premium of the petro-money over its zero-hedge rate for each date i, to rise, and each expected one-period real interest rate to fall.[23] The reaction of the total premium now and for intervals nearby is greater than for far-off intervals, due to the supposed greater price-elasticity of supply for far-off contingent incomes.[24] The increase in p_{et_i}, for each i, thus steepens the expected decline in the total premium of the currency's exchange rate over its zero E-hedge rate[25] (the rate which would prevail if the currency was not an E-hedge in any period), although it both starts from a higher level and remains above its previous projected path (before the increase in each p_{et_i}). This reaction of the total premium and its expected rate of decline are increasing functions of the degree to which E_{t_i} is a bad state. We have seen that a characteristic of hedge investments is their high price-sensitivity to changed market assessment of the probability of states of the world. In the extreme, it is possible for the hedge-characteristic of the petro-money to disappear if its cumulative supply (in real terms) has become so great as to remove all fear of an energy-crisis – so well are all investors protected by owning E-contingent income. Then E is no longer a bad state.

Despite the drop in the one-period real interest rates and the steepening of the expected decline in the total premium, the expected return per interval on the petro-money – taking into account the increased chance of energy crises occurring – certainly does not decrease and tends to increase for far-distant intervals. This follows from the earlier observation about the influence of positive price-elasticity of supply of x_0t_i-contingent income on the expected return from an x_0t_i-hedge.

Timing of Hedge Investment

Portfolios are continuously being created and destroyed. They can be created out of new savings, windfall gains, or inheritance. They can be destroyed by consumption and windfall losses. Should an investor choose a proportion for each hedge asset irrespective of the age of the portfolio? For example, should an investor designing a portfolio from scratch (that is, from cash) during a war crisis invest as high a proportion as 'older' investors in gold?

The theoretical answer, following from the principle of buying income contingent on each state up to that point where its expected marginal utility equals its price, is unambiguously positive. The determinants of the optimum portfolio today are future not past values of variables – estimates of the probability of each state occurring, and what income will be available there. The philosopher may indeed claim that bad news tends to rotate with good, and with patience, the newborn investor could buy hedges at a keener price. But if the Flood really occurs before the next bargain-sale of hedges, the latter's eventual occurrence would be of little consolation.

Is the investor who constructs a portfolio at a time of crisis less fortunate than one who constructs a portfolio at a time of calm? Certainly he will pay a high price for hedge-assets, but fairweather goods should be cheap. Whilst the price of income contingent on bad general states (and so the price of hedge assets) is likely to have risen proportionately more than the price of income contingent on good general states (and so the price of fairweather goods) will have fallen (see proposition 2 of previous section), income contingent on good states of the world is by definition in greater supply, and accounts for the greater proportion of total contingent income bought. The irrational, or lazy investor, who during good times does not buy income contingent on bad states of the world, and then in times of crisis scurries into hedge-assets, loses heavily from his neglect, for he will be topping up his holding of hedge-assets just when they become exceptionally expensive.

The proportion which fairweather goods and hedge-assets represents in the investor's portfolio will vary over time, according to changing present values of the different state-variables and changing probability distribution of their values in future intervals. At times of crisis, when one or more bad general states are awarded high probability estimates, hedge assets will represent a higher proportion, in value terms, of the total portfolio, than at more peaceful times.

The change, over time, in the proportion of hedge and fairweather assets, is brought about in part by valuation adjustments and in part by quantity adjustments. At the point of a significant change in views about the future, marked by the upgrading of the probability of a bad state, x_0, occurring, income contingent on state x_0, and so x_0-hedges, are marked up in value. Similarly, X-fairweather goods are marked down in value. So long as the investor does not disagree with the changed probability assessments of the market, and if the elasticity of supply of x_0-contingent income with respect to price is zero, there would be no need to transact. By being passive, he would find that although weightings of hedges and fairweather goods in his portfolio would have changed, expected marginal utility of income would remain equal to its price in all time-states.

In reality, the supply of income contingent on state-variable x taking value x_0 is likely to be price-elastic in some degree, especially for far-distant intervals. Following the above change in views, the supply of income contingent on x_0 in future intervals would increase. For example, if x_0 describes energy-catastrophe, and the chance of its occurring increases, then so would the supply of oil-equities. As the new supply came to the market, the investor would have to transact, buying sufficient new income contingent on x_0 to ensure that the expected marginal utility of income contingent on x_0 remained equal to its price. Here, the increased proportion of hedges in the portfolio would be brought about partly by price change and partly by quantity adjustment.

In practice, the supply of income contingent on several bad states – war, international banking crisis – is very price-inelastic; gold is the principal hedge asset with respect to these and it has a very low supply elasticity with respect to price. Income contingent on good states, in contrast, is usually price-elastic; increased prospects of economic recovery or boom would herald usually large growth in new issue volume of equities.[26] Thus, valuation changes often play a greater, and quantity changes a lesser, role in adjusting the proportion of hedge assets than they play in adjusting the proportion of fairweather goods, following a significant change in the market's views about the future. Bad news investment is often more passive in nature than is good news investment.

In addition to being sensitive to state-variables of universal relevance, an impure hedge asset may be sensitive also to state-variables which enter the reality of only one group of individuals. Such hedge assets may have to be managed actively in a portfolio. Consider gold for example. This is boosted in value by the increased chance of war or revolution in any region. An increased chance of revolution in Thailand would lead to increased gold hoarding in South-East Asia, as the probability of gold yielding monetary services in that region (in the event of revolution occurring) would have increased. Yet the resulting rise in the gold price would throw out of equilibrium portfolios of investors elsewhere in the world, for whom the probability of gold yielding monetary services had not increased. At the increased price placed on unchanged expected income, these investors would reduce their holdings of gold. Thus the gold investor must watch to adjust his gold investments when their popularity fluctuates in regions other than his own.

Not only the investor, but also the supplier of hedge assets, may be concerned by how far a general change in the portfolio proportion for hedge assets is accomplished by quantity changes and how much by valuation adjustments. For example, a country which supplies a hedge currency (i.e. a currency which yields high income in most possible realities where one or more state-variables assume bad forms) would suffer least economic disruption if exchange rate appreciation or depreciation – due to changed valuation of future contingent incomes – caused little change in its current account (as a proportion of GNP) and so in the fortunes of its export-industry. But low sensitivity of the current account to the exchange rate is equivalent to low price elasticity of supply for the hedge currency, which is supplied principally by the country running a combined deficit on long-term capital and current account, and so increasing indebtedness to the rest of the world. In turn, low price-elasticity of supply for the currency means – if it is a principal vehicle for trading a particular type of contingent income – that a change in the proportion of that type of hedge in the international portfolio will have its counterpart principally in valuation rather than in quantity adjustment.

The Swiss franc and British pound may be compared as hedge currencies – the former as a hedge against war, US inflation, and banking crisis and the latter as a hedge against energy catastrophe. As there is no market in pure hedges, it is not possible to confirm whether the price of war, US inflation, or banking-crisis-contingent income is more volatile than that of energy-catastrophe-contingent income. *A priori*, that depends on the price-elasticity of supply of the group of assets that produce war, inflation and banking-crisis-contingent income, relative to that of the group of assets that produce energy-catastrophe-contingent-income:[27] further, the amplitude of fluctuations in the probability of each type of bad state is relevant. However, a given degree of volatility imposed on the national currency's international value by its hedge properties would impose greater cost on the British than on the Swiss exporter. For British exports face a more price-elastic demand than do the more specialist Swiss exports. Thus pounds as energy hedges may be in more elastic supply than Swiss francs as hedges against war, US inflation and banking crisis.[28]

Elasticity of supply of hedge investments, and their degree of purity, can be dependent on institutional arrangements. In the heyday of the Gold Standard, 1890–1914, investors could exchange their domestic money at a fixed rate for gold which was effectively a package of pure hedges against several bad general states. Gold promised pecuniary income only in those possible realities where the domestic currency was forced off gold – and these could be typified by one of the state-variables of war, banking liquidity or social order, taking an extremely bad value. The values of many particular state-variables relevant today to the value of gold, and so reducing it to an impure hedge asset, were irrelevant in the days of the Gold Standard.

At times of political crisis under the system of the Gold Standard, private hoarding of physical gold would increase. The central banks, to maintain their currency on gold, would run down their gold reserves and push up interest rates – so hoping to cool hoarding. Once the currency had sunk to its lower gold point, the supply of gold became almost infinitely elastic with respect to its price: the central bank would sell as much gold as was necessary to defend the national currency from falling below its gold point.

This high elasticity of the supply of hedges in the form of gold (in the days of the Gold Standard) should not be mistaken for a high elasticity of supply of income contingent on the bad general states described. Nor should a fixed price for gold be interpreted as a fixed price for income contingent on these states. Gold has two sources of income contingent on bad states. First, in conditions of worldwide monetary breakdown, the stock of privately held gold would assume the functions of money. An increase in the supply of gold, by adding to the stock, reduces the potential monetary services of each unit of gold, although not necessarily in the same proportion: for the more widespread are gold holdings the more adequately may stocks of gold substitute for the services of paper money in one of the bad states. Whilst the ceiling price per ounce of gold would remain defended by official sales, contingent monetary services yielded by each ounce of metal would become more expensive as these are diluted between a larger quantity of above-ground supplies. The contingent monetary services from a given portfolio-holding of gold are reduced by the gold sales, and the rational investor must participate in the general wave of gold-hoarding in order to restore equilibrium. Indeed, the representative individual would re-build holdings of contingent monetary services above their previous level – given the increase in their availability. This positive elasticity of supply of contingent monetary services (with respect to price) means that the upward potential of their price is less than in a world of fiat monies (monies which are inconvertible into gold), where the short-run supply of gold is very inelastic.

Second, so long as a major part of the world's currencies remained on gold, each unit of gold represented a fairly constant amount of international purchasing power. Thus gold, like foreign currency, offered residents almost certain income contingent on a localised war, defeat by a foreign power, or domestic revolution.[29] This type of contingent income could be increased by official sales of gold, and was fixed in local currency price so long as the domestic money remained pegged to gold. If these localised bad states increased in likelihood, the investor should have participated in the resulting wave of gold hoarding, given the increase in the expected marginal utility of income contingent on them from an unchanged portfolio holding of gold.

In summary, the hedge investor in gold under the regime of the Gold Standard should be more active in transacting than his counterpart in a world of fiat monies – he should take advantage of the increased supplies, made available by official gold sales, of income contingent on bad states. Further, the greater price elasticity of supply of contingency services of gold under a Gold Standard than under a fiat money regime makes their price considerably less volatile there. The hedge investor should find the environment of the Gold Standard kinder than that of its fiat-money alternatives.

Hedging Income-redistribution

So far we have discussed trading income contingent principally on values of state-variables whose movement implies large aggregate gains or losses to the world economy, with the gains and number of gainers being much smaller than the losses and number of losers or conversely. However, the movement of many state-variables has little implication for aggregate economic welfare whilst implying large distributive changes. For example, movement of the state-variable of 'weather in the coffee-producing area of Brazil' redistributes income between coffee consumers and coffee producers, whilst causing little change in aggregate incomes.

Income contingent on the movement of distributive state-variables (changes in the value of which have large distributive relative to aggregate effects on income) is traded principally in an interpersonal market, where offsetting potential gainers and losers create hedges for themselves through mutual exchange. To take the coffee example, producers can sell coffee forward to consumers at a fixed price, thus buying income contingent on possible realities (i.e. combinations of state-variables) where the coffee-price would be very low and hence where their 'natural endowment' would be depressed. Consumers, by buying coffee forward from the producer, are themselves buying income contingent on possible realities where their own real endowment would be depressed. Thus both parties to the forward contract obtain income in possible realities where the level of the coffee price would be such as to depress their incomes.

If there were great asymmetry between the numbers of gainers and losers from the movement of a state-variable, then the scope for interpersonal trading of contingent income would be reduced. For example, for many consumers of a commodity, it represents a very small part of their shopping basket, and no clear identification of movement of its price with realities where natural endowment of income is low can be made. Then producers must buy income contingent on a low commodity price from investors who do not consider themselves as thereby obtaining a hedge against a bad reality. The producer may then have to pay a premium over actuarial value for income contingent on a low price. Further, if the movement of the commodity price showed positive correlation with an aggregative state-variable (changes in the value of which have large aggregate relative to distributive effects on income) taking a good value, the premium would be especially large – for buyers of forward contracts would be reducing their income contingent on a bad general state of the world. The commodity producer buys effectively income contingent on a low price by selling forward future output to investors who regard those forward positions as part of their portfolio of 'good news' goods. The need to obtain hedges in this way, rather than through mutual creation of hedges, adds to the cost of capital for the commodity production process. General investors must be found not just for providing capital to finance production but also to back a commitment to buy the product forward.

Income contingent on the value of aggregative state-variables is obtained predominantly from partaking in physical investment rather than from interpersonal forward contracting. There are very few individuals whose naturally endowed wealth gains from an aggregative state-variable taking a bad value and their total gains are small. Thus, the size of the premium which income contingent on the bad states of the world would obtain if only interpersonal hedges were available would be much larger than if physical production of hedges could occur. Then investors would have the alternative to provide hedges for themselves through buying a share in expanded physical investment rather than buying a share of fixed supplies of contingent income from those whose natural endowment is already skewed towards yielding high income contingent on the bad state. Similarly, widespread investor demand for income contingent on good values of an aggregate state-variable (for example, economic boom) is satisfied predominantly by the purchase of equity stakes in expanded physical investment, rather than by those with a naturally high endowment in such states of the world (owners of family enterprises) selling a part of their income contingent on them to the rest of the population.

The state-variable 'conditions in the energy market' can be taken as an example of an aggregative state-variable.[30] Public and private investors in OPEC nations have a naturally high endowment in the state of energy crisis, but their gains there are greatly outweighed by losses of economic output in the oil-consuming world. If income contingent on an energy crisis could be bought only from residents in energy-rich countries (for example, by non-residents lending a petro-money to residents of its country of issue), the premium of its price over actuarial value would be extraordinarily high. Instead, a large amount of income contingent on energy crisis is produced for residents in oil-consuming countries from direct physical investments in oil production and exploration.

The state-variable 'belligerency' is perhaps the purest type of aggregative state variable. In the state of the world 'general war' there may be assumed to be almost no gainers and huge aggregate losses. Thus income contingent on the state of general war is obtained preponderantly from physical holdings of gold rather than from any interpersonal insurance.[31]

Limits to Hedge Investments

In discussing income contingent on different possible realities, we have postponed the problem – largely philosophical in nature – of the distinction between particular and general reality. Thus, we have stated that reality can be described formally as a vector $(x_1, x_2, \ldots, x_N)$ where there are N state-variables x_1 to x_N, and each can take values between 0 and 1.[32] But these state-variables fall into three categories: personal, group and universal.

A *universal state-variable* is one whose value is significant to the aggregate level of income or consumption, or distribution of consumption between different groups considered worldwide. Examples include the variables of 'belligerency', 'level of economic activity in the global economy', and 'food supplies'. Most often universal state-variables are aggregative rather than distributive in nature.

A *group state-variable* is one whose value is significant to the level of income, level of consumption, or distribution of consumption, of an identifiable large group. Thus the state-variable 'political colour of the British Government' has relevance for British residents but is without importance in many parts of the world. Group state-variables can be found of both distributive and aggregative nature.

A *particular state-variable* is one whose value is significant to the level of income, level of consumption, or distribution of consumption, for only one or a few individuals. Examples include the state-variables 'health of individual *i*', 'taste for work of individual *i*', 'rainfall on the land of farmer *X*', 'weather in holiday resort *Y*', 'perceived beauty of product *Z* from viewpoint of individual *i*'.

By trading in hedge assets and fairweather goods, or by transacting in forward commodity markets, the individual aims to re-arrange what income he would enjoy contingent on different possible common or group realities. *Common reality* is a vector containing all universal state-variables; *group Y reality* is a vector containing all state-variables relevant to *Y*'s members but not of universal relevance; *personal reality* of individual *i* is a vector containing all state-variables relevant to individual *i* and his family but not of universal or group relevance.

Income contingent on a small proportion of particular state-variables may be traded with insurance companies. Where a group of particular state-variables can be combined for different individuals such that the value total of these variables is highly predictable, then insurance is possible. Thus insurance companies group the state-variables of 'health of *i*, *j*, *k*, . . . ', and promise income contingent on any one of them assuming a bad value.

However, only a small range of particular state-variables are the subject of contingent income trades. This is due to both transaction cost and moral hazard considerations. For example, an employee may wish to buy income contingent on the state-variable 'location of demand for his services', so that if the location moved far from its present situation – implying a loss in real income due to removal costs – then he would receive an income bonus. But costs of an insurance company calculating for a given worker the risks of his changing location of the work would be large relative to any sum insured.

Moral hazard problems arise where the probability distribution for each value of the state-variable is influenced by the trading of contingent income-claims.[33] Thus if an entrepreneur could insure several state-variables relevant to personal success – for example, consumer taste for a new product which he is introducing – his incentive to try the utmost to market it may be diminished. An often-quoted example of moral hazard relates to life insurance, where insuring the life of a non-relative is in many countries outlawed for fear that *X* holding an insurance policy on *Y* creates a risk that *X* will murder *Y*. The 'moral hazard' problem is, of course, not relevant to universal or group state-variables, as no individual – with the exception of a Napoleon – can influence what value they take.

Inability to trade income, contingent on what value many types of particular state-variables take, limits the individual's ability to trade income contingent on what value universal and group state-variables take. A coffee producer's output, for example, is dependent on the values of many particular state-variables – level of frost in his locality, degree of pestilence, luck in finding good labour: he cannot therefore quantify at all precisely his level of income for each given coffee price, although possible realities with a low price will usually be poorer than those with a high price. The coffee producer is likely to sell forward a volume of output far below his expected level of crop for fear that movement of particular state-variables may cause his output to fall by a large amount below expectation, and that he would then find that his losses were magnified by having to buy coffee in the spot market, at a price possibly far above the spot price, to meet obligations under forward contracts.

Similarly, an entrepreneur may wish to buy slump hedges for delivery in one year's time to insure his expected wealth accretion. But the level of his forward purchases cannot be made contingent on the value of particular state-variables which will influence the level of his wealth in one year. A coffee consumer may buy coffee for delivery in one year, to insure against a state where the coffee price was very high, but these purchases cannot be made contingent on his retaining his taste for coffee. He buys less coffee forward than if he was certain that his taste would not change.

Thus non-insurability of many particular state-variables limits the scope for defensive investment, even when many indirect methods exist of trading in income contingent on bad general states. We will see in Chapter 4 that these limits are particularly severe for the small saver for whom particular state-variables are relatively more important and general state-variables relatively less important in the determination of income than for large savers.

Notes and References

1. Such claims, in the terminology of the previous chapter, are described as combination-prospects.
2. There are N identities for $i = 1$ to N, $E(S_i) = \sum_{J=1}^{N} w_J^i x_J$. Providing the identities can be transposed in matrix alegbra to produce N identities with each x_J expressed as a function of the $E(S_i)$'s only, the weights given to each $E(S_i)$ for x_J, are the proportion in which the securities must be added to produce a pure x_J-hedge.
3. This possibility of a security being both a good news and a bad news good is excluded from the two-parameter model, where a good news good is one with a positive beta and a bad news good is one with a negative beta (see Fama; end-note 6, Ch. 1).
4. Natural endowment refers to those assets owned by the individual before he enters into market exchange involving securities. An example of a person naturally endowed with bad news goods would be one living in a country specialising in the production of energy, or gold. Another example would be someone with the capability to enter occupations whose income is proof against bad news.
5. This section may be omitted in a general reading without loss of continuity – see pp. xiv, 40.
6. See J. Hirshleifer, *Investment, Interest and Capital* Prentice-Hall, Inc., 1970) pp. 215–41, for a development of the theorem.

7. See Hirshleifer, op. cit., pp. 252–3, equation (16).
8. These relationships state that the marginal rate of substitution between the utility of income from the x_0-hedge and utility of present consumption must equal the price (measured in terms of present consumption) of the x_0-hedge; similarly for X.
9. Where consumption is measured in terms of a given quantity of consumer goods.
10. This assumption is described as time-independence property of the intertemporal utility function – see Hirshleifer, op. cit., p.253. This time-independence is a simple case only; complementarity is possible.
11. In the simple world described, $(p_{x_0} + p_x = 1)$. An increase in probability of state of the world x_0 must then equal the decrease in probability of state X, and S_{x_0} rises by more than S_x falls.
12. An analogy exists here with conventional insurance business where individuals insure a particular bad state of the world (e.g. ill-health, fire). The event insured at the date on which the policy is taken out always has a small likelihood of occurring.
13. Where good news increases the probability of the good state of the world occurring by the same absolute amount as bad news increases the probability of the bad state of the world occurring.
14. It is assumed that consumption in the present period, C_0, is not sensitive to the changed probability assessment of p_{x_0}.
15. By Taylor's expansion, $V'_{c_x+e} = V'_{c_x} + e\,V''_{c_x}$ (approximately).
16. See K.J. Arrow, *Essays in the Theory of Risk-Bearing,* (North Holland, 1974) pp. 95–8. The principle of increasing relative risk aversion is shown to follow from the necessary boundedness of the utility function from above. An implication of the principle is that if both wealth and size of a bet are increased in the same proportion, the willingness to accept the bet should decrease. A related implication is that wealth-elasticity of demand for risky assets is less than unity.
17. See Note 16.
18. The assumption is made that C_0, consumption in the present period, is fixed.
19. This increase in $p_{x_0t_i}$ would cause $S_{x_0t_i}$ to rise in the same proportion if the supply of x_0t_i-contingent income was fixed.
20. The differing result is due to the supposed fixity of income contingent on war but the supposed elasticity (with respect to price) of energy-crisis contingent income.
21. For $E(r_{x_0t_i}) = \dfrac{p_{x_0t_i}}{S_{x_0t_i}} = \dfrac{p_{x_0t_i}}{p_{x_0t_i}V'_{c_{x_0t_i}}} \times V'_0 = \dfrac{V'_0}{V'_{c_{x_0t_i}}}$
22. N is given in expanding the intertemporal utility function:

$$V(C_0, C_1) = V_0 + \frac{V_1}{1+N}$$

23. This sharing of the increase in each S_{et_i} between the expected real interest rate and premium of the exchange rate over its zero-hedge rate is essential to maintenance of full employment in the domestic economy.
24. The implicit assumption is made that even if p_{et_i} showed some rising tendency with t_i the total premium would still be expected to decline with

i due to increasing supplies of income contingent on *E* at t_i.

25. At any time, given the extra assumption in Note 24, the market must expect the premium to be on a declining trend, due to S_{et_i} falling as i becomes more distant.
26. Scope of active management may be reduced by new equities being supplied indirectly to the market – through the capitalisation of retained earnings, rather than through a new issue in the equity market.
27. It appears that hedge assets which produce income contingent on energy crisis are in more elastic supply than those that produce income contingent on war. For oil equities and energy monies are more elastic in supply than gold, the principal asset producing war-contingent income. This should depress the price volatility of the first type of contingent income relative to the second.
28. This judgement about relative elasticities must be tempered by the general tendency of island-currencies to be more inelastic in supply, *ceteris paribus*, than currencies of small continental countries (see p. 158).
29. Indeed, this quality of gold or foreign currency of offering income contingent on defeat in war led Friedman to advocate that central banks should sell foreign currency to defend their own currency during a war crisis (see M. Friedman, 'The Case for Flexible Exchange Rates' in *Essays in Positive Economics* (University of Chicago) pp. 157–203).
30. Indeed, all state-variables which take values that can be identified as a bad or good general state (see Chapter 1) are aggregative rather than distributive in form.
31. See Chapter 1, p. 4.
32. See Chapter 1, p. 3.
33. For a full analysis of reasons for non-existence of many types of insurance, see K.J. Arrow, *Essay in Theory of Risk-Bearing* (North Holland, 1974) Chapter 5.

3 The Rentier on the Defensive

A rentier is a passive investor who lives on the earnings from capital. His entire income is derived from assets on which the income yields are outside his control. Examples include equities, bank deposits, and other securities. Real estate is also a favourite investment with rentiers, although its income derived depends to some extent on the efficiency of estate management. The straight rentier, as distinct from the trader or financier, does not attempt to make speculative profit from trading opportunities in the market.

The rentier does not earn a wage in the labour market, nor does he generate self-employed income from entrepreneurship. This feature has caused some political economists to deride the rentier class. Keynes, in *The General Theory*, welcomed the heralded 'euthanasia of the rentier'. It is not the purpose here, however, to enter into diatribes about the normative justice or injustice of the distribution of income. Such arguments are based inevitably on a mixture of emotional and personal circumstance. Rather, the subject to be explored is how the rentier should safeguard his portfolio against the risks to which it is exposed.

Exposure of the Rentier to Income Redistribution Risks

Being entirely dependent on non-labour sources of income, the rentier is exposed acutely to the risk that the distribution of income will change in favour of labour. The rate of profit (and the expected real rate of interest) is more sensitive than the real wage-rate to the course of the business cycle. Secularly, capital's greater exposure than labour's to income-distribution risk arises out of the smaller share of earnings from capital than from labour in national incomes. A transfer of x per cent of national income from capital to labour (due, for example, to an increased supply of capital relative to labour) has a much smaller proportionate effect on the real wage rate than on the rate of profit.

Exposure of the rentier to income redistribution risks (and to other risks to be discussed in subsequent sections) depends on whether the rentier expects to be a transitory or permanent member of the rentier class. In order to understand this distinction, it is helpful to identify the principal motives behind the holding and accumulation of wealth.

First, individuals build up their own pension fund, which will provide earnings later on in life when their labour earnings will have dwindled. They may insure the fund, by buying annuities from an insurance company, against the risk of their life-span exceeding normal expectations.

Second, individuals save to provide legacies for their children. Some portion of an investor's portfolio may be identified as a 'legacy fund'. The accumulation of this fund may be insured against the risk of early death, although 'moral hazard' problems described below limit the scope of many other types of insurance.

Third, the saver may have as one purpose the building-up of a 'nest-egg'. As we saw in the previous chapter, many types of personal state-variables are uninsurable – due to the problems of transaction costs and moral hazards. To some extent, therefore, individuals insure themselves by setting savings aside into a nest-egg, from which funds are drawn when the personal state-variable takes specified bad values.

Fourth, part of a portfolio may be identified as a 'working-life income fund' – a fund which provides income for the investor in the period prior to normal retirement age.

The *permanent rentier* intends to live from the gradual run-down of the 'working-life income fund', whilst earning sufficient return on the other three funds to maintain (or provide) an adequate pension fund, a nest-egg which is 'comfortable' in size for both him and his dependants, and a legacy of sufficient size that his inheritors will receive funds of similar real size (including a working-life income fund) to funds he owned at the same age. Thus, the second and third funds must yield sufficient cumulative income to replace the initial setting-up of the 'working-life income fund' and the 'pension fund'.

The *transitory rentier*, in contrast to the permanent rentier, does not see his basic task as the generation of new savings to replace those which he sets aside into his 'working-life income fund' and 'pension fund'. Instead, a prime motive for his saving during working-life is often the building up of a personal pension fund, which is then consumed in retirement. The retired person living in large part from earlier savings fits the definition of rentier, but he and his family are transitory rather than permanent members of the rentier class.

The permanent rentier, being concerned with the accumulation of wealth out of the earnings of capital, and the provision of personal income over a long period of time, is particularly exposed to the risk of the rate of return to capital falling. The transitory rentier, whose aim is to provide for consumption in his post-retirement lifetime out of the run-down of wealth, is less exposed to that risk. For example, a transitory rentier with a 10-year life expectancy and personal pension-fund of $200,000 will find his expected annual income less sensitive to the rate of return to capital than the annual income of the permanent rentier with a 40-year life expectancy who inherits $10 million, which he wishes to pass on intact to his heirs.

An 'income-redistribution' hedge is an asset which gains in value when the state-variable 'share of labour in national income' rises in value. We saw in Chapter 1 that such assets are likely to command a premium as those with large purchasing power in the contingent-income market would be anxious to buy income contingent on a state where capital suffered at the expense of labour.

In practice, hedges against income redistribution must take the form of assets which are especially popular with labour or of equities in enterprises whose product is sold principally to those who stand to gain from income redistribution in favour of labour. Residential property designed for middle or low-income occupants is one such hedge asset. Another example is equities in retail stores selling to the non-luxury market and shop rents in locations where such stores are concentrated.

The state-variable of income redistribution must be specified in terms of country of reference – for example, the distribution of income in the USA. The values of the state-variables 'distribution of income in country A' and 'distribution of income in country B' are likely to be positively correlated, but not perfectly. Thus, in advanced economies, the share of labour has risen everywhere, but by significantly different amounts, since the turn of the century. By spreading his investments between different economies, the rentier can reduce his exposure to the risk of income redistribution.

Income redistribution can be brought about by tax changes in the country of residence of the investor rather than by any change in pre-tax factor incomes. For example, the Government of country A may increase taxes on capital and reduce taxes on labour. The rentier will be anxious to obtain income contingent on such tax-redistributive policies being put into effect. International diversification will again provide some protection in so far as tax-policies do not change identically in each country at all times, and investors can place funds outside the reach of their own tax jurisdiction. Even so, rentiers are likely to have a substantial proportion of their portfolio within their own political and tax jurisdiction. Hedges against tax-induced income redistribution in their own country are likely to command substantial premiums.

To understand the type of assets which become tax hedges against income redistribution, allusion must be made to the concept of tax arbitrage. In a given tax jurisdiction A, both individuals and assets are ranked into distinct tax brackets. Individuals are commonly ranked into successively higher tax brackets according to their level of income. Assets are ranked into tax brackets in part according to ease of deriving tax therefrom and in part arbitrarily. Thus assets whose income is derived in kind rather than in cash (for example, collectables and housing) fall into very low tax brackets. Assets whose income is largely in the form of capital gain, which is infrequently realised, are similarly taxed at a favourable rate. Assets whose income is entirely paid in cash (e.g. bank deposits) fall into the highest tax bracket. Examples of arbitrary distribution of assets between tax brackets include the exemption from tax of pension-fund and life-assurance assets.

Tax brackets of assets are identified by the proportion of their income which is added to the tax payer's taxable income on which the tax rate of the tax bracket to which he belongs (at the margin) applies. In general, assets in different tax brackets are priced so that high tax-bracket assets appeal predominantly to low tax-bracket investors whilst low tax-bracket assets are bought principally by high tax-bracket investors.

Now if tax brackets for investors' income became more progressive, then the yield on low tax-bracket investments would fall; investors up-graded into a higher tax bracket would be sellers of high tax-bracket investments and buyers of low tax-bracket investments at unchanged yields. Equivalently, high tax-bracket investments would fall in price relative to low tax-bracket investments. Investors can thereby obtain a hedge against a tax-induced redistribution of income by buying assets in a low tax bracket: for in the event of tax changes in a progressive direction, such assets would produce a bonus income in the form of capital gain. Similarly, by issuing liabilities in the form of high tax-bracket securities, the investor obtains income contingent on a switch of tax policy towards more progression.[1] The best hedges against tax-induced income redistribution in country A are those whose price is very sensitive to movement of the state-variable tax-progression in country A, and very insensitive to other state-variables. Thus a low-coupon short-maturity bond is a better tax hedge than an equity with a low dividend yield or a collectable.

An alternative hedge against the state-variable 'tax progression in country A' taking a bad value is the purchase of real estate in the most popular tax haven for residents of country A. Thus property in the Channel Islands for the British resident, and property in Andorra for the French resident, are tax hedges – albeit impure. In the aftermath of a Socialist Government coming to power in France, it could be expected that Andorran property would gain in value. The affluent rentier, by holding residential property investment in the tax haven, obtains income contingent on a progressive change in the tax regime of his own country. Some tax-havens do not have a national catchment area, but attract the wealthy rentier from a wide selection of tax jurisdictions. Real estate, in such tax havens with universal appeal, is a hedge against some type of weighted average of state-variables 'tax-progression in country x_i' (for $i = 1$ to N, where there are N large economies) taking a bad value. The weights will be particularly large for very large and rich economies, especially those which are close geographically. Thus Monte Carlo is a tax haven with a universal appeal based on climatic and scenic features, for which tax-rates in the nearby countries of France, Germany, and Italy have especial relevance to real-estate prices. The Channel Islands, in contrast, are not naturally attractive and their clientele is predominantly British, who derive convenience yield from being close to home.

Tax havens may be ranked for each investor according to their benefits in kind, including natural facilities and closeness to country of origin. Those with the largest incomes will gravitate to those offering the greatest natural facilities (e.g. Monte Carlo): far-off islands and towns in the middle of mountain ranges tend to be relevant tax havens for the rentiers with smaller incomes.

Real estate in a universal appeal tax haven is not the only example of a hedge against an increase in the rate of tax progression, on average, in major OECD economies. Non-luxury collectables, such as consumer-durables and housing, are low tax-bracket investments in many different tax jurisdictions. However, they are very impure hedges against increased tax progression given the number of other state-variables to which their prices are sensitive.

The Rentier's Exposure to a Vanishing of Investment Opportunity

From the age of Ricardo and the Classical economists onwards, the idea of an over-abundance of capital and dwindling of new investment opportunities can be found scattered across the economics literature. The idea became popularised beyond the confines of academia.[2] In the twentieth century, the notion was picked up by Hansen and Keynes. These economists believed, with the world fully discovered, markets opened up, and slowing population growth, investment opportunities were vanishing. Hence, if full employment was to be maintained, then real interest rates would have to fall to zero. In consequence, Keynes foresaw

> enormous social changes resulting from a gradual disappearance of a rate of return on accumulated wealth. A man would still be free to accumulate his earned income with a view to spending it at a later date. But his accumulation would not grow. He would simply be in the position of Pope's father, who when he retired from business, carried a chest of guineas with him to his villa and met his household expenses from it as required.[3]

It is possible, in principle, to conceive of a world where the equilibrium real rate of interest would be negative. The reader who doubts this should refer himself to Fisher's example of sailors stranded on a desert island[4] whose only resource is a given fixed stock of figs. The figs remain palatable indefinitely, but there is no way of preventing rats from eating one quarter of the stores each year. Then for every four 'real' dollars saved this year, only three are available next year: the real rate of return to capital is −25 per cent.

The existence of a fiat money would not prevent the emergence of a negative real interest rate in Fisher's example. For a given nominal stock of fiat money, the price per fig, as their supply diminishes, would rise. Thus, fiat money which bore no interest would itself yield a negative real return of −25 per cent.

Similarly, in a more complex economy, again with a fixed nominal stock of money, a negative real interest rate could emerge. A vanishing of investment opportunity and fall in the real rate of profit available would lead to an increased demand for money (assumed to be in non-interest-bearing fiat form) and a decreased demand for enterprises' trading assets (and hence for goods which are inputs into investment projects). Thus the increased demand for real money balances would be satisfied by an immediate fall in the price level. However, the gradual erosion in private real wealth due to the prevailing negative real rates of return would reduce the demand for real money balances. Hence the rational investor would expect the price level to rise: this expectation would cause fiat money to yield a negative real return.[5]

In an inflationary context, where money supply expands at a higher rate than the equilibrium demand for real money balances, then money is no obstacle to the emergence of negative real interest rates. A vanishing of investment opportunities would lead simply to a fall in nominal interest rates relative to the inflation rate.

In only one type of model economy would the emergence of a negative real interest rate be impossible. This would be where all goods could be exchanged at zero transaction costs, could be stored at zero cost, were subject to zero risk of obsolescence and to zero relative price risk, and did not deteriorate with age. Then each investor by holding a store of goods would, in effect, own a riskless asset of zero real return. If, therefore, the rate of return on physical investment fell to low levels, there would be a surge in demand for consumer goods (riskless securities). The riskless real rate of interest could not fall below zero. The model economy described is, of course, a moneyless economy; money would serve no purpose better than would the direct ownership of inventories of consumer goods.

Let us return to the monetary economy, where the rentier must be aware of the risk that the real rate of return can fall to negative levels. What would realities in which investment opportunity had vanished be like? Would they be strange, like in Alice's adventures in the *Through the Looking Glass*, or would they bear great resemblance to the realities with the positive real rate of return?

Low or negative real interest rates would influence the physical and social landscape in the following respects.

First, the existing building stock would be replaced at an accelerated rate, and by buildings which had a much longer duration. Thus, over the long run, the average age of the building stock would increase. Further, the stock and quality of residential building would increase; for a fall in the real interest rate to low or negative levels would reduce the value of present in terms of future income. Reconstruction of a present old building which promised a given reduction in maintenance costs and improved (more up-to-date) facilities over a long period of time would become more attractive. Further, in choosing between a long-life and short-life reconstruction, the low interest rate would tend to make the investor favour the former given the greater valuation of far distant cost savings. After the old buildings were gradually replaced by the new generation of long-life buildings, the rate of replacement would fall far below its previous level, and the average age of the building stock would increase. Lastly, the vanishing of investment opportunity would not impact directly on the level of house rents, and so a fall in interest rates, by causing house prices to increase, would stimulate an expansion of physical investment in housing stock. In time, the increased supply of housing would be accompanied by a falling level of house rent. The above comments about buildings may be extended to other consumer durables. Automobiles and washing machines, for example, would be replaced at an accelerated pace by a new generation of longer-life equipment. In the long-run the average age of these items at any time would increase.

Second, in the area of agricultural investment, the optimum maturity of certain types of assets would increase. For example, a favourite problem in the theory of finance is when to cut down a forest to sell for timber.[6] The timber value of the forest grows at an increasing rate, at first, with maturity; then at a decreasing rate, and finally beyond a far-distant maturity, the timber value begins to fall. The optimum maturity – that is the optimum lifetime for the forest, at the end of which it should be cut down for timber – is that for which the present value of the proceeds, at the given interest rate, is a maximum. That optimum life is shown, in the literature, to increase as the given interest rate level is lowered. More esoteric examples than the forest would include the maturity of wine and of cheese (for example, Roquefort). At low or negative real interest rates, a greater proportion of wine would be held to mature into vintage wine, and the proportion of quality vintage cheeses should increase.

Third, investment in human capital would be likely to increase in intensity. So long as the vanishing of investment opportunities were not accompanied by a large drop in the prospective differential earning advantage of trained (skilled) labour over unskilled labour, then a low or negative real interest rate would encourage labour to invest in itself, given the increased valuation of future income returns.

Fourth, conspicuous consumption by the wealthy would increase. Given the decrease in the rate of return on physical investment projects, the attractions of purchasing consumer-durables would increase. Collectables – for example Persian rugs, master paintings, fine porcelain, antiques – would become a popular investment with the wealthy as their yield (including returns in the form of aesthetic enjoyment) would look relatively attractive, especially as these returns continue over very long periods of time (indeed centuries), and a lowering of interest rates increases the valuation of far-off income enjoyment. Given that the supply of collectables is price-inelastic (indeed, the supply of certain antiques may be fixed), their prices would be sharply higher in a low-return world.

Fifth, the rentier class would become decadent (i.e. unable to reproduce itself). With a zero or negative real rate of return, the rentier would not be able to replace, out of earnings from capital, the 'working-life income fund' which he subtracted from his initial endowment. Further, the size of 'working-life income fund' drawn to provide a given size of annual income would increase. This inability to replace consumed capital could in turn lead to rentiers having smaller families, in order to spread their diminished residual wealth less widely.

Sixth, the life-time pattern of saving and consumption would tend to change. It would be most efficient for wage-earners to build up their pension fund (out of which they would draw capital during their retirement to supplement what other pensions they may enjoy) in the years immediately before retirement, rather than spacing over a lifetime saving towards pension provision. For savings made at the age of 30 would contribute much less than the same real saving made at age 58 to the value of an accumulated pension fund at age 60. Similarly, it would be more efficient to save late rather than early in working-life towards providing a legacy. In a world with a negative or low real rate of interest, we would thus expect to witness the young 'living it up' whilst the near-retirement worker would be saving very hard.

Seventh, self-insurance against personal state-variables taking bad values – the provision of a nest-egg fund – would become more difficult. A nest-egg fund is aimed to provide income contingent on a wide spectrum of time-states, many of which are far into the future. Yet a low or negative real interest rate makes the securing of income in far-distant states especially expensive.

In summary, an age of negative real interest rates and vanished investment opportunities would be marked by the features of a building stock which was old and of long prospective life; old, but long-life, automobiles and other equipment; cheap house-rents and thereby spacious living; aged forests and a good supply of vintage wines and cheeses; a large supply of educated labour and widespread postgraduate training; conspicuous consumption by the wealthy; a widespread interest in collecting 'objets d'art' and a particularly high valuation being put on these; a decadent rentier class, which had low fertility and had become successively poorer in each generation; high-spending by the young in the population, with the 50 to 60-year-olds living frugally and saving hard – hence consumer products would be largely tailored to the tastes of the young; there would be a widespread feeling of insecurity due to the difficulty of providing for personal disasters which may occur in the far-distant future.

The rentier may buy income contingent on a vanishing of investment opportunity in several ways, some of which may be deduced from the above summary of what a world with a negative real interest rate would be like, and the nature of consumer taste there. For example, collectables suggest themselves as a hedge against a vanishing of investment opportunity; their potential for yielding aesthetic pleasure is not sensitive to those factors which influence the secular rate of return on industrial capital, and so their price would be relatively high in possible realities where the rate of profitability were low.

Given the expansion of the building stock associated with the vanishing of investment opportunity, land should be a good hedge against such an eventuality. Further, if increasing long-run marginal costs apply in the construction industry, then existing buildings themselves (exclusive of the land element) should gain in value in the aftermath of the change in investment climate.

If the fall in the real rate of return on investment originates in diminished investment opportunities in the commercial and industrial sector, not in the agricultural sector (for example, there may be no decline in the fertility of the soil, accompanied by a decline in technological progress in industry and commerce) then agricultural land should perform strongly in price to bring its yield into line with sunken yields elsewhere. In modern advanced economies it is the investment opportunities in industry rather than in agriculture which are the dominant influence on the overall rate of return to be earned on capital. Thus, if there is little reason to expect investment opportunities in agriculture to be highly correlated with those in industry, then agricultural land should offer an expected positive income contingent on the transition from a reality with abundant industrial investment opportunities to one with few such opportunities.

The increased level of conspicuous consumption, and consumption of long-life high-quality durables, should favour business enterprises specialising in the sale of such items. Equities in these enterprises should provide income contingent on a change in investment opportunities in aggregate. However, these equities are also very sensitive in value to tax-induced changes in the distribution of income, and this counts against them as hedge assets.

Whether equities themselves provide a hedge against decreased investment opportunity turns on whether the anticipated profitability of projects already entered into is simultaneously downgraded. If not, then equities in corporations which already have many projects on-stream, stretching over many years, would gain in price from the diminished supply of new projects offering similar returns to investors.

Bonds with very long maturities and a fixed coupon should show often a handsome gain as the transition is made to a world with low or negative real rates of interest. In practice, in a high-inflation world with high nominal coupons, the effective maturity of bonds is short, and their inflation risk high – they are very impure hedges.[7]

In summary, the rentier should be especially interested in investments in land (in commercial and residential areas), in agriculture, in housing, in collectables, in long-term fixed-rate bonds and equities of enterprises which have entered into a core of highly profitable long-term investment projects. However, all these investments are very impure hedges against a diminishing or vanishing of investment opportunity, as they are also sensitive to many other state-variables, and often to a greater degree.

The Rentier's Exposure to the Risks of Inflation and Social Revolution

The rentier has typically a significant proportion of his portfolio invested in bonds and deposits. This phenomenon is due in part to the function of bonds as a hedge against slump (a reality in which the rentier suffers particularly hard due to the fall in the share of profit in national income), and against the vanishing of investment opportunity. Further, the 'permanent' rentier is typically very wealthy – and it follows from certain necessary properties of individual utility functions that the wealthy should be expected to hold a larger share of their portfolio in low-risk assets than do the less wealthy.[8] Low-risk assets take the principal forms of bank deposits and government bonds.

Even a large proportion of the rentier's so-called real assets can become casualties of high inflation or hyperinflation, as any reader of the histories of the great inflations in central Europe after World War I, will realize. For example, Bresciani-Turroni[9] recounts how during the German hyperinflation small groups of large shareholders took advantage of financial chaos to push through capital reconstruction schemes that robbed the smaller shareholder. The rentier, who was not in the position of having a controlling interest in any corporation, suffered. Investments in real estate where the tenant had a long lease fixed in nominal terms became next to worthless.

Unlike the wage-earner, the rentier does not possess an endowment of non-marketable wealth (human capital) which is well protected against inflation. Labour contracts, unlike financial contracts (for example, between borrower and lender), are rarely enforceable with respect to both parties. If inflation suddenly takes off, labour unions would normally insist on the breaking of long-term wage agreements which had not provided for frequent adjustment to inflation of the wage rate. In contrast, a landlord who had leased a building at a fixed rate for three years, or a lender of money at a fixed rate for five years, has no legal right in practice or in principle to re-negotiate the terms of his contract should inflation accelerate to unexpectedly high levels.[10]

The greater violability of property rights over physical and financial capital (of which the rentier's wealth wholly consists), than of those over human capital or labour services, exposes the rentier to an especially high degree to the risk of social and political change. Gold stands out, together with certain collectables (including stamps), as an asset whose realisable value for the present owner is not dependent on a set of property rights established in law. Such assets thus lose value to a lesser extent than do most others in the transition to a society where private property rights are abrogated. Their residual value (that is, the income potential which their owner would enjoy in an otherwise property-less society) is highly valued – especially by rentiers.[11]

Rentier Survival in a Petro-economy

Since the revolution in the pricing of oil in 1973, the proportion of domestic energy consumption which is satisfied by indigenous production – and how this ratio changes over time – has had significant implications for macroeconomic variables in each country. It can be shown that residents of an economy with growing oil revenues (due either to a rising volume of energy production or to a continuing rise in the real price of energy) should tend to enjoy an exceptionally low real rate of return on capital (where real rates are measured with respect to domestic purchasing power).

Consider such an energy-rich economy. Growing oil revenues, *per se*, cause the equilibrium relative price of traded to non-traded goods to tend downwards.[12] For if the country's balance of payments is to remain in equilibrium, a growing source of one type of traded goods production (here in the form of indigenous energy supplies) must be matched by a contraction of production of other types and a switch in consumption patterns in favour of traded goods (and away from non-traded goods). The relative price change plays an essential role in this adjustment.

Today's exchange rate reacts not just to changes in the present level of energy revenues but is a function also of their expected level in the future. If the revenues were expected to rise, then speculators would bid up the spot price of the currency realising that its future exchange rate must be at a premium over purchasing power parity such that the relative price of traded and non-traded goods is consistent with long-run balance of payments equilibrium. This uplift of the spot exchange rate, due to speculators anticipating adjustment in the structure of the country's trade necessary to the maintenance of balance of payments equilibrium, has economic impact in the present.

The anticipatory movement of the exchange rate leads to a deterioration in the petro-economy's non-energy trade before the improvement in its energy balance actually occurs. The implied short-term deterioration in the overall current account is a source of speculative holdings of the petro-money. The exchange rate appreciation depresses aggregate demand in the petro-economy, as the non-traded goods sector suffers from a loss of custom, and shrinking profit margins in the traded goods sector hurt investment activity there. Thus, if full employment is to be maintained during the period (often of several years) when the exchange rate has risen in anticipation of a far-off energy revenue bonanza, some offsetting stimulus must be present.[13]

One stimulus could be provided by an increased propensity to spend by residents of the petro-economy, who realise that the present value of future tax savings that will result from increased oil revenues has added to their wealth. But such discounting of future tax savings is likely to be very imperfect. In the absence of explicit stimulation by budgetary means (increased government expenditure or reduced taxation), the real rate of interest must fall to maintain a level of economic activity consistent with full employment. In turn, the lowering of the real interest rate relative to the world average limits the advance of the spot exchange rate and the amount of deflationary influence to be offset.

Thus the rentier in the petro-economy with prospective rising net energy revenues is likely to find that the real rate of return on investments becomes depressed. Indeed, he will wish to hedge against a steepening of the time-profile of energy revenues – due either to the expected rate of energy price rises increasing or to unexpected success in domestic oil (and other energy) exploration – which would lead to the current real rate of return falling further. By buying energy-crisis hedges – purchasing, for example, oil equities or gold – he can hedge a fall in the real rate of return induced by a steepening in prospective energy price rises.

Hedging a fall in the real rate of return due to successful exploration in the rentier's country of residence (Ruritania) may be effected by buying equities in oil corporations with particularly heavy exposure to projects in Ruritania. Alternatively, the rentier may borrow a foreign money and take a long position in the Ruritanian money (crowns), expecting to make an exchange profit in the event of new energy finds. The 'traditional' hedges against a vanishing of investment opportunity – domestic real estate, in particular – should be represented highly in the portfolios of Ruritanian rentiers: for the energy base of Ruritania increases the exposure of its rentiers to the risks of a fall in the real rate of return.

As we have seen, diversification internationally provides the rentier with hedges against domestic political change, and unexpected acceleration of domestic inflation. But the Ruritanian rentier, by investing in international monies (which are most often not petro-monies) exposes himself to both a high degree of real exchange risk and a large loss in the event of an energy crisis or of a steepening of the expected growth of energy revenues in Ruritania.

The Ruritanian crown's real exchange rate is likely to be more volatile than that of energy-neutral monies due to the importance to the former's value of conditions in the energy market and to the greater price-volatility of hedge-investments than of neutral or fairweather ones.[14] The Ruritanian faces an especially unfavourable trade-off between reducing inflation risk by diversifying into low-inflation international monies and assumption of real exchange rate risk. If an energy-crisis were to occur, the Ruritanian would find that the value of his portfolio of international monies would slump in terms of purchasing power inside Ruritania (due to the importance of non-traded Ruritanian goods in his shopping basket); in contrast, the resident of a non-petro-economy would find that the value of the international portfolio fell in real domestic value by only the price-level rise attributable to the energy price rise.[15] Further, by investing in an international money portfolio, the Ruritanian rentier would suffer a loss if prospective energy revenues in Ruritania increased due to successful new exploration or due to greater pessimism (from the viewpoint of consumers) about the price of energy in the future – events which would be accompanied by a fall in the real rate of return on investment, and where the rentier could ill afford a loss.

Yet there are strong motives in favour of international diversification for even the Ruritanian rentier. He must, however, be careful to offset his resulting increased exposure to the risk of vanishing investment opportunity[16] or of energy crisis. He may do this by increasing even further holdings of gold and oil equities, especially those in corporations whose stakes in Ruritania represent a large share in their assets.

The rentier, finding his real rate of return to investments squeezed due to the prospect of strongly rising national energy revenues, can gain relief by switching his consumption as much as possible to internationally traded goods and even by ultimately emigrating. It is the steadily rising price of non-traded in terms of traded goods in Ruritania that erodes the real rate of return from the viewpoint of Ruritanians; because the nominal interest rate on crowns equals that on any other currency (say, dollars) plus a margin equal to the expected differential rate of inflation of internationally traded goods when measured in crowns rather than in dollars. But the margin by which the rate of inflation (in crowns) of non-traded goods in Ruritania exceeds that of non-traded goods in the USA (the issuer of dollars) will be greater than the similar margin for traded goods.

Scope for switching consumption from traded to non-traded goods is, however, limited. Common forms of non-traded goods consumption – for example, house rent, transport services, and public goods – are not easily replaced by foreign goods. Instead, to improve substantially the real rate of return obtainable, the rentier could emigrate to a country of residence which was not rich in energy, and so look forward to a lower rate of inflation on non-traded goods consumption there relative to the nominal rate of return on his portfolio.

Emigration would become a realistic option only when the price of non-traded goods in the particular energy economy, Ruritania, had risen above that in the new potential home country. If, before the oil bonanza, Ruritania had been a poor country, with the price of non-traded goods there being very cheap by international comparison, then emigration would not usually become attractive unless the bonanza were huge. As a tendency, the rentier should emigrate from petro-economies to energy-poor economies. A petro-economy does not provide a kind environment for the rentier.

In practice, in the post-1973 age, there has been an observable pattern of rentier emigration from energy-rich economies to energy-poor economies whose national currency appeared cheap relative to most measures of purchasing power parity. In the mid-1970s oil-rich Arabs flocked to London, attracted by the very cheap pound of that time, and pushed from their own countries by the very high rate of inflation of non-traded goods there (in particular, of residential property). By the late 1970s, when the pound had 'taken off' as a petro-money, Arab rentiers moved on in large numbers to the USA, where growing dissatisfaction with US energy policy – amongst other concerns – had led to the dollar weakening and non-traded goods in the USA being cheap by international comparison.

It is still too early to tell whether the pound's petro-status and the prospect of the equilibrium real rate of return on investments in terms of UK purchasing power being far below the OECD average will set off a wave of rentier emigration from the UK. In 1979/80 real interest rates were held at very high levels as part of the British Government's policy of deflation, and so the dilemma of the rentier in a petro-economy was postponed. One factor which has restrained rentier emigration from Britain has been her relative poverty compared to that of other major OECD economies, and so the level of non-traded goods prices started from a base in the mid-1970s that was low by international comparison.

The Public Rentier

In addition to the private rentier, it is possible to identify rentiers in collective form. Examples include the rentier-nations – foremost amongst which are the low-absorbing countries in OPEC.[17] The OPEC rentier-nation lives from the rental income on oil currently produced (the so-called OPEC 'oil tax') and on income from accumulated financial investments. Its principal assets fall into two categories – financial investments and oil under the ground.

As rentiers, OPEC nations are very sensitive to the risk of vanishing of investment opportunity in the world. If the real rate of interest and the rate of profit were to fall to low or negative levels, then each OPEC state would see advantage in reducing the rate of depletion of oil under the ground, on which the rate of return relative to that on other assets would have become even more attractive. Collectively, the reduction in the rate of production by OPEC would cause the price of oil to surge and for their revenues to balloon – so inelastic is the demand for oil. In turn, increased OPEC revenues from oil tax, matched by decreased real incomes in the oil-consuming world, would increase the supply of savings in the world economy – given OPEC's higher marginal propensity to save out of income than the oil-consuming world's.

Thus, it is possible that the world supply of savings could be a decreasing function of the rate of profit (or real rate of interest); although savings for each individual may be a rising function of interest rates for given income, the distribution of income between OPEC and oil consumers is itself a function of interest rates. A fall in interest rates can have a greater influence on world savings through the channel of income distribution than in the opposite direction through individual incentive to save.

Indeed, if the distributional consequences for OPEC and oil consumers were very great, the world supply of savings, for given non-oil output, may be more elastic (in a negative direction) with respect to interest rates than would be the demand for capital. This possiblity is illustrated in Figure 3.1, where SS is the world savings schedule, for a given level of non-oil output, II is the marginal efficiency of investment (demand for capital) schedule, and r is the real rate of interest. A diminishing of investment opportunity is illustrated by II shifting to the left to II′: for any given cut-off rate of profit there are now fewer acceptable projects. The intersection point of II′ with the saving schedule is at a higher real rate of interest than previously. Thus it is possible that a diminishing of investment opportunity, in a world where OPEC oil revenues are a large proportion of world income, and where OPEC's marginal propensity to save out of income is considerably higher than for oil-consumers, could call for a raising of interest rates if full employment in the world economy is to be maintained. The raising of interest rates would cause each OPEC state, acting individually, to wish to increase oil output. The aggregate increase in output would cause aggregate oil revenues to fall sharply and world savings to decrease which would balance the decrease in overall investment opportunity.

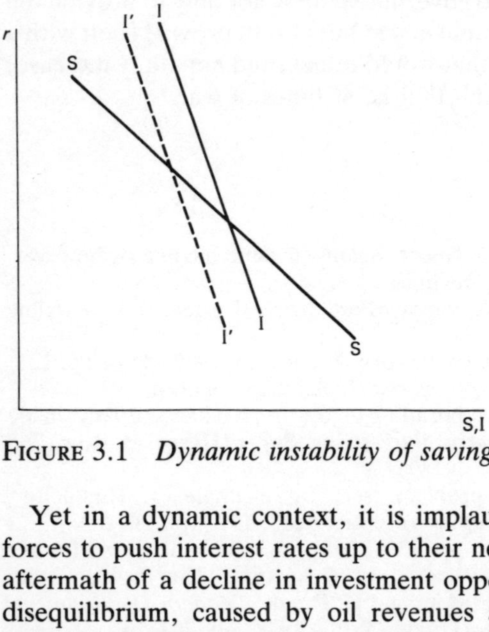

FIGURE 3.1 *Dynamic instability of saving due to OPEC*

Yet in a dynamic context, it is implausible that there would be forces to push interest rates up to their new equilibrium level in the aftermath of a decline in investment opportunity. Instead, dynamic disequilibrium, caused by oil revenues and savings ballooning as interest rates fell yet further, would be likely.

Other examples of the public rentier include a nation which derives significant investment earnings from abroad as a proportion of national income. Britain, in the nineteenth century and up to 1914 was a rentier nation. In the contemporary world, the USA and Switzerland are important rentier nations. It should be expected that rentier nations would have a strong interest in the preservation of international peace. In a state of war they would be cut off from important foreign income. Further, because war and the rundown of foreign investments would force particularly severe adjustment on the rentier nation, its official international reserves should be heavily directed to war-hedges, notably gold.

Official international reserves are, in part, a form of communal hedge investment. Many small savers cannot afford, given high transaction costs, to buy hedges against energy catastrophe, war, deterioration in the national terms of trade, and many other bad realities. Yet by holding reserves, the government would be able to provide its citizens with extra income in these bad realities by financing the concomitant trade deficit through running down international reserves. Further, the state itself would be a large importer in times of war, and its demand for reserves would grow sharply. By investing in hedge-assets the government aims not only to provide the small investor with a communal hedge but also to provide itself with a stock of means of payment that would retain (and hopefully increase) its value when most needed – that is, at times of war.

Notes and References

1. The offsetting of interest payments against taxable income is, however, strictly limited in most tax-regimes.
2. See, for example, Chekov's Ivanov where the rentier bemoans the falling return on capital.
3. See J. M. Keynes, *The General Theory* (Macmillan, 1965 edition) p. 221.
4. See I. Fisher, *The Theory of Interest* (Macmillan, 1930) p. 191.
5. This account is a slight elaboration of the 'real balance effect' made famous by Patinkin in *Money, Interest and Prices* (Harper & Row, 2nd edition, 1965) Part 1.
6. For an account of this problem, see, for example, J. Hirshleifer, *Investment, Interest and Capital* (Prentice-Hall, 1970) pp. 82–5.
7. For elaboration, see Part 2, pp. 131–2, of present volume. For a further treatment of the concept, see S. M. Schaeffer, 'The Problem with Redemption Yields', in J. Lorie, and R. Brealey *Modern Developments in Investment Management* (Dryden Press, 1978) pp. 702–26.
8. See K. J. Arrow, *Essays in the Theory of Risk-bearing* (North Holland, 1974) pp. 99–105. Low risk is defined here in terms of the asset's contribution to the volatility of the portfolio's returns. The proposition here does not conflict with that in the next chapter, where small savers are found to place a larger share of their portfolio in hedge assets than do large savers.
9. See Bresciani-Turroni, *The Economics of Inflation* (Kelley, 1968) pp. 253–85.
10. There are, though, historical incidences of renegotiation. In the final phase of the German hyperinflation and its aftermath, German courts sanctioned claims in equity that nominal contracts should be revalued. See Bresciani-Turroni, pp. 320–3.
11. Collectables' real value is reduced in the transition, for no longer would

there be a wealthy class to buy them. But the rate of reduction is less than for other assets, and so they enjoy a premium valuation.

12. Goods may be divided into two basic categories: traded and non-traded. The former, due to low transport costs, enjoy an international market in each part of which the price must be similar. The latter enjoy a domestic market only and sell for potentially very different prices in different countries.
13. If the increased oil revenues had only a small rent-content, and were mainly matched by exploitation and exploration costs, then the influence on the exchange rate may be small, and its depressing effect on economic activity offset by increased demand for goods and services by the energy sector. This discussion is implicitly about prospective revenues in net terms.
14. This proposition is proved rigorously in Chapter 8.
15. Thus if a 50 per cent rise in the energy price fed through to a 2½ per cent rise in the overall price-level in most non-oil OECD economies, then the portfolio would fall in real domestic terms by around 2½ per cent.
16. Due to increased prospective oil revenues and hence depression of domestic real interest rates.
17. A low-absorbing OPEC nation is one for which oil represents almost 100 per cent of export revenues, and for which the propensity to spend out of revenues is low: thus it has huge holdings of investments accumulated out of surplus revenues.

4 Little Saver, What Now?

The little saver is handicapped typically in two major respects. First, transaction costs bear on him particularly heavily: in most markets these fall (in per unit value terms) as the size of transactions increases. Second, the greater part of his wealth is likely to be held in non-marketable or very illiquid assets – principally in the form of human capital and residential investment. In short, the little saver is in a mesh, from which the escape has to be mainly through enlargement of wealth.

The predicament of the small saver can become particularly acute at times of economic shock.[1] In the aftermath of the shock, investment is likely to be redirected from enterprises specialising in one type of economic activity to those specialising in others more suited to changed circumstances. The necessary portfolio reconstruction imposes more costs on the little than on the large saver. Where the shock is institutional or monetary – for example, a change in tax rulings or a change in the long-run inflation rate expected – existing financial instruments (for example, securities) can become obsolete in form. In an age of rapid institutional change and repeated monetary shocks, a tendency should be expected for the maturity of financial instruments to shorten, so reducing the risks of obsolescence. But as we shall see below, it is the small saver who is especially penalised by a shortening of maturities.

Transaction costs, expressed in annual equivalent terms over the life of the instrument, tend to be lower for long-maturity than for short-maturity instruments. Further, the rate at which transaction costs (in annual terms) fall with maturity is similar whether large or small transactions are being considered. But as transaction costs 'eat up' a larger proportion of the real returns on the small saver's than on the large saver's portfolio, their similar rate of decline (in percentage terms) with maturity has greatest significance for the little saver.

For example, consider an investment in a 1-year Euro-dollar deposit and compare it with another in a 5-year Euro-dollar bond. Assume that both have an expected real annual rate of return (prior to transaction costs) of 1 per cent per annum. As an illustration the annual equivalent transaction costs for the large investor in buying the deposit and bond respectively could be 12½ and 10 per cent of the expected annual real return (corresponding approximately to ⅛ and ½ per cent of the initial capital sum). The smaller investor could face annual equivalent costs of 50 and 40 per cent of the expected annual real return (corresponding approximately to ½ and 2 per cent of the initial capital sum). Thus by extending the maturity of investment from 1 year to 5 years, the small saver obtains a 20 per cent increase in annual net real yield, whilst the large saver obtains only a 2.77 per cent increase.

As we saw in Chapter 2, the breakdown of the international gold standard and subsequently of the gold-dollar exchange standard has made hedge investment more hazardous. Today the investor must construct a portfolio of impure hedges to protect himself against a major disaster such as war, US hyperinflation, or world slump. In the gold standard era, a holding of gold would have been a far less impure hedge than it is today against war or US hyperinflation, and fixed-rate bonds would have been a less impure world-slump hedge than today. The small saver could have been broadly content without spreading the scope of hedge investment beyond gold and fixed-rate bonds. Today, the changed nature of hedge investment, involving wide diversification between various impure hedges, has imposed a special burden on the small saver, for whom transaction costs can be penal.

Now it can be shown from certain propositions about behaviour under uncertainty that the small saver should invest usually a larger proportion of his portfolio in hedge investments than does the larger saver (for a formal derivation see the next section below). Thus the small saver suffers doubly from the increased difficulty of buying income contingent on bad states – not only are such purchases particularly expensive for him to effect, but they form a particularly high share of his investment activity.

Hedge Investment by Rich and Poor[2]

Consider a simple world where reality is described by one state-variable only, x, which may take alternative values of x_0 and X, where x_0 is a bad general state, and X is a good general state. Assume further that the natural endowment of the rich investor in state of the world x_0 and X is aY and Y respectively, whilst that of the poor investor is ay and y respectively, where y is less than Y.

To discover the relative preferences of the rich and poor man for hedge investments, it is necessary to determine for each man the respective ratios of the expected marginal utility of natural endowment in the good state of the world to that in the bad state of the world. Equivalently, if $U(y)$ is a utility function – assumed to be of identical form for rich and poor – how does the function

$$F(y) = \frac{p_{x_0} U'(ay)}{p_x U'(y)}$$

(the ratio of expected marginal utility of endowment in the poor state to that in the rich state)[3] change with y – the wealth bracket of the individual considered? (p_{x_0} and p_x are the probabilities of state of the world x_0 and X occurring respectively).

Differentiating $F(y)$ with respect to y. We get:

$$F'(y) = \left(\frac{U''(ay)}{U'(y)} - \frac{U'(ay)U''(y)}{U'(y)^2}\right)\frac{p_{x_0}}{p_x}$$

Thus $F'(y)$ is less than zero if $-U''(y)/U'(y)$ is less than $-U''(ay)/U'(ay)$. Now $-U''(y)/U'(y)$ is a measure of absolute risk aversion, which is a decreasing function of income,[4] and so $F'(y)$ is less than zero. This implies that the ratio of expected marginal utility of income in state x_0 to that in state X is higher for small values of y than for large values of y. Thus at an equilibrium price in the contingent income market, the small saver must have increased the proportion of income he enjoys in x_0 to that in X to above a, whilst the large saver must have reduced the proportion to below a.

Human Capital – Problems of Diversification

An important property of human capital is non-diversifiability. A doctor, with $150,000 invested in his upkeep and training to date, cannot ordinarily sell shares in himself for general ownership, and thus reduce his exposure to specific (non-diversifiable) risk. In contrast, if he held $150,000 in material wealth, he would be most unlikely to hold it in one asset. Instead he would attempt to wash out specific risks, and be left exposed only to general market risk, by diversifying his wealth between a broad range of assets.

But the problems of 'moral hazard' prevent the diversification of human capital. If our doctor above diluted equity ownership of his own human enterprise, he would have less motivation to make it a success. Further, in free economies, labour contracts are in general unenforceable with respect to the employee. Even if the human capitalist promised to constrain his behaviour according to guidelines as published in a prospectus accompanying the issue of equity in himself, the constraints would prove unenforceable. Heavy transaction and information costs would impede the marketing of equities in human labour ventures. In Chapter 2, similar problems were discussed in the context of buying income contingent on the values of personal state-variables.

Inability to diversify the specific risk of human capital explains why labour-capitalists (individuals whose wealth is wholly or largely in the form of potential income from their own labour services) may be as anxious as rentiers to buy slump hedges, despite the share of labour in national income being less sensitive than the share of capital to the business cycle. In a slump, the risk of unemployment for each worker is higher than normal, and unemployment entails a period of zero return to human capital (probably negative if considered net of depreciation); in contrast, the investor with a diversified portfolio would find that only a small proportion of assets owned directly or indirectly became idle.

The labour-capitalist's exposure to specific risk can be heightened by the holding of a stake in residential property. Clearly the labour-capitalist with a high proportion of his overall wealth invested in his own home has a poorly diversified portfolio. Risk could often be reduced by renting rather than buying his living space. Even so, three considerations suggest why residential property should figure prominently in a portfolio – albeit by less than would result from ownership of 100 per cent of the equity in one's own home.

First, an equity stake in residential property provides income contingent on the bad general state of housing shortage (see Chapter 1). Diversification of the stake between a wide spread of properties lowers the impurity of this type of hedge. Second, consumption of residential space may figure particularly prominently in the individual's shopping basket, as for an individual with a large family or with spacious tastes. For him the state-variable of space-availability taking a low value would be a particularly bad state of the world, and it would be efficient for him to buy income contingent on a space-shortage by investing directly in the physical stock of housing (usually in his own home). The state-variable 'space-availability' is aggregative rather than distributive, in the terminology of Chapter 2. Thus hedges against space-shortage are derived principally from physical investment in housing rather than from interpersonal transactions. Third, an individual's income may be particularly sensitive to the level of house rent in one location. For example, if house rents rose strongly, relative to elsewhere, in his present location, the tenant could be faced with the prospect of moving, which could entail high relocation costs being incurred, a possible diminution of labour income, and many non-pecuniary disadvantages.[5] A stake in local housing can thus provide income contingent on the movement of a fairly particular state-variable.

The hedge function of residential real estate with respect to 'space-availability' should, in itself, lower the expected yield on housing relative to that on neutral (non-hedge) investments. The counterpart premium valuation put on housing is responsible for a larger-than-otherwise allocation of resources towards housing and for a bloated housing stock. This enlargement of the stock of living space makes events that would decrease the net supply of space less awesome. An analogy exists in the energy market, where a premium valuation put on oil equities stimulates oil exploration and makes disruption of energy supplies in any region less awesome. Investment can make a bad state of the world less bad.

Yet for the small saver, even taking into account the above hedge considerations, the optimum share of residential property in his portfolio is likely to be less than would result from ownership of 100 per cent of the equity in his home, and the optimum geographical spread of his investment in residential property is likely to extend beyond his present neighbourhood. The institutional constraints that have promoted home ownership have had particularly grave effect where the price of a man's labour services and the price of residential property in his location are very highly correlated. In this case, the hedge-type arguments for a stake in local real estate are least. The wage earner who owns residential property whose price is correlated closely with the wage level for his own type of service risks suffering unemployment or a wage cut together with a capital loss on his property simultaneously.

This powerful argument against home ownership is unfortunately often most valid in areas where the attractions to potential landlords of investing in houses to rent are least. For in certain non-metropolitan areas where one type of economic activity is predominant (and thereby the wage rate of most labourers and house rents are highly correlated), there is a low rate of population turnover (i.e. a static population). Hence there could be long periods of non-occupancy for residential properties, between one tenant vacating and the finding of a new tenant. The landlord could, of course, charge a rent sufficiently high to compensate for the risk of lengthy periods without rent. By so doing, however, he would suffer from 'adverse selection', attracting as tenants that part of the local population which are likely to have the shortest period of residence.[6,7] Those who are reasonably confident about staying in the neighbourhood for a long time could economise by buying their home rather than paying a high insurance premium against inoccupancy to the landlord.

In general, the price of residential property is positively correlated with the share of labour in national income. This attribute was shown, in Chapter 3, to make residential investment attractive to the rentier. Yet the same attribute makes residential investment less attractive to the individual for whom labour-income is very important. It is somewhat paradoxical that house investment should represent typically a much larger share of the portfolio of the small saver than of the large saver.

Human Capital – its Different Forms

Earnings to labour may conceptually be divided into three streams. First, the individual must receive a wage to offset at least the disutility of his own work effort; if that is all he receives, he is termed a labourer. Second, he should earn hopefully an amount, in excess of the above disutility payment, to provide a return (including compensation for depreciation) on capital invested in his education and upbringing.[8] Third, he may earn a surplus, described as human rent, over and above the disutility payments and the provision for amortisations and interest on the training and upkeep fund. Recipients of the second or third category of income are termed labour-capitalists, although if they have very large portfolios of non-labour capital they may be considered as rentiers.

Corresponding to the last two income streams, there are two distinct components of human capital. First, there is the original 'training and upkeep fund', which is built of educational and maintenance costs plus interest thereon in the years before the individual entered the labour market, minus repayments since then. This fund is valued at the lower of cost or market value. If, for example, the individual has suffered illness or other misfortune, there may be little prospect of the costs sunk in previous years being matched (in present value terms) by revenues in excess of disutility payments. Second, there is rent capitalisation. This is the residual present value of the individual's future earnings after offsetting the value of the 'training and upkeep fund' and compensation for disutility of work in each period. The basis of rent capitalisation is special ability.

What is termed 'pursuit of a career' means effectively the maximisation of rent capitalisation. But maximisation in the very imperfect labour makets is no easy achievement. Transaction costs are huge. Knowledge of the labourer's (or labour-capitalist's) ability and the intended nature of employment are not shared evenly between buyer and seller. In large organisations, political costs and benefits are likely to play a major role in determining earnings of labour in managerial positions.

Often the labour-capitalist of outstanding skill will find that to maximise his rent capitalisation he must establish his own enterprise. This would be true if his ability were outstanding in a field where there is only one potential employer of his full range of skills. In his capacity of employee, he would be paid only the value of his services to the nearest competitor employer – for that would be sufficient to keep him in his present employment. But by opting for self-employment he may hope to capture a part of the employer's surplus value derived from his own labour.

It is not necessary to assume an employer with some degree of monopoly power in a particular segment of the labour market to derive a surplus value element which the labour-capitalist could hope to capture through self-employment. It is sufficient to assume a more unequal distribution of employment opportunities than of human ability in a particular skill. Suppose the top 35 per cent of foreign exchange dealers could be divided into three grades of ability – 5 per cent in grade 1, 10 per cent in grade 2, and 20 per cent in grade 3. Suppose further that the top 35 per cent of banks that would profit most from having good dealers fall into three categories, according to the amount of extra profit potential which could be exploited – 2½ per cent in category 1, 7½ per cent in category 2, and 25 per cent in category 3. Then banks in category 1 would have to pay grade 1 dealers only as much extra profit as the latter could earn for category 2 banks. The wage rate for each grade of dealer is determined by their marginal productivity, which for grade 1 dealers would be determined in category 2 employment. Category 1 banks would derive surplus value from grade 1 dealers.

Examples of the derivation of surplus value from labour can be found in agriculture – a favourite roaming ground of the Classical economists. There is a general tendency for marginal man to farm marginal land, whilst the ablest farmers farm the richest lands. The absolute extra yield which the good farmer can obtain (per acre) over the bad farmer is assumed to increase with the natural fertility of the soil; neither the good nor the bad farmer would reap any crop from a desert patch, but their differential produce could be huge in the Rhone valley. Thus, in a free market for agricultural rents, the able farmer could out-compete the less able farmer in bidding for fertile land.

Now, if the distribution of top farming talent were less unequal than that of fertility of farmland, then the landlord of the most fertile land would capture in rent the full difference in productivity of his land, compared to the next most fertile, as farmed by the most able farmers. If, in contrast, the distribution of top farming talent were more unequal than that of fertility, then the landlord of the most fertile land would capture in rent only the difference in productivity of his land compared to the next most fertile as farmed by grade 2 or grade 3 farmers. Then top-grade farmers themselves would capture the full rent potential of their special ability.

The rent-capitalisation component of human capital is likely to be more sensitive to the movement of personal state-variables and less sensitive to the movement of general state-variables than is the 'training and upkeep' fund. The value of the latter can be insured to some degree by the purchase of hedges against such bad states of the world as war, slump, or hyperinflation, and by the purchase of one special type of fairweather good – one which thrives on the share of profits rising in GNP. This fairweather good should be a popular investment for labour, as it yields income contingent on realities where real wages are depressed at the expense of profit. However it is difficult to identify a good which is sensitive to the state-variable of income distribution without also being significantly influenced by the level of economic activity. Thus a portfolio of equities may gain, *ceteris paribus*, from a rise in the share of profits in GNP, but it would suffer a loss of value in a state of slump, where labour's natural endowment would be low and of especially high specific risk (given the high risk of labour being unemployed in times of slump).

It is more difficult to insure the rent capitalisation than the 'training and upkeep' component of human capital. A top doctor cannot buy an asset which yields income contingent on his quality differential with the 'average' doctor narrowing. Transaction costs and moral hazard inhibit such insurance being available. Thus human capital in the form of rent capitalisation is exposed doubly to specific risks – not only to that of unemployment, but also to that of diminution in its standard of quality. The high variability of returns on human capital – and the constraints on diversifying away this risk – are likely to make the investor, for whom human capital is a large share of his wealth, less willing than the rentier to bear riskiness of returns on his portfolio of material assets. This aversion to bearing risk will be particularly noticeable for labour-capitalists who face a significant chance of unemployment, whose rent capitalisation is volatile in value, and who own residential property of which the value is highly correlated with that of their own labour services.

Human Capital – its Insurance

A major specific risk of human capital is due to the uncertain length of human life. The labour-capitalist is unsure of the length of his working life, which can be cut short by death or illness. If the prospective income from his human capital has a bearing on the welfare of others about whom he is concerned, then the individual would wish to buy income contingent on death or illness. The normal vehicle for this is the insurance contract. The rentier, in contrast to the labour-capitalist, need not bear the cost of life assurance, for he does not hope to produce income through his own labour.[9]

Although the rentier and labour-capitalist have conflicting interest in life assurance, they have similar interest in buying annuities for their post-age-of-retirement years. They may wish to buy income contingent on their life being much longer than its normal expectations; in that personal reality, their own accumulated pension fund may dry up, and they would then have to either draw on the legacy fund for their heirs or suffer poverty.

Human capital itself is subject to inflation risk, but only to a small extent. Wages are fixed for periods of time in nominal terms, and can thus suffer erosion from higher-than-expected inflation during the given period. Indeed, vivid examples of this type of erosion are given by Bresciani-Turroni in his history of the German hyperinflation, where even with weekly indexation of the wage rate, its real value was seriously eroded by the end of the week when it was paid.[10] In a less esoteric context, Modigliani has shown that even in an economy where wage rates are 100 per cent indexed to the inflation rate, but adjusted only at set intervals, an acceleration of the inflation rate reduces the average real wage.[11] However, in the longer term, a secular acceleration of inflation would be accompanied by a shortening of the labour-contract interval.

Life insurance, except in conditions of hyperinflation, is rarely indexed, and when effected over long periods of time, is subject to a high degree of inflation risk. To understand fully the nature of the exposure to inflation risk, an analysis of the nature of the insurance contract is required (see below). It emerges that human capital, insured against early death, where insurance is specified in nominal terms, is exposed to significant inflation risk.

The simplest type of life-assurance contract is a spot 1-year (or less) term-assurance. Here the individual life is insured against death at any time during the next year. A 5-year term-assurance, in contrast, provides for payment contingent on death at any time during the next 5 years, and can be considered as a combination of a spot 1-year policy on a life aged say 40 years now, plus a 1 year forward 1-year policy on a life aged 41, plus a 2 year forward 1-year policy on a life aged 42, etc. Thus the insured gains if the actuarial standard of his life declines by more than foreseen by the insurance company during the life of the contract;[12] he loses in the converse situation.

In a long-term term-assurance policy (say 25 years for a 40-year life), it is common practice for the annual premium to be quoted as an equal amount each year. Yet the forward premiums on the 1-year contracts rise with age. Thus premiums in the early years of the conventional 40-year policy must be set above the 1-year spot-rates for policies to provide a fund out of which to pay towards much higher spot premiums later on. The nature of saving is illustrated in Figure 4.1, for a sum of $20,000 insured. The broken lines indicate the net sum insured each year after deducting the fund which the insurance company has accumulated out of excess premiums (the annual premium minus the relevant spot premium) to date. It emerges that the net sum insured decreases at first, then increases towards maturity. The advance deposit fund (see Figure 4.1.) may be considered as also fulfilling a margin requirement – guaranteeing to the insurance company that forward contracts will be honoured. But as the value of human capital should deteriorate sharply in value towards retirement, this implicit increase in the sum assured as the term-policy approaches maturity is undesirable, assuming the purpose of the contract is to insure the value of human capital against the risk of death.

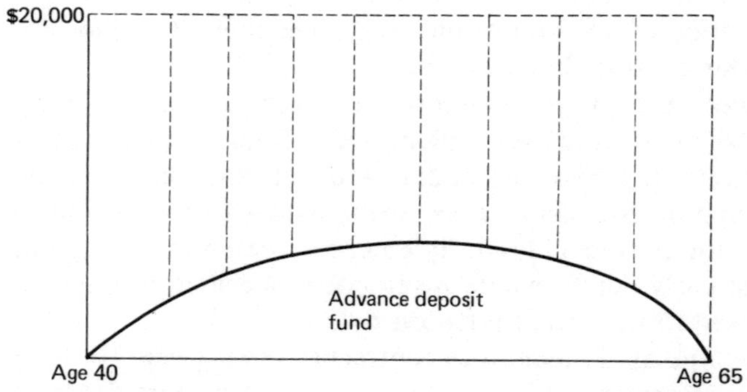

FIGURE 4.1 *Term assurance: the advance deposit fund*

An endowment policy promises a fixed sum contingent on the holder's death or maturity of the policy, whichever occurs sooner. Thus the endowment policy is equivalent to a spot 1-year term assurance, plus a series of forward 1-year term policies, plus a savings programme. The pattern of savings and annual implicit term-policy is illustrated in Figure 4.2. Savings are accumulated out of the excess of the premium in each of the early years over the spot premiums that would be charged for successive 1-year policies. In the late years of the policy, part of the interest on the savings accumulated to date plus the new premium payable meet the cost of the implicit 1-year current spot life assurance.

An endowment policy, in contrast to the long term-policy discussed earlier, provides declining assurance with age – a desirable feature. However, the savings component of the endowment policy is considerably larger than for the term-policy and it is offputting to many investors to have a large chunk of their savings managed (at high management costs) by an indifferent insurance company.

Ideally, the labour-capitalist would buy, say at age 30, a 1-year spot term-policy for an amount related to the value of his human capital

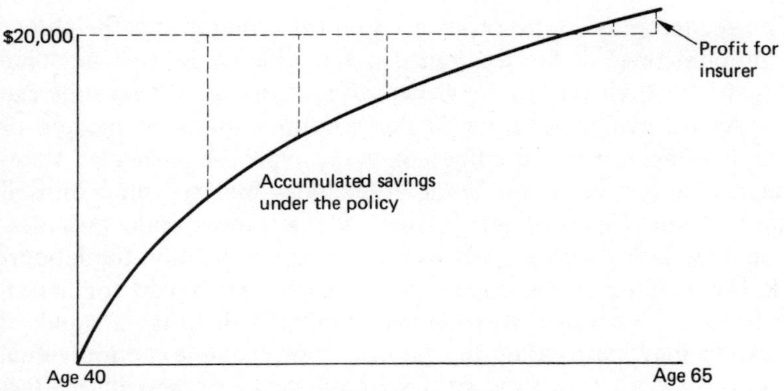

FIGURE 4.2 *The endowment policy*

today. In addition he would buy forward 1-year policies for each successive year related to what the expected value of his human capital would be then. But there are two major uncertainties that complicate the choice of the annual sum to be assured.

First, sums assured are expressed in nominal terms, yet the individual (who does not suffer from money illusion) wishes to insure his human capital according to how much it is worth in terms of constant purchasing power. Thus he must base his purchases of forward life assurance on an estimated inflation rate. If that estimate proves too low, then later in life he may find that he wishes to top up the amount to which his life is insured. But at that time his life may have become actuarially sub-standard and possibly uninsurable. Higher-than-expected inflation reduces the real value of his life-risk protection gained to date; inflation uncertainty exposes the real value of his human capital, even when insured, to health and life risks.

Inflation imposes a further cost on the labour-capitalist. This arises from the convention that term policies provide for a fixed nominal sum insured each year, and hence a declining real value. Yet it is probable that in the early years of working life, as the labour-capitalist approaches his years of peak earnings, that the value of his human capital increases; the dependence of others on the value of his human capital is likely also to be increasing, as his family commitments become more extended. Thus in order to buy forward the desired amount of insurance in mid-working life, the labour-capitalist would have to over-insure by a large margin during his early working life.

The second major type of uncertainty that complicates the choice of optimum level of life assurance is the wide range that personal state-variables relevant to the growth of human capital over time can take. As we saw in Chapter 2, the non-tradeability of income or goods contingent on the values of many types of particular state-variables limits severely the scope of the individual to protect himself against the movement of aggregative and distributive state-variables. An analogy holds with respect to life assurance. Ideally, the labour-capitalist would buy life assurance for each year ahead for a sum equal to the then value of his human capital (valued for a standard life-expectancy appropriate to that age). For example, an individual of age 40 would buy forward 1-year policies to come into effect successively at the beginning of each year until retirement, and for sums contingent on the rate of growth in the value of his human capital. But the insurance company writing such a policy would have to make an estimate not only of the individual's mortality risk, but also the probabilities of his capital value falling into different bands for each age. For a large population, the insurance company would not have to measure this probability very precisely for each individual, providing that income distribution between high and low earners remained fairly constant over time. However, redistribution of income has at times been significant. Further, the difficulties of determining into which band the value of human capital falls at the date of a claim are immense.

The individual would also like to make his forward purchases of life assurance contingent on how much the welfare of those for whom he is concerned would lose through a reduction in the value of his human capital, whether due to death, illness, or obsolescence. Thus someone unmarried at age 25 may wish to buy life insurance in each successive year where the amount insured is contingent on whether he is yet married and how many children he has. Although the insurance company may derive relevant probability estimates from general statistical information for a whole population, there is a problem of inequality of knowledge. The insured knows better than the insurer what are the risks of personal state-variables described above taking given values. Thus the insurance company would find that its population of insured had more unfavourable probability parameters – and by a margin that was unascertainable in advance – than had the population as a whole.

Insurance Costs Bear Heavily on the Small Saver

Each individual attempts to ascertain what significant losses may occur contingent on the movement of certain personal state-variables. How much would the value of his human capital fall contingent on illness or on being thwarted in his career? How much would his wealth decline if his home went up in smoke? Having determined these losses, the question then must be posed as to what proportion of the loss should be insured.

The provision of insurance services is not costless. The insurance company charges a premium significantly higher than the mathematical expectation of loss. It is out of this margin over the true premium (the premium which would equal the mathematical expectation of loss) that the substantial administration costs of the insurance company are paid, and a return paid to the equity shareholders. Because the possible realities in which the insurance company will 'pay out' are low-income states for the individual, where the marginal utility of income is high, he is prepared to pay over actuarial value for income there. But it is most unlikely that the optimum level of insurance – where the expected marginal utility from increasing the sum insured equals its price (the premium) – equals exactly the potential loss.

The risks of human capital loss or the home burning down are particularly significant for the small saver, for whom those assets represent a large share of his portfolio, and for whom realities including illness or house-destruction are ones of very low relative real incomes where the marginal utility of income would be very high. Certain types of risk associated with home and human capital are the subject of insurance contracts.

Thus the small saver should typically insure a higher proportion of potential losses through fire, health, or death, than the large saver. This imposes an extra cost on the small saver since all insurance, of any type, is bought at sizeable margins over mathematical expectation of loss. A wealthy rentier, who need not insure human capital, and who should insure only a small proportion of relevant assets against specific risks, pays a low contribution to the upkeep of insurance companies (where contribution is measured relative to size of wealth). The small saver is less fortunate.

Notes and References

1. This may be defined as where at least one important state-variable changes in value by a large amount.
2. This section may be omitted in a general reading – see pp. xiv, 74.
3. p_{x_0}, p_X are the probabilities of state x_0 and state X occurring.
4. See K.J. Arrow, in *Essays in the Theory of Risk-bearing* (North Holland, 1974) Chapter 3. Arrow shows that decreasing absolute risk aversion implies that 'risky' assets are superior goods, and that decreasing absolute risk aversion follows from the axioms of choice under uncertainty.
5. Implicitly considered here is a reality where demand for the individual's labour and local rents are not highly correlated.
6. Leases are assumed to be standard, with break-clauses periodically.
7. For another example of 'adverse selection', consider the banking industry. In a competitive system, the bank which did not charge clients a fee for each transaction would find that it attracted those individuals with a high turnover rate on their account.
8. For example, a graduate from private school and university could easily have had $150,000 invested in his training, upbringing, and interest obligations incurred thereon, by age 25. A subsequent 40-year life, with a 10 per cent real rate of return, would require annual labour earnings of $15,333 (in real terms) in excess of disutility of work.
9. The rentier may still buy life assurance for tax purposes, or to insure those whose welfare concerns him against non-pecuniary losses contingent on his death.
10. See Bresciani-Turroni, *The Economics of Inflation* (Kelley, 1968) pp. 300–20.
11. See F. Modigliani and T. Padoa-Schioppa, 'The Management of an Open Economy with "100% plus" Wage Indexation', Princeton, *Essays in International Finance,* No. 130, December 1978.
12. In the event of death, the forward contracts become annulled.

Part II

The Practice of Hedge Investment

5 Real Estate

Real estate is regarded commonly as an inflation hedge. We have all heard how 'bricks and mortar' retain value in an age of fast-depreciating paper monies. In the present chapter, the inflation-hedge function, together with other possible hedge functions of real estate, are examined. Different types of real estate – residential, commercial, and agricultural – are distinguished, which are in turn further subdivided according to quality.

Valuation – a General Formula

With some simplification, property may be considered as an asset which produces a stream of rents over time. In nominal terms these may grow at a rate of $g_t - d_t + p_t$, where g_t is the growth rate of real rents measured for newly completed property of similar type, p_t is the rate of inflation, and d_t the rate at which the open market rent falls on an existing building below that on a newly constructed one due to obsolescence. All variables are measured over the discrete interval of time, t to $t+1$, and are each drawn from distinct probability distributions – g, p, and d. In addition, associated with a property is a stream of outgoings – principally in the form of maintenance charges, legal and negotiation fees. The latter can be particularly heavy where the landlord and tenant are separate, and least when the property is occupied wholly by its owner.[1] The value of a property is the sum of the present value of incoming rents less the present value of the stream of maintenance charges and fees. In the context of state-preference theory, rent contingent on each possible reality at time t is multiplied by the market price of income there. Thus if property were essentially a fairweather good, producing highest income in realities where aggregate incomes are high, the expected rent at each time t would be discounted at a high rate in calculating present value. If, in contrast, property had important hedge characteristics, then expected rent inflows would be discounted at a lower rate.

In contrast to the incoming cash flows from rent, the stream of maintenance charges and fees should not show any particular association with bad or good realities. These outgoings in each time-interval can be regarded either as the outcome of a gamble whose odds are the same in whatever reality occurs (for example, legal and other professional fees) or as known with certainty (for example, various maintenance charges). Hence their expectation, in each period, should be discounted at a rate near the riskless rate of interest – lower than the rate used to discount rental inflows (unless the property is a hedge asset).

An arithmetic example will demonstrate that transaction costs (fees and professional charges) are not trivial. Consider investment property where the landlord and tenant must negotiate a new base rent each 3 years. Suppose negotiation costs averaged 10 per cent of the new rent agreed, and that this shows an initial yield of 8 per cent on the capital value of the property.[2] Further, suppose the expected real rate of return from property (net of depreciation and tax) were 1 per cent per annum. Then every 3 years negotiation costs would absorb 80 per cent of the expected real income from the property.

In practice, as suggested implicitly in the above example, rents are not renegotiated each year to reflect what rent the property would obtain in an open market. The negotiation costs of such an agreement would be extremely offputting. Instead, rents are often fixed, usually in nominal terms, for periods of 3 to 7 years. A property subject to such a lease-arrangement can be described as a series of annuities, each of say 5 years' maturity, whose annual payment is set at a notional level equal to what a willing landlord and tenant would contract for the benefit of using the specified space for 5 years. If there were also a market in 1-year lettings, then the value of the 5-year annuity must, in equilibrium, equal the present value of the prospective 1-year rents over 5 years. Even where a spot market in 1-year rents does not exist, both tenant and landlord should form implicity an expectation of what these would be when appraising whether to pay (accept) a given level of annuity payments.

Now consider the relationship between the nominal yield of the property immediately subsequent to a rent review, expressed as the new level of the annuity payment (the annual rent) divided by the property's market value, and the expected real rate of return on the property. A rise in the inflation rate should, for a given expected real yield on the property investment, increase the nominal yield: both the landlord and tenant realise that the real value of payments under the 5-year annuity will decrease at a more rapid rate, and hence agree to a higher nominal starting rent. It is possible, though, that an acceleration of inflation could lead to a fall in expected real yields on property if it were regarded as an inflation hedge and investors sought to buy extra income contingent on realities of high inflation. Superficial evidence in the British commercial property market shows nominal yields falling secularly during the period 1965-80, with inflation rising. A falling expected real rate of return, due to the growing recognition of property's inflation-hedge qualities, would appear to have outweighed the influence of higher inflation itself on the level of nominal yields.

Properties for which maintenance and negotiation costs are high (expressed as a proportion of gross rents) should promise, *ceteris paribus*, a greater nominal net yield than those for which they are low. This follows from the generally lower discount rate used for converting future maintenance and negotiation costs to present values than that used for converting prospective gross rents. Thus residential properties with high service charges should show a higher nominal net yield (nominal rent, net of maintenance charges, expressed as a proportion of capital value) than those which are self-contained with very small fixed outgoings.

The present value of each set of annuity payments is dependent on the creditworthiness of the tenant. Where the tenant becomes delinquent, in the course of the annuity contract, the landlord is faced with the prospect of both a period of non-occupancy and a rent which may be below the current annuity payment (due to an interim fall in rental values). In addition, a change in tenancy would probably impose an extra set of negotiation and transaction costs on him. A poor-quality tenant must thus pay a higher nominal annual rent than a high-quality tenant for the same property – especially where long leases are being considered. The differential should be proportionately less significant on property which is easily lettable than on one for which a period of non-occupancy could be prolonged. In sum, a prime tenant should obtain a comparatively low nominal rent, especially on property which is not prime and where the lease is long-term.

In Britain, leases are typically very long-term contracts with maturities of 20 years or more, broken by rent reviews at say 5-yearly intervals. A long lease shifts the burden of risk of periods of non-occupancy from landlord to tenant – and most effectively where the tenant is of prime credit standing. In addition, a clause that rent revisions at review dates may be upwards only is standard in British leases. The clause shifts a part of the risk of the return on the property investment from the landlord to the tenant – even if the market rent fell below the current rent, specified in the lease contract, the tenant has bound himself to pay the latter for the duration of the lease. Again, this shifting of risk from landlord to tenant is more effective for a tenant of high credit rating than for one of poor credit rating; but unlike in the case of shifting of risk of non-occupancy, it is not less important with respect to prime than to secondary properties. The stipulation of a minimum rent should lower the landlord's expected real yield from property ownership and lower its nominal yield.

Now the value of the minimum-rent clause to the landlord is diminished by the advent of high inflation. For then the real value of the minimum rent can fall sharply from one rent-review date to the next. One special attraction of the good quality tenant is in consequence diminished. The landlord suffers in two principal ways from an unanticipated acceleration of inflation. First, the real value of the present-running 5-year annuity is reduced. Second, his exposure to the risk of the property's value changing is increased through the diminution of the protection of the minimum-rent clause. Non-indexation of depreciation allowances can subject property investment to substantial further inflation risk. For if depreciation deductions against tax are allowed at only *x* per cent of historic cost per annum, the proportion of real depreciation which is offsettable would fall as the price level rises – and so the post-tax real rate of return on the property is depressed cumulatively. Thus a building which cost $100,000 to construct in 1975, may now cost $200,000 to replace. But if the annual depreciation allowance of $2500 remains fixed, despite the depreciation measured on a replacement cost basis having risen to $5000, then the rate of tax on the net rent (rent less depreciation at replacement cost) would have increased.

The above characteristics of common types of investment property illustrate that they are more exposed to inflation risk than are properties where the tenant is the owner. The owner-occupier does not risk loss through inflation eroding the value of a 5-year annuity, nor through the protection from a minimum-rent clause being eroded. He may, like the pure investor, suffer from non-indexation of depreciation allowances. The particular inflation-hedge characteristics of residential property are examined in the subsequent section. Then we return to different types of investment property, their hedge characteristics, and how these should influence their respective expected rates of return and nominal yields.

Residential Investment

For many types of residential investment a rental market does not exist. The danger of long periods of non-occupancy between tenancies, high transaction costs, high enforcement costs[3] (ensuring that the tenant carries out covenants stipulated in the lease), tax-incentives commonly given to owner-occupation, and rent controls, often prevent a rental market from emerging. Even so, in his purchase decision, the potential owner-occupier must calculate the prospective rental stream which he would have to expect from a tenant to justify paying, as an outside investor, the market price. He must assess whether these rents could in fact be obtained. Then, as consumer, he decides whether he would choose to be a tenant of the given property.

Without information on rent levels it is difficult to analyse trends in nominal yields and use these as an indicator of trends in the expected real rate of return on residential property. In the USA, in contrast to the UK, an active rental market exists, about which detailed statistics are collected. Table 5.1 presents an index for residential rent and house prices for the period March 1979 to 1980, a period marked by heightened anxiety about inflation. It can be seen there that rents moved ahead at a less rapid pace than house prices. As this occurred at a time when the US economy was slowing down and hence the prospective growth in the level of real rents must have been falling, and when real interest rates were rising strongly, the figures are suggestive of an increased premium being awarded to the inflation-hedge properties of residential investment. It has been suggested that during the period house ownership – in contrast to renting – came to have a social status attached. Supportive evidence of a grown hedge premium was provided by a report of the Mortgage Bankers Association in 1980, showing that \$1 invested in a house in 1968 was worth \$1.29 in constant purchasing power by the beginning of 1979: the same dollar, if it had been invested in common stock, would have been worth 78½¢. Thus residential investment appears to have thrived in the decade starting from the dollar's first break with gold in

1968 and marked by subsequent mounting inflation and public awareness of inflation risks.

TABLE 5.1 *House prices and rents in the USA, 1979–80 (3-monthly, at annual per cent rate)*

		Rents	*House prices*
1979	March	3.6	11.1
	June	8.2	14.8
	September	10.2	17.4
	December	9.0	18.8
1980	March	8.3	11.6

SOURCE: *Federal Reserve.*

In the UK the absence of a rental market means direct evidence about hedge premiums is available only directly from data on house prices. This is displayed in Table 5.2 where it can be seen that in the period end-1971 to end-1973 a large inflation-risk premium developed on residential investment. This was subsequently slashed in the recession of 1974–76, to recover in 1977–79. Again, during the Great Recession of 1979–81, the inflation premium on housing was

TABLE 5.2 *House prices in the UK (percentage increases over previous year)*

	House prices	*Retail price index*	*Ratio of house prices to average earnings*
1970	10.1	7.5	3.29
1971	22.1	8.0	3.58
1972	33.0	7.8	4.05
1973	23.0	12.0	4.82
1974	9.0	18.0	4.23
1975	7.0	18.7	3.62
1976	7.0	16.1	3.48
1977	12.0	12.0	3.45
1978	23.5	10.2	3.55
1979	19.8	19.8	3.75
1980	16.8	15.8	3.65

SOURCE: *Financial Times.*

reduced. Over the period 1970–80 as a whole, house prices in real terms rose by 10–15 per cent more than real disposable incomes, and this may be suggestive of an increased awareness by investors of the real value which housing would retain even in realities where inflation were very high.

In order to qualify as a good inflation hedge, the real value of housing would have to be particularly sensitive to the level of inflation, without being highly sensitive to other state-variables. Indeed, there are reasons to believe that the values of a diversified portfolio of housing would be less sensitive to the movement of most general state-variables (other than inflation) than would be a portfolio of equities. Housing has the nature of a wage-good, for which real incomes of labour are a principal determinant of value. As we have seen in Chapter 1, the fluctuations in aggregate labour incomes are likely to be less than those in income from non-human sources of capital. So widespread is home ownership, and so important is the homeowner politically, that many types of political risk are less relevant to residential property ownership than to equity ownership. Further, technological progress and changes in consumer taste are typically very slow for residential property, unlike for the products of many industrial and commercial enterprises. Property values are, however, sensitive to the state of finances of local government (both in general and particular) given the importance of property taxation (which takes the form of a consumer tax on rent whether paid to a landlord or imputed to the owner-occupier) as a source of local revenue.

Given that residential property (in aggregate) has a low sensitivity to many general state-variables, why should it have a particularly high sensitivity to the rate of inflation? The explanation centres on the deterioration in the quality of monetary assets that occurs in the transition from low and stable rates of inflation to high and unstable rates of inflation. From being a near-riskless asset in the former reality, money moves to being a risky asset in the latter. The implicit destruction of low-risk assets, that occurs in the transition, increases the riskiness of the set of investments from which each saver constructs his portfolio. The power of net holding of money and bonds to dilute the riskiness of investment (direct or indirect) in given physical investment opportunities is reduced, and so demand for low-risk physical investment increases whilst that for high-risk investments decreases. Residential real estate, being considered a low-risk asset, gains from this shift in asset demand that accompanies the increase in inflation rate and inflation risk.

Residential property's inflation-hedge properties are based also on tax considerations. In most fiscal regimes, capital gains on house property (where owner-occupied) are exempt from tax. As the real rate of capital gains tax, when set as a fixed proportion of nominal capital gain, rises with the inflation rate, the value of capital gains tax exemption also rises. Further, the real tax rate on traditionally low-risk nominal assets, such as bank deposits and treasury-bills, is a steeply rising function of the inflation rate in non-indexed tax regimes. Thus, in realities where inflation is high, and the real rate of tax on nominal assets very burdensome, the price of residential property, which is regarded as a low-risk physical asset, is likely to be especially high – driven up by investors trying to switch out of highly taxed nominal assets into low-risk physical assets which are less heavily taxed.

Yet residential property is a lumpy asset. As we saw in Chapter 4, the small saver who invests in property assumes a high level of specific risk; he does not invest in a hypothetical well-diversified portfolio of residential properties where specific risk is 'washed out', but in a particular property whose value depends on a host of highly particular rather than general state-variables. Thus investment in one's own home is a considerably more impure inflation hedge than an investment in a diversified portfolio of residential properties.

The switch in demand, between nominal assets and residential property, is the basis of the latter's inflation-hedge characteristic. Yet because of the lumpiness of residential investment, the switch in demand can be effected by only a few marginal purchasers – for a large body of investors already own their own home, and could increase their investment in real estate only by buying a second home which would represent a large proportion of their portfolio. The main shifts in demand for residential real estate that would occur in the transition to a state of high and variable inflation would be likely to take four forms.

First, some present tenants of house property would choose to switch to owner-occupation. Second, some younger investors, who have not yet bought their own home, would accelerate their entry into the house market. Third, some wealthy investors may choose to buy a second house, in a vacation area, and so switch away from renting space in hotels. Fourth, some investors would decide to trade up – they would reduce their holding of nominal assets (or increase their nominal liabilities) and switch from lower-quality to higher-quality homes or from less spacious to more spacious homes: they would be prepared to accept a lower marginal utility from their 'consumption' of living space, given residential property's heightened service as an inflation-hedge.

The third and fourth forms of shifts are likely to be highly dependent on the level of economic growth. In a state of stagflation, luxury-type spending, whether on second-homes or on quality accommodation, is unlikely to be buoyant. Further, inflation can be associated with cost-push pressures and a fall in the rate of profit and top incomes – developments which would depress demand for luxury accommodation. The first and second switches are less dependent on the level of economic activity and growth. This suggests that residential property, designed for occupation by middle-income groups, should be a purer inflation hedge than homes providing quality accommodation.

Specific risk is not equally important for different types of property. An apartment of standard design in a desirable central location of London or New York is of lower specific risk (that is, less sensitive to movement of particular state-variables and more sensitive to the movement of general state-variables) than is a one-off luxury penthouse designed to the tastes of a particular owner. The value of the latter is highly dependent on the tastes, incomes, and personal state-variables of a very small number of potential purchasers. The value of the former is dependent, rather, on general state-variables of inflation and real incomes; the existence of a large spread of potential buyers and sellers for each standard unit effectively diversifies away any influence of non-general state-variables on price. Thus the standard apartment is the preferred inflation hedge. In subsequent sections and chapters we shall repeatedly find that standardisation is an important property of hedge investments. The one-off rarity, whether a stamp, a Leonardo da Vinci, or a Bayeux tapestry, is not a good hedge investment.

We have already seen how non-luxury residential property can be a hedge against a fall in the rate of profit and against a redistribution of national income from capital to labour. Residential property of certain types may also be a hedge against energy shortage, whilst other types are fairweather goods with respect to energy supplies. An increase in energy costs should cause rents in a city centre to rise, and rents in suburbia to fall, due to the increased savings in transport costs that result from central rather than suburban living. Most urban dwellers should be anxious to obtain income contingent on an energy crisis; however, the owner of residential property in the city centre would enjoy an income bonus contingent on an energy crisis, due to the windfall gain that would then be realised on the value of his home, and does not share the general concern about energy crisis. The city-centre tenant, in contrast to the owner of residential property in the city centre, is as exposed as the suburban tenant to increased energy costs: he would find that his rent would rise by an amount of similar order to the increased transport costs paid by the suburban dweller in his journeys in and out of the city centre. The owner of residential property in suburbia would be doubly hit by energy crisis. Not only would his real income fall, but the value of his home would fall also. Increased rents in the city centre would, in the long run, lead to increased living accommodation being built there (as higher prices made it economic to construct higher apartment houses). The increased supply of living space would cause rents in the city centre to moderate, whilst rents on the city periphery would fall below their levels prior to the energy crisis. Expectations of this path of rental adjustment would cause the value of homes on the city periphery to fall in the wake of an energy crisis.

A major negative feature of residential property in most forms is its illiquidity. Transaction costs are high, and time needed for disposal may be lengthy. One-off properties in highly desirable locations enjoy the most liquid market. At any time, there should be a large number of potentially interested buyers, and the property can be sold in a full auction house. However, one-off desirable properties are very impure hedge assets.

Being a lowly taxed asset in some respects (zero capital gains tax and flat-rate local tax on imputed rental value), residential property can perform as a tax-hedge, gaining in value from an increase in the degree of progressivity of the tax structure or the loading of tax on other capital assets. However, luxury-type property is likely to be an unsatisfactory tax-hedge; the particularly great reduction in real disposable incomes of top earners due to the tax change may depress their demand for luxury accommodation despite property's attraction as a lowly taxed asset (relative to other assets).

In the long term, the real value of residential investment is highly dependent on the rate of economic growth and of population growth. The emergence of an inflation premium as low-inflation realities give way to high-inflation realities is in the nature of a once-and-for-all adjustment. But the difference between economic growth of 2 and 4 per cent per annum, and its implication for the growth in demand for living space and hence rents, is likely to be of greater cumulative importance for real property values than whether the annual inflation rate lies in a 5–10 or 10–20 per cent band.

Commercial and Industrial Investment Property

Despite equity prices falling sharply in real terms both in the US and in the UK during the decade of the 1970s, prices (in real terms) of commercial and industrial property advanced. Real rents advanced also, but by less than property prices, and there was an overall falling pattern of nominal investment yields. These trends are illustrated in Table 5.3. The fall in nominal yields occurred despite an increase in the inflation rate, and the consequential erosion of the protection gained by minimum-rent clauses. The increase in inflation led to a general shortening of periods between review dates; in Britain the rent became subject to reviews every 3 or 5 years, in contrast to every 21 years as previously. The increased frequency of review dates was a downward source of pressure on nominal yields as it reduced the potential erosion by inflation of the real value of annuities fixed periodically.

Although the failure of nominal yields to rise despite higher inflation may be ascribed in part to the shortening of rent review

TABLE 5.3 *Rent index for the UK (adjusted for inflation)*

	1965	*1969*	*1972*	*1973*	*1974*	*1975*	*1976*	*1977*	*1978*	*1979*	*1980*
ICHP rent index	100	123	144	188	189	157	139	127	136	138	135
Shops	100	119	150	178	180	152	142	136	156	163	156
Offices	100	131	155	223	217	171	143	123	128	126	124
Industrial	100	113	116	135	152	138	131	124	126	130	129
Prime commercial nominal yields (per cent)											
Offices			$4\frac{1}{2}$	$4\frac{3}{8}$	$6\frac{1}{4}$	$6\frac{1}{2}$	$5\frac{1}{2}$	$5\frac{3}{4}$	$4\frac{7}{8}$	$4\frac{1}{2}$	$4\frac{1}{2}$
Shops			$4\frac{5}{8}$	$4\frac{3}{8}$	$6\frac{1}{4}$	$6\frac{1}{2}$	$5\frac{1}{2}$	$5\frac{1}{2}$	$4\frac{5}{8}$	$4\frac{1}{4}$	$4\frac{1}{4}$
Industrial			$7\frac{3}{4}$	$6\frac{7}{8}$	$8\frac{7}{8}$	$8\frac{3}{4}$	8	7	$6\frac{1}{2}$	$6\frac{1}{4}$	$6\frac{1}{4}$

SOURCE: *Investor's Chronicle* and Hiller Parker (ICHP).

periods it is probable that an increased inflation-hedge premium on investment properties was also responsible. Like residential property, many types of industrial and commercial property are considered to be of low risk and become highly sought after when high and variable inflation reduces sharply the real return on net holdings of money and bonds and increases its variability. The low risk of commercial and industrial property is based on the demand for space by users being of low sensitivity to the business cycle and yet being fairly elastic with respect to price. Low sensitivity of demand for space to the business cycle follows from the volume of labour employed and machines owned fluctuating by less than output over the business cycle, and the assumption that demand for space is closely linked to the number of workers and machines to be provided with working accommodation. Further, there are assumed to be heavy transaction costs (in the form of legal and relocation expense) of changing space usage over the business cycle. Price-elasticity of demand for space follows from the importance of rent levels to space expansion plans of individual enterprises.

The importance of the level of economic activity and price-elasticity of demand for space is illustrated in Figure 5.1. A dip in economic activity causes RR, the demand schedule for space, to shift horizontally to RR′ – at each level of nominal rent, the demand for space falls by amount x. The flatter is the RR schedule – equivalently, the more price-elastic is the demand for space – the less does rent fall, for a fall in demand for space by given amount x. The supply of space is assumed fixed, at amount Q, over the time-period considered.

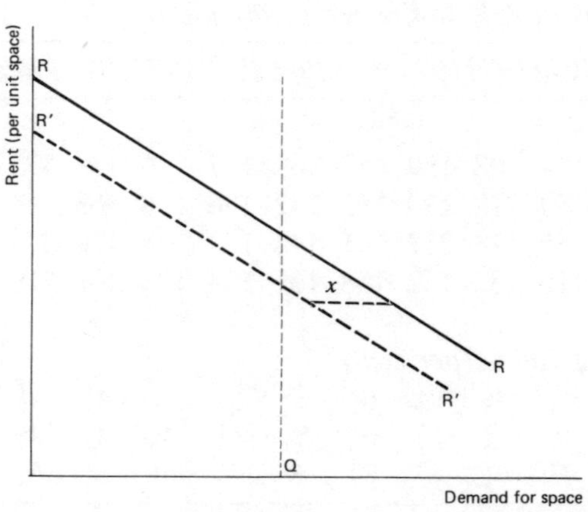

FIGURE 5.1 *Demand for space and the business cycle*

Empirical evidence for a lower cyclical sensitivity of real rents than of trading profits in industrial and commercial corporations is at best sketchy. In Table 5.4, figures are given for the real rate of return on trading assets in the UK. Income from real estate is less volatile than shown by the ICHP index, for that is made up from data on new lettings, whilst actual income is derived from a series of annuities.

TABLE 5.4 *Rates of return on trading assets of industrial and commercial companies (excluding oil profits)(per cent)*

	Pre-tax real	*Post-tax real*
1971	8.9	5.1
1972	9.3	4.9
1973	8.8	6.1
1974	5.2	4.3
1975	4.7	3.6
1976	5.1	3.8
1977	5.8	4.2
1978	5.9	4.5
1979	4.1	3.5

SOURCE: *Bank of England Quarterly Bulletin*, June 1980.

In principle, commercial real estate being of fairly low cyclical risk compared to equities should be sought after as a low-risk alternative to nominal assets at times of high and variable inflation. As for residential property, the investments with low specific risks should be preferred as hedges, although the investor in commercial property will typically have greater scope than the home-owner to diversify these away.

In general, property whose value has a large land content is less pure as an inflation hedge than property with a small land content. This is due to the greater potential volatility of real prices of land than of building costs (in real terms). Supply of land in given key positions, whether in the centre of a shopping or banking area, or at a crucial transport juncture, is fixed; whilst that of buildings is variable especially where their rate of depreciation is high. For example, compare a shop property in London's Bond Street or New York's Fifth Avenue, with a warehouse property in an industrial area on the edge of a city. The premium of the value of the Bond Street shop over its replacement cost (adjusted for depreciation), representing land value, is highly variable and equal to the capitalisation of the future differential in rents between Bond Street and a location at the margin where property value equals replacement cost. During periods of strong economic growth, accompanied by expansion of shopping space, rents in the top position in the city centre where land supply is fixed would rise sharply relative to rents in the growing shopping areas at the margin where land is in elastic supply.

In contrast to Bond Street, supply of land in most industrial estates (other than at key positions in a transport grid) is elastic, and the premium of the warehouse's value over replacement cost is small: hence the variability of overall property value should be less in industrial estates than in Bond Street. A strong growth in demand for warehouse space would undoubtedly lead to an upward trend in warehouse rents; but at higher rent levels, the supply of newly constructed buildings situated in almost equally good positions could increase, albeit via the re-zoning of some areas as industrial from their previous usage. As this new supply came on-stream, the rental levels would recede somewhat. Similarly during a period of slump in demand for warehouse space, warehouse rents would fall sharply; but this would tend to be reversed in the medium and long term, as space shrank due to natural wear and tear and decisions not to replace old buildings, given that values had fallen below building costs.

For warehouses, the average life is much smaller than for other types of building, due to their typically less durable structure and a faster rate of technological progress in their design. Even over medium periods of time, an elastic supply of space should ensure that values remain close to replacement cost, except in certain key distributional centres (for example, near an airport or motorway junction) where supply may be inelastic. Thus rents of warehouse properties in non-key positions should be less variable than for a portfolio of top-situated shops, over medium-term periods of time, and should be more particularly sensitive to movements in replacement costs which in turn should be closely linked to the movement of a general index of prices.

Investors are aware of the different supply-elasticities which typify different categories of real estate. Thus in conditions of strong economic growth, nominal yields (based on new lettings) are likely at first to fall by less on industrial buildings (or on shops and offices in marginal locations where there is a good supply of extra land) than on top-situated shop-property. Investors realise that the immediate rise in rents will be more sustainable where relevant land supply is fixed (as for a top-located shop) than where supply is variable, at least in the medium term.

Sensitivity of industrial warehouse rents to short-term cyclical factors is likely to prove greater than of rents for most other types of space. Demand for warehousing space is linked to the level of industrial production and inventories, both of which are more volatile over the business cycle than is national income. Demand for retail and office space is linked rather to consumer spending and public expenditure, which are usually among the more stable components of national income.

As in the residential property market, one-off high-quality commercial real estate is a very impure inflation hedge, although it has the undoubted attraction of high liquidity. There would always be a potential audience at an auction for top retail property. The rental value of a top shop, besides being highly sensitive to the rate of economic growth, is also sensitive to particular state-variables. The distribution of talent for retail management has relevance to shop rents; for suppose that large strides were made in retail management by a few retail groups and that these could be exploited most effectively in top locations where retail turnover is highest – so increasing the potential trading profit of top locations compared to marginal locations. If the number of retail groups which could exploit the new technique in a city centre were greater than the supply of top-located space, then the landlord of such top retail property would gain an increase in rent from the new innovations. The rent increase would equal the increase in the differential profit that could be exploited on top compared to secondary retail property. If, in contrast, the new retail management technology were developed effectively only by one or two corporations, then they rather than the landlord would capture ensuing growth in trading income.

In the 1960s and 1970s the development of supermarkets was one main form of technological innovation. The technology of supermarket operation was potentially most profitable (relative to the old style of retailing) in large retail spaces in town-centre locations. Many large groups were aware of the new techniques, but the supply of large units in top positions was very scarce. Hence the rents for this category of shop shot up relative to those for secondary locations or for units of small size. Investment in retail property of prime quality (defined to include the characteristics of large floor area and central location) proved highly successful. Success was due not primarily to the perception of inflation-hedge characteristics in top retail property investment, but to economic growth and technological innovation –

both of which increased the rent on top properties compared to those at the margin.

The value of commercial properties can be sensitive in different directions, depending on their type and location, to movement of the state-variable of energy supplies. Sensitivity of values would often be observable only over medium to long-term periods, and energy costs are only one of many relevant influences. Retail property in the city centre would be likely to be diminished in value by substantial rises in the price of energy, whilst suburban retail property would be likely to receive a boost in price. The profitability of retailing in the town centre would be cut both by the fall in effective purchasing power due to the higher transport costs that the great mass of suburban shoppers must pay to travel in to the centre, and by the rise in the wage that must be paid there for retail labour. The retail labour force is drawn typically from suburbia, and the increased cost of travelling into the centre makes them willing to accept a lower wage locally whilst insisting on a higher wage (before deduction of transport costs) in city-centre employment. The lowered retail wage in suburban shopping districts combined with switching of consumer demand away from the city centre would boost profitability of suburban retailing and rents in the town centre would fall relative to those on the periphery.

In general, the distribution of population between the city's centre and its suburban areas is related closely to income distribution. The differential in annual rental value between residential property in the town centre compared to that on the periphery is much greater than simply the extra annual transport cost which the average suburban dweller incurs compared to the city-centre dweller. Transport costs time as well as money. The highly paid worker is willing to pay a greater premium to avoid loss of time travelling to work than the lowly paid worker. Not only can the highly paid worker use that time to achieve a higher rate of earning, but also he is able to pay a higher amount to avoid the non-pecuniary costs associated with commuting. Living centrally permits the avoidance of high costs in terms of time and money of using entertainment facilities concentrated in the city centre. Further, the city-centre dweller is more accessible to being visited by others – again possibly a source of non-pecuniary return.

The concentration of the wealthy in the city centre, and their potential gains from property prices rising there in the aftermath of a substantial rise in energy prices, means that shops specialising in luxury items, and situated in the city centre, should not find that aggregate demand is reduced significantly. They may, however, suffer a contraction in profit margins due to the higher cost of labour which is drawn predominantly from the suburbs.

Office rents should demonstrate the same tendencies as shop rents in the aftermath of an abrupt change in the price of energy, but to a lesser degree. The increased supply of labour in suburban areas and its reduced supply in the city centre would increase labour's cost to central offices, whilst reducing its cost to suburban offices. Unlike for shops, however, the demand for the services of centrally located and suburban located properties should not be affected differentially by the increase in energy costs. Hence the differential between central and suburban office rents should not be doubly squeezed by adverse influences on demand in addition to those on costs.

The distributional impact of energy price increases on warehouse property is the reverse of that on office and shop property. Warehouses situated near key junctions centrally situated in the national or international economy gain in value whilst those in periphery areas and far from key junctions and autoroute systems lose in value. Transport costs are a crucial variable in the decision of management as to where to place a warehouse, especially where its use is for distributional purposes. The significant widening of the differential transport costs incurred between using a central and periphery warehouse, that would occur in the wake of an energy crisis, would lead to a significant increase in the differential between their rents.

In Britain, some confirmation of the above hypothesized response of warehouse rents to energy crisis can be obtained from the behaviour of rents in the aftermath of the 1979–80 doubling of the oil price. Warehouse rents in the 'golden triangle' extending from Reading to London Airport and South Basingstoke continued to advance, whilst elsewhere rents were falling – in part due to an increase in the incidence of transport costs.

The expected real yield from commercial property ownership would appear to have fallen by 1980 to very low levels in the UK, even from the viewpoint of the tax-exempt investor. For consider a newly let prime office building in 1980 yielding a nominal return (first year's rent divided by capital value) of 4½ per cent with the rent being subject to reviews every 5 years. Assume further that investors expected inflation to run at an average 12½ per cent per annum. Then the building would promise a real rent which declined by 12½ per cent annually for the first 5 years then to be refixed for another 5 years at a rent equal to the then market level for newly let properties of similar description. This revised rent in real terms may be above or below 1980 levels but, given the lack of optimism about economic growth, it may be assumed that the revised rent, in real terms, would be close to 1980 levels, and possibly somewhat below, due to intervening obsolescence.

Assuming a real interest rate of close to zero, the annuity equivalent, in terms of 1980 pounds, of the promised rental stream for the first 5 years would be approximately 80 per cent of nominal rent. The annuity equivalent, expressed in real terms (base 1980), of the nominal rent payments, represents 3.6 per cent ($\frac{4}{5} \times 4\frac{1}{2}$) of capital value. Depreciation, at replacement cost, is commonly taken at between 1 and 2 per cent per annum (properties with a high proportion of value attributable to land could have an even lower depreciation rate), leaving a net income yield of around 2 per cent. In addition, every 5 years, agency fees equal to around 0.5 per cent of the then value of the property are incurred in negotiating rent reviews, and every year management costs of around $12\frac{1}{2}$ per cent of the real rent are incurred. Ignoring income tax, a net expected real yield of 1.35 per cent per annum remains, on the assumption of no growth in real rents for newly let properties of similar types. This 1.35 per cent expected pre-tax real return should be compared to a prospective 4.1 per cent pre-tax real return on trading assets owned by UK commercial and industrial enterprises.[4] Given the assumption of zero growth, it would appear that the market acknowledges that real estate is less of a good news good than are trading assets and places some premium on its inflation-hedge properties.

Another consideration relevant to explaining the lower expected real yield on real estate than on enterprises' trading assets is the problem of employing an agent. Owners of real estate can be their own managing agents: they control directly the budget for maintenance, repairs, and professional fees, and have complete control over gross income receipts and their re-investment. In contrast, the owner of equities must ordinarily employ agents (effectively corporate personnel) to manage the underlying trading assets and cash flows therefrom. He must be aware of the risk that the agent (corporate management) will not pay back capital to the owners if the prospects for profit in the corporation's field of activity should deteriorate relative to elsewhere. Indeed there may be tax penalties and legal restrictions on doing so.[5] Further, corporate management see their own livelihood threatened by a decision to repay capital and reduce their corporation's size.[6] In contrast, an owner-manager of a portfolio of commercial real estate investment has complete control over re-investment of income, and may invest depreciation funds outside commercial property if his view of its attractions changes, and so decrease his commitment to that field of investment.

So far, comparison has been made of pre-tax returns. For the taxable investor, the differential between the net yields on real estate and on enterprise assets can be larger than for the tax-exempt investor. Consider the investor whose relevant tax rate is 50 per cent, and assume that – as in Britain – depreciation on buildings (except for certain industrial structures) is not deductible against taxable income: depreciation on trading assets held by a corporation (with the exception of real estate) is, in contrast, tax-deductible. On the prime office property described above, the given investor would earn a real return of −0.25 per cent; on trading assets owned by a corporation – assuming that he bought shares in a corporation with a low dividend pay-out ratio, that depreciation at replacement cost is deductible against corporate taxable income which is taxed at 50 per cent – the investor would earn 3.5 per cent (see Table 5.4). The tax-exempt investor would buy shares in corporations with a high dividend pay-out ratio, but would be subject to a 30 per cent tax rate withheld on dividends. Thus the tax-exempt investor must compare a real return of up to 3.8 per cent on trading assets owned by a corporation with a 1.35 per cent real return on the office property owned directly. The tax-exempt investor would avoid purchasing shares in corporations with significant holdings of real estate – whether occupied by the corporation for trading purposes or let to outside tenants – as its net real yield would be diminished by being passed through the corporation rather than being extracted directly from a tenant.

The apparent comparative advantage of equities to the tax payer may be offset by the more generous expense deductions that can be made against income from property than against income from equities for taxation purposes. The potential of expense deductions to reduce tax is not relevant to the tax-exempt investor.

Investment in Agricultural Land

In the UK nominal yields (rent divided by capital value) on agricultural land have been typically at least 1½ percentage points below those on commercial and industrial properties. For example, in mid-1980, tenanted farmland showed nominal yields of $3\frac{1}{4}$ per cent compared to $4\frac{1}{2}$–$4\frac{3}{4}$ per cent on prime office and shop investment. Superficially the difference approximates annual depreciation on the latter (due to both wear and tear, and gradual technological obsolescence) which does not bear on the owner of tenanted agricultural land, but does bear on the owner of commercial property. Yield comparison is, however, more complicated. For prime shop or office property values are likely to have a particularly high land content, and land is not subject to deterioration. A prime shop in Bond Street or a prime office in the City of London may be subject to depreciation annually of only around $\frac{1}{4}$–$\frac{1}{2}$ per cent of annual value.[7] Such properties, together with the narrow range of warehouse properties on which depreciation is tax-deductible, should be especially attractive to the taxable investor.

Agricultural land's value should, *ceteris paribus*, be boosted by economic growth. Let us take the case where economic growth results from a fast rate of productivity advance in the industrial and commercial sectors – the most important components of GNP in the OECD area – without any productivity advance in the agricultural sector. The increased rate of productivity growth and hence of real wages in industry and commerce would cause the real wage paid by agriculturists also to rise faster – assuming that the supply of farm labour would be responsive to the higher wages obtainable in the towns (we assume no productivity growth in agriculture). The margin of cultivation should expand: the supply of food is fairly price-inelastic and as the demand for food increases, albeit slightly, with incomes, food prices are pushed up and real wages in terms of food fall. The expansion in the margin of cultivation would cause the productivity differential between prime and marginal land to increase and hence prime rents would move upwards.

Consider the alternative case where agricultural productivity advanced by the same percentage, x, each year as did productivity in industry and commerce. Then the differential between the productivity of soil on top land and soil at the present margin (were it to remain unchanged), in combination with a given amount of labour and capital, should increase by the same percentage, x. The increase in the supply of food from an unchanged amount of land would be likely to exceed the increase in demand for food due to the rise in aggregate real incomes (given that income-elasticity of demand for food is assumed to be especially low) and the price of food would fall. In consequence, the price of food would be on a falling trend and this would cause the margin of cultivation to recede somewhat – but the differential between the productivity of the soil on prime land and on land at the contracted margin should still be greater than previously. Hence agricultural rents on prime land may rise but by less than the general increase in productivity.

Although agricultural land is definitely a fairweather good with respect to secular economic growth based on productivity advance, it should be less sensitive in value to the pattern of cyclical growth than is commercial and industrial property. For over short periods of time, demand for food is hardly sensitive to income levels, whilst being sensitive to many non-economic variables – in particular, to the state of weather, the degree of pestilence, and to supply and demand conditions in the centrally planned economies. The low or zero correlation between food prices and the business cycle should in turn translate into a low correlation between agricultural rents and the business cycle.

Agricultural land has been regarded traditionally as a war hedge. Modern war would probably be accompanied by a mixture of food rationing and higher prices for agricultural output. The owner of agricultural land has direct access to food output, and his personal consumption of food would be unconstrained by rations. Further, subsidies would be likely to be given to domestic producers during war-time, and the margin of cultivation extended. The extensions would widen the differential between the productivity of soil at the margin and on top land and so top rents would be increased.

Agricultural land is a hedge also against the bad general state of food shortage, where a growing population not matched by productivity increases in agriculture would cause the real price of food to rise. It is a poorer hedge, however, than commercial and industrial property, against inflation. The behaviour of food prices is often dissimilar to that of a general index of consumer prices, and yet food prices are a major determinant of agricultural rents. The price of agricultural land has proved to be more volatile than that of commercial and industrial property, and hence it has less appeal as a low-risk alternative to monetary assets at times of high and uncertain inflation.

The low sensitivity of the value of agricultural land to the business cycle, together with its positive correlation with the state-variables of belligerency and food shortage, should depress its expected yield relative to that on commercial and industrial property. The poor quality of inflation hedge provided by agricultural land should have an opposing influence on its yield differential with commercial property. Actual nominal yield differences, quoted above, would suggest that agricultural land is awarded a very slightly higher hedge 'rating' than commercial property. Both are essentially convertible news goods, responding positively in value to sustained economic growth in addition to providing their stated hedge services.

Notes and References

1. This reduction in transaction costs is a significant factor favouring owner occupation. Unfortunately, the technology of building is such as to favour economies of scale, and buildings – especially in city centres – typically provide accommodation for many users. Even if each is an owner, as distinct from tenant, there are high negotiation costs incurred in management.
2. Initial nominal yield can be very much higher than the expected post-tax real yield on the property investment, for reasons explained below.
3. A lease creates a conflict of interest between owner and tenant, not present for the owner-occupier. The landlord is concerned that the property should be well-maintained, in order to extend its life – but this does not concern the tenant.
4. See *Bank of England Quarterly Bulletin*, December 1980. Comparison is made for non-geared assets.
5. For example, there are tight controls on the ability of corporations to buy back their own shares. Further, distribution to shareholders of accumulated profit attracts high marginal rates of tax, which often will be in addition to those already paid by the corporation itself.
6. Thus suppose that the expected yield on commercial investment, at the margin, were 4 per cent. The owner of equities in corporation X would face the risk that X's officers may continue to invest retained earnings at rates below 4 per cent. Further, 4 per cent may be below the cost of new equity capital, but the penalties are so great on the corporate sector paying back capital, that corporations are constrained to accept projects at prospective returns below what equity shareholders would supply new funds for.
7. The low depreciation on properties with a high land content is one factor responsible for the lower nominal yield on prime properties compared to secondary properties. Other factors include the greater liquidity of the prime property and the lower risk of periods of inoccupancy between tenancies. Also, during periods of economic growth, prime rents should grow more than rents on marginal properties.

6 Equities

A diversifed portfolio of equities thrives on good news. Its returns are especially high in realities where there is economic boom. Yet at times it has been fashionable to suggest that a market portfolio should be a hedge against inflation. Certain sectors of the equity market are reputed to possess further hedge properties; oil and Swiss bank equities are perceived as energy hedges, and armaments shares as war hedges. These claims can be assessed more fully once certain principles about the relationship of equity valuations to the total value of assets owned by the corporation are developed. This is the first topic of the present chapter.

Equity Valuation

A corporation owns a portfolio of trading and financial assets, including inventories, real estate, plant and machinery, and debtors. The market value of the corporation is the sum of the market values of its equities and debts outstanding. Under certain conditions, developed by Modigliani and Miller,[1] the market value of the firm depends only on the investment projects into which it has entered, and not on how its capital is structured. We start here by assuming that this separability of the financing and investment decision – the Modigliani and Miller Theorem – holds.

The market value of the corporation is in theory determined as equal to the present value of the income which it promises in each and every possible reality, where the prices of contingent incomes are determined as discussed in Chapters 1 and 2. In practice, the number of possible realities are immense, and many analysts have used a simplified two-parameter model, where the expected cash inflow in each period is discounted by a rate which is an increasing function of the covariance of the probability distribution of the cash inflow with that of returns on the market portfolio.[2]

The market value of the corporation may be conceived of as having three components. First, the *liquidation-value* component is what the corporation's assets would realise in the open market, if not sold as part of a trading concern. For a manufacturing concern, the liquidation value consists of the market price of real estate and net financial investments owned, plus what could be obtained for inventories, machinery, and debtors outstanding. Second, the *sunk-capital fund* consists of the present value of rents to be obtained on capital sunk in the enterprise.[3] The cost of investment in the sunk-capital fund is the cumulative difference between the cost of assets acquired and their resale value (as determined immediately after acquisition). Thus a firm which buys a specialised machine for $100,000, whose resale value is negligible, sinks $100,000 into the enterprise. It hopes thereby to obtain a stream of annual rents (net of providing the going rate of return on each category of market capital) from its trading activities that at least equals, in present value terms, the value of capital sunk. Third, *goodwill* represents the capitalisation of supernormal profits, or efficiency rents, expected in the future.

The sum of the three components – market assets, the sunk-capital fund, and goodwill – equals the market value of the corporation, which is in turn determined in the capital markets. The proportion of the three components differs significantly between various categories of enterprise. Thus a retail store chain may have a high proportion of its value attributable to market assets, principally in the form of prime retail properties, whilst a steel manufacturer may have a very large sunk-capital component. Bank enterprises contain significant sunk-capital components, made up of non-marketable loans (to borrowers such as little-known corporations, and high-risk governments in the developing world).

We may conceive of the purchaser of equities in corporation X as buying a levered share in X's market assets, sunk-capital fund and goodwill. The leverage depends on the extent to which the corporation has issued debt per unit of equity. The sunk-capital fund may be thought of as a series of risky bonds with different maturities. The purchase of each machine or other asset whose market value immediately following purchase is far below cost gives rise notionally to an issue of bonds by the sunk-capital fund. The issue is equal to the immediate shortfall in value below cost and is hopefully repaid (together with interest) out of rental income from the operating divisions using the non-market assets. But different assets have different physical lives and hence the bonds issued by the sunk-capital fund differ in their maturity. Unlike for conventional bonds, the rights of the notional bondholder in the sunk-capital fund expire at maturity. Once a machine has been scrapped, holders of that series of bonds in the fund which was issued against the promise of rent from the machine have a worthless asset. In contrast, holders of conventional bonds in a corporation still retain rights of repayment – albeit *vis-à-vis* a liquidator – if full repayment has not been made by maturity.

The above hypothetical breakdown of corporate value into three components is helpful in analysing the extent to which equities are fairweather goods, and their sensitivity to the movement of certain general state-variables. In conditions of economic boom, or fast economic growth, less efficient enterprises are able to enter industries and survive; the differential between the efficiency of the top and of the marginal enterprise in each industry widens. Thus the efficiency rents earned by most intra-marginal enterprises increase, as does the proportion of their total market value based on goodwill. Further, the frequency of write-offs on outstanding bonds of sunk capital funds should be reduced.

In conditions of economic slump, less efficient enterprises go to the wall, and the differential in efficiency between top and marginal enterprises narrows, as does the value of goodwill. Large write-offs are likely to be experienced by the owners of sunk-capital funds: the present value of expected income surplus to providing a normal return on market assets owned by the enterprise is likely to fall below the nominal value of bonds outstanding for the sunk-capital fund (that is, money paid into the sunk-capital fund less repayment to date).

In short, suppose we define the valuation ratio of a trading enterprise as the ratio of its total market value to the value of its market assets. At the bottom of an economic cycle, the valuation ratio will be low, reflecting the write-off of bonds in the sunk-capital fund and the diminished value of goodwill. It is possible for the valuation ratio to be less than unity, if penalties are present on the repayment of capital. Goodwill and the value of the sunk-capital fund are especially sensitive to the business cycle and secular growth trends, and so trading enterprises for which these account for a large proportion of value should often have the characteristics of fair-weather goods.

Suppose at the date of maturity of one bond series of the sunk-capital fund – marked by one set of machinery reaching the end of its economic life – the owners find that they have not yet been repaid in full, due to earnings having fallen below expectation. They may be offered sometimes a re-financing package – whereby they provide funds for replacing the machinery. They may hope that by doing so there will be a good chance of recovery of earnings in the future. Failure to provide funds for replacement could bring about substantial write-offs on other holdings of bonds in the sunk-capital fund which form part of the package of notional securities bought by the shareholder in corporation X. The machinery in question may be the key to the production process being undertaken. This possible commitment to further capital investment and the prolonged period of time which usually proves necessary to the winding-down of activity is attributable to the non-synchronisation of the expiry dates of assets bought by the sunk-capital fund. Thus, despite a downgrading of the aggregate income prospects of corporation X's trading activities, its equity-holders may be committed to new investment in them, a danger not relevant to real estate investment. Further, the short life of many assets owned by the corporation makes the corporation's total value especially sensitive to cyclical variables. In contrast, the long life of real estate reduces the importance of cyclical variables to its value determination. Both considerations should depress the expected yield on property relative to that on equities in general – or equivalently should tend to lead to a higher premium rating on property.

In the previous chapter, the comparative absence of the principal-agent problem was cited as an advantage of real estate investment. For equities, the problem's degree of importance was found to be dependent on the normal dividend pay-out ratio of the corporation. Where a corporation is committed to paying out a high proportion of its profits and seeking capital for new ventures via new issues of securities rather than through profit retentions, shareholders have little reason to be fearful that corporate officers will plough profits into new ventures whose prospective return is below the cost of new equity capital. Yet in most tax regimes, dividends are subject to higher-rate tax – especially for wealthy shareholders – than are retained profits. Thus tax considerations promote a higher tolerance level for potential misappropriation by corporate management of retained profits. In the absence of tax discrimination between distributions and retentions, the corporation which undertook to pay out a high proportion of annual profits should receive an especially favourable rating.[4] Corporations which tried to block their proposed set of investment projects from being subject to a vote of approval from the capital market – by minimising their dependence on new equity capital and by retaining a high proportion of profits – would be viewed with suspicion.

Equities as an Inflation-hedge

The decade of the 1970s demonstrated that a market portfolio of equities was in general a poor hedge against inflation, with world stock markets reaching cyclical low-points in 1974 and 1979 – both years of peak inflation. The record for the decade of the 1970s is shown in Table 6.1.

TABLE 6.1 *World stock markets and inflation*

	Stock market index in local currency, 13 December 1979 (1970 = 100)	*Consumer price index, end-1979 (1970 = 100)*
Japan	249	229
Canada	207	206
UK	143	336
France	114	235
USA	104	201
Switzerland	93	162
Germany	85	163
Netherlands	84	200
Italy	54	329

SOURCE: Capital International Index

Reasons for a secular decline in the real price of equities from 1970 onwards are not hard to find. Economic growth slowed in the OECD in the aftermath of the 1973 oil crisis, and the real rate of profit was squeezed by the combination of OPEC's grown oil levy and the tendency for real wages to rise by more than aggregate productivity. In consequence, the goodwill component of many corporations' values was reduced and part of their sunk-capital funds written off.[5] The sinking of capital prior to 1973 had been proved to have been based on over-optimistic assumptions about profitability, and valuation ratios fell.

Yet conventional wisdom of the early 1970s would have suggested that an acceleration of inflation would boost equity values (expressed in real terms), albeit relative to a secular downward trend. It was agreed that at times of monetary instability, investors would scurry from nominal assets into real assets including equity and real estate. But conventional wisdom failed to acknowledge that equities were in large part nominal assets; and that, further, investors would not switch indiscriminately into real assets as an alternative to money and bonds, but only into low-risk real assets. In addition, periods of high inflation tended to be associated with values for other state-variables – including government policies and cost-push pressures – which were unfavourable for profits.

Many of the market assets owned by the corporation have fixed nominal values whose real purchasing power would be eroded by unanticipated inflation. For example, a proportion of inventory at any time has typically been already sold where the sales contract specifies a fixed nominal price. Long-term contracts, where fixed nominal prices are quoted for future deliveries of goods, are common. Even though that part of inventory which has not been sold forward – non-committed inventory – is in principle a 'real asset', it may in practice be transformed into a nominal asset through the failure of corporations to adjust continuously their selling prices. If these were adjusted only periodically, then inventory would be in part a nominal asset. Suppose that inflation during the period between the posting of successive price lists were more than anticipated, then the real profits of the enterprise would be diminished. Equity shareholders realise that corporate management is sluggish in changing its routines – whether in inventory management or in costing – in response to an increase in the inflation rate; high inflation increases the danger of misappropriation of retained profits, with projects being undertaken in error due to failure to adjust capital-budgeting procedures.

The taxation of corporate income is at best only partially indexed. For example, depreciation allowances are typically non-indexed. It is a mistake to believe that provisions for initial allowances of 100 per cent against certain types of capital expenditure are equivalent to tax-indexation. For if the post-tax real rate of return on financial assets were a declining function of inflation, then the real deduction that must be made from profit each year, to provide a fund which would accumulate – together with interest – to provide sufficiently for capital replacement, would be an increasing function of inflation. Capital gains tax, both on asset realisations by the corporation itself, and on equity disposals by the shareholder, is rarely indexed. Hence the relative tax burden on equity investments, compared to that on housing or collectables or assets which are invisible to fiscal authorities, is increased by inflation.

As discussed in Chapter 2, and in the introduction to the present chapter, a market portfolio of equities has returns which are typified by higher volatility than those of certain consumer durables (including residential real estate) and some types of commercial property (excluding one-off prime examples). The advent of high and variable inflation rates would cause the demand for nominal assets to fall, the demand for low-risk real assets to rise, and the demand for high-risk real assets to fall. Investors would adjust to the vanishing of the opportunity to acquire nominal assets of zero or low risk by reducing their desired holdings of high-risk real assets and by increasing their desired holdings of low-risk real assets. The market portfolio of trading assets owned by the corporate sector is of higher risk than the real assets which would be sought as substitutes for monetary assets, and so the overall demand for enterprises' trading assets would be reduced by an increase in inflation risk.

Higher than anticipated inflation would be likely to trigger the enacting of avowedly anti-inflation measures by government. At one extreme, these could include price, profit and dividend controls – obvious negative influences on equity values. Alternatively, a policy of monetary restraint and fiscal deflation could be introduced; this would inflict losses on the goodwill and sunk-capital components of corporate value due to expectations of a reduced level of economic activity. Many types of real estate and of consumer durables are less sensitive in value than are equities to cyclical dips in the economy.

It has sometimes been argued erroneously that highly levered equities should prove to be a good inflation hedge. The reader will remember, from Chapter 1, that investors consider high inflation (which has not been fully anticipated) as a bad general state of the world, for real income from net holdings of nominal assets (represented by government debt in various forms) would be exceptionally low there. By buying inflation hedges – assets that produce relatively high income in realities where inflation is high – the investor insures his holding of nominal assets against unexpected acceleration of inflation. But by selling lowly levered equities for highly levered equities, the investor reduces implicitly his holding of net nominal assets and increases his holding of enterprises' trading assets; he does not thereby gain inflation insurance for a given net holding of nominal assets but reduces simply the net amount of nominal assets to be insured.

If inflation were to increase in unpredictability, we have seen that demand for low-risk real assets would be likely to increase whilst that for nominal assets and for high-risk real assets would be likely to decrease. One channel through which the changed pattern of portfolio demand could be effected would be the sale of nominal assets in exchange for highly levered equities in corporations whose portfolio of trading assets was of low risk. But given that the investor himself can 'lever' a holding of equities in a non-levered corporation whose value is of low risk, there is no reason to expect that the levered corporation would have a special premium value placed on it (compared to the non-levered corporations) during such periods of changing portfolio demand.

Even if factors such as non-deductibility of interest payments against personal taxable income were to violate the assumption that the investor could reverse on personal account any borrowing (or lending) transaction which could be effected by the corporation and on the same terms, competition between corporations engaged in low-risk enterprise to obtain a premium valuation by levering their capital structure would force the premium towards zero. Moreover, if the change in portfolio preferences were general, a change in corporate leverage ratios – which alters the gross but not the net amount of nominal debt securities outstanding – would not satisfy them: there would be no reason to expect a change in the degree to which the capital structure of low-risk corporations was levered.

In Chapter 1, the distinction was made between monetary and non-monetary sources of inflation. Equities are usually victims of some types of non-monetary source of inflation – energy shortage in particular (given that 'oil tax' falls, at least on impact, on profits). The two inflation bursts in the advanced industrialised countries during the decade of the 1970s had an important non-monetary source in soaring commodity and energy prices. Given the apparent high correlation (through time) between the state-variables of monetary and non-monetary inflation, equities should rarely perform well in realities where observed inflation is high.

Accounting problems that arise from high and variable rates of inflation are further responsible for dampening any latent enthusiasm among investors for equities as an inflation hedge. With a highly unstable unit of account, the interpretation and comparison of corporate performance becomes especially difficult. Although a large literature exists on adjusting accounts for inflation – and in Britain inflation-adjustment is now mandatory for large corporations – any method of adjustment falls far short of producing an ideal concept of real income. Investors must fear that the dissemination and authenticity of corporate information would fall as the inflation rate rose; this makes equities less attractive relative to simple real assets, such as property or commodities, about which information is not a decreasing function of inflation.

Evidence on the importance of information-loss to the behaviour of equities at times of high inflation can be found in historical episodes. Bresciani-Turroni recounts how the small investor was swindled by large controlling groups of shareholders during the German hyperinflation due to the breakdown of safeguards against corrupt practices and the meaninglessness of published information.[6] Indeed, by mid-1922, equities in real terms had fallen to 8 per cent of their October 1918 level. The complete failure of equities to provide protection against inflation was not due entirely to the breakdown of safeguards and loss of information. The loss of territory by Germany, the imposition of reparations,[7] and the fear of domestic revolution – aggravated by hyperinflation – all contributed to the collapse of equity prices in real terms. Bresciani-Turroni suggests that in the second half of 1922, and during 1923, equities became transformed into inflation hedges, rising in real terms, despite an ever-accelerating rate of inflation, up to the stabilisation of the mark at end-1923. The reason for the transformation was a ban imposed late in 1922 on the purchase of foreign exchange by domestic residents: until then, foreign monies had been the most widely used hedge against hyperinflation in post-war Germany.

In more recent times, the particularly poor performance of equity markets in the two major OECD economies which experienced the highest sustained inflation rates during the 1970s – Italy and Britain – may have been at least partly due to the deterioration in the quality of corporate information available, and the consequential growing domination of equity markets by inside dealers. A relation between inflation, information quality, and equity value cannot of course be proved. Other factors were at work in both Italy and Britain to depress real equity values – including fears of political instability and a sharply falling share of profit in national income due in large part to acute wage–cost pressures.[8]

Hedge Sectors of the Equity Market

Although an investment in a diversified portfolio of equities is very much in the nature of a fairweather good, individual sectors of the equity market have attracted attention in respect of their hedge properties. These include bank shares as an inflation-hedge, oil shares as an energy crisis-hedge, Swiss shares and armaments shares as war-hedges. We examine each of these in turn.

The idea that bank shares can be a hedge against inflation is derived from the observation that in most countries banks do not pay interest on sight-deposits. Hence at times of high inflation, when a high rate of inflation is expected to continue, and nominal interest rates are also high, the real revenue obtained from sight-deposit business is likely to be particularly high. The revenue per period equals the difference between the average earnings per dollar on the banks' assets minus the cost of servicing sight deposits per dollar. Now when nominal interest rates, expected inflation, and actual inflation are all 1 per cent per annum, the real revenue from sight deposit business is clearly much less than when nominal interest rates, expected inflation, and actual inflation, are all 15 per cent, say. In the transition from a reality of low actual and expected inflation to one of high actual and expected inflation it may be expected that bank shares, in real terms, would receive a boost from the market coming to expect an increased flow of real earnings from sight-deposit business.

Yet the inflation-hedge property of bank shares, based on banks' potential revenues from sight-deposit business, must be qualified by a number of observations.

First, revenue from sight-deposit business is a direct function of the level of nominal interest rates, and indirectly of the level of expected inflation due to the high correlation of inflation and nominal interest rates. Thus sight-deposit earnings would not gain from an inflation which was unanticipated – unless news of higher-than-anticipated inflation during the immediate past period led to a rise in inflation expectations and in nominal interest rates. In a monetary inflation where nominal interest rates lagged behind inflation expectations which in turn lagged behind actual inflation, prospective earnings from sight-deposit business would be linked only loosely to actual inflation rates.

Second, taxation bears especially heavily on banks at times of high inflation. In most fiscal systems, partial adjustment for inflation is made to assets such as inventory and machinery when calculating taxable income. Nominal assets, in contrast, are taxed at an increasingly burdensome rate as inflation rises. For example, with a corporate tax rate of 50 per cent, inflation at 1 per cent per annum, and an average nominal rate of return of 3 per cent per annum on the banks' loans and investments, the real post-tax rate of return would be $\frac{1}{2}$ per cent; if the real pre-tax rate of return were to remain unchanged, but inflation and the nominal rate of return were to move up to 10 and 12 per cent respectively, the real post-tax rate of return (on the bank's assets) would fall to −4 per cent, and the rate of tax as a proportion of real earnings would rise to 600 per cent from 75 per cent. Most of the banks' loan and investment portfolio is financed typically by deposits, but some part is financed directly by equity issue. Equity capital so invested is subject to taxation which becomes ferocious at high inflation rates – a negative factor for bank equities as an inflation-hedge.

Third, union wage-negotiators for bank labour often cite the current year's profit performance as justification for real wage-rate rises. Yet real wages tend to be rigid downwards. Thus long-term prospects for profit are likely to be affected adversely by a transitory increase in the inflation rate.

Fourth, real revenue from sight-deposit business is not a monotonically rising function of nominal interest rates and of expected inflation. As both rise, an increasing incentive is created to economise on the holding of non-interest-bearing deposits and currency. Indeed, it can be shown that beyond a certain level of nominal interest rate and expected inflation rate, the potential real revenue falls, due to the increasing rate of economising on holdings of sight deposits and currency.[9] Further, at high and sustained inflation rates the forces of monopoly or collusion that allow banks not to pay interest on sight-deposits are likely to be weakened.[10] Thus real revenue from sight-deposit business is likely to diminish as a source of inflation protection to bank shareholders as inflation reaches very high levels.

Fifth, banks hold a portfolio of government bonds usually unmatched by fixed-rate borrowing. Hence they suffer losses when nominal interest rates and inflation expectations rise. These losses may be aggravated by the general tendency of banks to borrow short and lend long. Even when long-term loans are subject to a floating rate of interest, with rate re-fixings at, say, 6-monthly intervals (as is common in the Euro-market), it will normally be found that the average roll-over period of the banks' deposit base is shorter. Thus the general practice of liability and deposit management tends to subject banks to income and capital losses on their loan and investment portfolios at times of increasing inflation expectations, and these offset – at least in part – prospective earnings from current-account business.

Sixth, in the transition to extreme inflationary conditions, actually realised nominal earnings from sight-deposit business, per dollar of deposits outstanding, may fall. This could occur if inflation far exceeded expectations; then nominal interest earnings, derived from that portion of bank assets financed notionally by the issue of sight-deposits, could fall short of the dollar costs of servicing those sight-deposits. Thus a bank may have budgeted that its $20 million of sight-deposits will earn, during the next 3 months, $1 million in nominal interest from being used to finance fixed-rate 3-month lending. The bank's management may, further, have budgeted for servicing costs of $0.5 million to be incurred in handling transactions on the sight-deposits. If, however, inflation were suddenly to take off, with the price-level doubling in 3 months, then realised earnings, net of servicing costs, from sight-deposit business would be near-zero. This type of consideration is relevant, of course, only in conditions of hyperinflation.

Historically bank shares have proved to be hedges neither against hyperinflation nor against high inflation. During the German hyper-inflation,[11] gold-equivalent book value of the leading seven Berlin banks was reduced by 61 per cent: banks had used their own capital in lending to customers at nominal interest rates which lagged far behind inflation. Further, the banks had suffered heavy losses of capital in the aftermath of Germany's defeat, as a result of forced closures and liquidations of foreign branches, and of sequestration of securities and properties held abroad. The mortgage banks lost an even greater proportion of their capital than the leading Berlin banks, due to laws which obliged them to invest largely in fixed-rate form and for long periods of time.

In more normal conditions, econometric research both in the USA and UK has shown that bank shares' prices are highly correlated to the value of the market portfolio.[12] Given that the market portfolio itself has not proved to be an inflation-hedge, neither are bank shares likely to prove so, given the high correlation of their returns with those of the market. Though earnings from sight-deposit business have been an increasing function of inflation over its range experienced during the 1970s in the USA and in Britain, other factors – in particular, movement of the business cycle and the international flow of funds – have dominated both actual and anticipated overall profit performance.

There are three reasons in theory why oil shares should receive a fillip in value from a sharp rise in the oil price. First, the value of oil inventories owned by the oil companies would be increased in value. Total stocks of crude oil and products held by oil corporations in Europe, Japan, and the USA, averaged over 2½ billion barrels in 1980;[13] each $4 rise in the oil price would have generated inventory profits of at least $10 billion. Second, oil prices on the free market in Rotterdam tend to lead price rises by OPEC producers. In the interval of time during which spot-prices are above official ones, oil companies would realise arbitrage profits from selling contract oil, bought under contract from OPEC, in the free market. Third, the value of oil which the oil corporations own under the ground would increase. Not only the value of proven reserves but also of unproven reserves rises. There would be an increase in the potential profits from further exploration on lands presently owned by the oil corporations.

During the oil crises of 1979 and 1980, oil shares certainly performed as energy crisis-hedges (see Tables 6.2 and 6.3). Gains of over 100 per cent were common for oil shares between the beginning of 1979 and the end of 1980,[14] and the gains were concentrated in the periods of sharply rising spot oil prices. This behaviour of oil shares was more marked in the second than in the first oil crisis of 1974. At that date oil prices were still strictly controlled in the USA, whilst early in 1979 a 2-year programme for the phasing out of controls had been announced. Further, the US oil majors still had, in 1974, substantial assets in the Middle East, and the increased tensions there which had themselves been a political source of oil price rises had also brought into reality the threat of nationalisation.

TABLE 6.2 *USA oil equities' price ($ per share)*

	1979		*1980*	
	High	*Low*	*High*	*Low*
Atlantic Richfield	$41\frac{1}{2}$	28	71	$38\frac{3}{4}$
Conoco	$48\frac{1}{2}$	17	70	$41\frac{3}{8}$
Exxon	$60\frac{1}{4}$	$48\frac{3}{4}$	$83\frac{5}{8}$	$52\frac{3}{8}$
Gulf Oil	$36\frac{7}{8}$	23	$46\frac{1}{4}$	$32\frac{7}{8}$
Mobil	$58\frac{1}{2}$	$36\frac{1}{4}$	81	$51\frac{1}{2}$
Shell Oil	$29\frac{1}{2}$	$14\frac{1}{8}$	$62\frac{1}{2}$	$27\frac{3}{4}$
Standard Oil (California)	62	$34\frac{1}{4}$	$101\frac{3}{8}$	$53\frac{3}{4}$
Texaco	$31\frac{1}{4}$	$22\frac{1}{8}$	$44\frac{3}{4}$	$28\frac{1}{8}$

SOURCE: *The Petroleum Economist.*

TABLE 6.3 *USA oil company earnings (million dollars)*

	January–June 1979	*January–June 1980*	*Percentage change*
Atlantic Richfield	502.6	860.9	+71
Conoco	377.6	578.2	+53
Exxon	1785.0	2955.0	+66
Gulf Oil	540.0	759.0	+41
Mobil	867.0	1533.0	+77
Shell Oil	501.0	780.0	+56
Standard Oil (California)	726.0	1162.0	+60
Texaco	641.0	1103.5	+72

SOURCE: *The Petroleum Economist.*

Indirect confirmation of oil shares' hedge-property comes from the fairly low correlation of their values with that of the market portfolio. For example, the London Business School, in its 'Risk Management Service', measures the beta-coefficient of sectors of the *Financial Times* index with the overall index, based on observations of market data over the past 5–7 years. The oil sector had a beta-coefficient of only 0.66 for the period 1973–80, despite the capital structure of oil corporations having an especially high leverage ratio.[15] Over the same period, movement of the oil price in Rotterdam was a powerful factor in determining price behaviour of the oil sector relative to that of the market as a whole.[16]

A rise in the oil price is, of course, not unambiguously good for all parts of an oil company's business. The major oil companies are involved substantially in downstream activities, including the refining and distribution of petroleum products. In the late 1970s downstream earnings accounted for around 25 per cent of total earnings of the oil majors. Yet earnings from downstream activities are cyclical – with margins on refining reaching its peak at the top of the business cycle when there is least unused capacity. A large hike in the real oil price reduces demand for oil products, both directly, and indirectly via an induced world recession. Oil companies with a very small downstream component should, *a priori,* be purer oil crisis-hedges than those with significant downstream activities.[17]

Oil companies are far from being a pure energy crisis-hedge. We have seen how their earnings are significantly dependent on cyclical factors. Further, they are subject to the movement of certain state-variables – in particular, rates of taxation, whether in the form of product tax, windfall profit tax, or a surcharge on local production by an OPEC member. An abrupt change in the rate of tax, if it occurred at the same time as energy crisis, would dampen the protection given by oil shares against falling income on most assets.[18] Other particular state-variables include the rate of oil-finds for the particular company considered. Thus the investor buying income contingent on an energy crisis should hold a portfolio of oil shares, together with other hedges against energy crisis, including petro-monies; he would reduce thereby the variance of income in possible realities marked by energy crisis.

If the market had grounds to suspect that a windfall profits tax would be imposed on oil and gas companies in the event of an energy crisis, the hedge property of their equity would be diminished. The prospect of a windfall profits tax – however necessary from a political viewpoint – has the unfortunate side-effect of raising the cost of equity finance for the oil companies and so reducing physical investment in projects which would produce especially high pay-offs in energy crisis. The danger of a windfall profits tax limits the scope of oil and gas exploration to alleviate the fear of energy shortage by increasing the minimum level of energy supplies.

In the event of a major war, many investors believe that Switzerland would be one of the few countries which would be able to remain neutral. Thus, assets owned in Switzerland are less subject to war-risk than are those in most other lands. Further, assets owned by Swiss residents in countries at war would be subject to less risk of confiscation, either during war or in its aftermath, than would be assets in the same lands held by foreigners resident in belligerent countries. Residence should be interpreted here to include the corporate form; assets held in France by a Swiss corporation may be viewed as of lower political risk than assets held in France by a German corporation. In the event of an intra-European war, German foreign (and domestic) assets would probably be confiscated, whilst those held by the Swiss corporation would be untouched as neutral property.[19]

Residents in belligerent, or potentially belligerent, countries can obtain a war-shelter by investing abroad via the vehicle of a Swiss international. Thus an Englishman wishing to buy a share in the food industry in Continental Europe would see lower war-related risk in doing this via buying a share in Nestle, Hero (or some other food multinational based in Switzerland), than via buying shares in an English food multinational. In consequence, the cost of capital to the Swiss multinational should be especially low, due to the potential income-yield of its securities in a state of war, and on this score the Swiss corporation has a comparative advantage in 'going international' over say, the French or German corporation.

This comparative advantage of the Swiss multinational cannot be diluted by the non-Swiss multinational borrowing in Swiss francs. Empirical evidence suggests that interest rates in the domestic Swiss capital market may have been depressed secularly by the importance of hedge considerations for investors.[20] But Swiss franc bonds issued by a non-Swiss corporation are not a war-hedge, and franc denominated bonds issued by top-rated non-Swiss sovereign names have yielded typically as much as one percentage point more than top Swiss cantonal names.

The attraction of Swiss equities to the international investor is due to more than war considerations: Switzerland's reputation for low inflation is also a source of its equity market's popularity. We have seen that equities are not in general inflation-hedges, and indeed that equities of corporations investing in high-risk enterprise activities are fairweather goods which gain from low inflation. The low chance of high inflation in Switzerland means that equities there are less exposed to the risk of downward adjustment due to portfolio shifts out of equities and into real estate and consumer durables in the wake of an increased inflation rate.[21] Further, in so far as tax is charged on the multinational on a consolidated worldwide basis by the government of the country in which its headquarters are situated, it is beneficial that the inflation rate there should be low. The tax-charge in real terms is less subject to the risk of upward distortion due to high inflation in a traditionally low-inflation country like Switzerland than in other countries, and this is appreciated by international investors.

Indeed, Swiss equities in the late 1970s acted as an impure US inflation-hedge. At times when market expectations of inflation in the USA received a jolt upwards, the relative attraction of investing in equities issued by multinationals with a low inflation base in Switzerland compared to investing in equities of US multinationals increased. Further, real interest rates and bond yields were depressed on francs during the mid-1970s, by the aggravation of US inflation expectations and consequential foreign inflows into the Swiss money; the Swiss equity market itself received a boost from the falling yield on alternative assets issued in the Swiss capital market.

Dividend yields on Swiss equities are typically very low by international comparison. The bulk of investors in Swiss equities are *'de facto'* not subject to capital gains tax, but are subject to withholding tax on dividends; Swiss corporations respond by packaging an especially high proportion of their income in the form of capital gain rather than in the form of dividends. Capital gain on equity holdings has as one component retained earnings which are subject to corporate income tax. However, in Switzerland, the effective rate of tax on retained profits has been significantly below that on dividend payouts.

One particular section of the Swiss equity market deserves special attention for its hedge properties. Swiss bank shares should yield particularly high income contingent on international banking crisis and on energy crisis. For Swiss banks have only slight exposure to debtor countries in the non-oil developed countries, and should gain custom if fears were to grow about the safety of Euro-banks, particularly of German or US nationality, with large exposure to these areas. Further, as much as 25 per cent of OPEC deposits in the Euro-market are placed on a fiduciary basis with Swiss banks who earn commission thereon. OPEC countries and private investors value the anonymity and possibly keener terms obtained by using a Swiss bank as agent, rather than placing funds directly in the Euro-market themselves. Thus, if the oil price rose sharply and OPEC revenues rose simultaneously, Swiss banks could look forward to large prospective revenues from increased fiduciary business.[22] Swiss bank shares should then perform strongly, and indeed this was the experience in 1980, a year of huge OPEC surpluses.

Enterprises specialising in the production of armaments should gain directly from increased military expenditures, which are symptomatic of an increased risk of war. Thus armament equities should yield especially high income in realities where war risks are high, and during periods of war itself.

Certainly armaments equities have performed particularly well at times of international tension. US corporations specialising in armaments, such as General Dynamics, Honeywell, and Boeing, were market favourites during the build-up of military expenditure for the Vietnam War in the late 1960s, again in the aftermath of the Russian conquest of Afghanistan in late 1979, and during the East European crises of 1980, together with the election of Reagan as US President on the ticket of a tougher policy towards the USSR. But all these war crises have been associated with general strength of the US market index, and hence armaments-equities cannot strictly be termed as hedge assets. Movement of the state-variable 'belligerency' in the direction of war – over the range of its values taken in recent history – has tended to be associated with increasing not decreasing aggregate income.

For more extreme movements of the state-variable 'belligerence', into a range near world war, there is fortunately no evidence of how armaments equities would perform today. 'War profits' would be likely to be tightly controlled in principle, if not in practice. Further, the risks of nationalisation of armament firms would surely increase. Armament firms typically have a diversified product range extending into many areas beyond the military, and their revenues from these non-military sources would be curtailed severely in a war economy – reducing the prospective gains to the equity-holder contingent on war.

We must conclude that equities in armament firms should provide income contingent on exacerbation of international tension within the range known in recent years. But high international tension has been a state of greater income abundance than one of low international tension. The likelihood of movements of the state-variable 'belligerency' in the direction of war not being monotonically a 'bad thing' (from the viewpoint of those with important purchasing power in world equity markets) prevents us classifying armaments shares as hedge assets. Their income prospects may compare favourably with those of most other assets, albeit depressed, in situations of much greater war-danger than we have experienced in the recent past; but that is unproven.

Notes and References

1. M. Modigliani, and M. Miller, 'The Cost of Capital, Corporation Finance, and the Theory of Investment', *American Economic Review,* vol. 48 (June 1958) pp. 261–97. An important assumption is that individuals can lever their portfolios on the same terms as the corporation can lever itself. An investor buying an equity seeks to obtain a share in its portfolio of assets, including trading opportunities. If the corporation's leverage ratio is different from the investor's preferred one, he can correct for this by borrowing or lending on personal account.
2. See W. Sharpe, 'Capital Asset Prices: A Theory of Market Equilibrium under Conditions of Risk', *Journal of Finance,* vol. 19 (September 1964) pp. 425–42, for the original development of the two-parameter model.
3. Conceptually, the operating divisions of a corporation may be viewed as leasing equipment from the sunk-capital fund. A default on a lease commitment could arise from premature obsolescence, for example, and this would lead to a portion of the sunk-capital fund being written off.
4. According to Modigliani and Miller's famous article on dividend policy, see 'Dividend Policy, Growth and the Valuation of Shares', *Journal of Business*, vol. 34 (October 1961) pp. 411–33, the dividend decision is irrelevant to the market value of the enterprise; but they assume the absence of taxation, and ignore principal-agent problems.
5. For evidence of the profit squeeze, see *OECD Economic Outlook,* December 1978. Except in the UK, a further profit squeeze did not occur in the aftermath of the second oil crisis in 1979–80.
6. See Bresciani-Turroni, *Economics of Inflation* (Kelley, 1968) p. 255.
7. In the German press there was frequent comment about 'the invisible mortgage' weighing on German industry because of the payment of reparations which contributed to the uncertainty of the future income from shares.
8. For example, in Italy the operation of *'la scala mobile'* effectively prevented a diminution of the real wage, even when the terms of trade moved in a sharply adverse direction.
9. See M. Friedman, *The Optimum Quantity of Money* (Macmillan, 1969), Chapter 1.
10. For example, in the USA in the late 1970s, restrictions on the non-payment of interest on sight-deposits were increasingly 'got round'. Finally in 1980, a Monetary Control Act came into force which provided for eventual phasing-out of interest rate ceilings.
11. See Bresciani-Turroni, *op. cit.*
12. For example, the 'Risk Management Service' of the London Business

School shows that the beta-coefficient for the UK clearers is approximately equal to unity and that their specific risk is low.

13. For the world as a whole outside Comecon, oil stocks in the second half of 1980 reached 5 billion barrels. For statistics see various issues of the *Petroleum Economist.*
14. During the same period, the Dow Jones Index (in which oil shares have a significant representation) rose by nearly 35 per cent.
15. Beta is a coefficient heavily dependent on the coefficient of correlation between returns on the given security and on the market portfolio.
16. For evidence on this, see Vickers da Costa Ltd, *United Kingdom Research,* 9 October, 1979.
17. Indeed stockbrokers' research analysts do attempt to pinpoint these different categories of oil companies. See L. Messel & Co., *Oil Review,* January 1980.
18. One example is the increase in taxation of oil companies and plans to decrease foreign ownership of energy-resources that were announced in Canada in late 1980, in the middle of the Iran–Iraq war. The announcement detracted transitorily from the appeal of US oil equities as inflation hedges.
19. This consideration is of course much less relevant today than in the period, say, before World War II.
20. For evidence of the low real rate of return on domestic francs, see R. Z. Aliber, 'Attributes of National Monies and the Interdependence of National Monetary Policies', in R. Z. Aliber (ed.), *National Monetary Policies and the International Financial System* (University of Chicago, 1974).
21. It is assumed here that the Swiss themselves are a principal source of demand for Swiss equities – and hence Swiss inflation risk is highly relevant to their pricing.
22. For example, at end-1979, fiduciary deposits placed by Swiss banks were approximately 50 billion francs. One year later, with the huge OPEC surpluses of 1980, fiduciary deposits had doubled. On these deposits, commissions of $\frac{1}{4}$–$\frac{1}{2}$ per cent of capital value were charged.

7 Bond Markets

The high and volatile inflation rates of the 1970s have increased greatly the perceived risks of investing in fixed-rate bonds. Long-term yields on dollar bonds, which started the decade at near 7 per cent, finished the decade at near 14 per cent; sterling bond yields moved from 9 per cent to near 17 per cent over the same period. Fixed-rate bonds, once viewed as near-riskless assets, ended the decade as highly volatile investments.

Yet top-rated fixed-rate bonds still provide important hedge properties against slump and against banking crisis. Specific sectors of the bond market possess additional hedge properties – Swiss bonds as hedges against US inflation; commodity bonds as hedges against various commodity shortages; indexed bonds as hedges against inflation. We shall examine each of these in turn.

Slump-hedges

As an economy slides into slump, top-rated fixed-rate bonds are likely to show extraordinary returns, and this is the source of their slump-hedge property. Falling interest rates typify a slide into slump and cause fixed-rate bonds of top quality to show capital gains. Yet the insurance against slump offered by bonds is made very uncertain by the advent of high and variable inflation. For then the real return from bonds in each period would become highly dependent on changes in inflation expectations, and these may dwarf the influence of the level of economic activity on bond prices. At best, fixed-rate bonds are a fairly impure slump-hedge.

The investor looking to buy income contingent on a world slump should find bonds denominated in a low-inflation international money particularly attractive, even when he would thereby assume exchange risk against his own money. For capital gains generated by a fall in interest rates (both spot and forward) are greatest for bonds of long effective maturity, and the longest effective maturity bonds are found in low-inflation monies.[1] Further, low-inflation bonds, whilst being more sensitive to the level of world economic activity than are high-inflation bonds, should also experience less volatility on account of changing inflation expectations. Non-residents of the country of issue of the relevant low-inflation money do, however, assume exchange risk when they buy bonds in that denomination. Even so, if real exchange rate volatility is small relative to inflation volatility in the investor's own country, then the low-inflation bond should prove a less impure slump-hedge than domestic bonds.

For example, if world slump brought an equal drop in nominal interest rates in Germany and in Italy (with the Italian inflation rate and nominal yield on bonds being far above those in Germany), then Deutsche mark-denominated bonds – having the longer effective maturity – would show a larger capital gain than the high coupon (and thereby shorter effective maturity) lira bonds. Given a much lower inflation volatility in Germany than in Italy, and limited prospective volatility of the real lira–mark exchange rate, Deutsche mark bonds should prove less impure than Italian bonds as a hedge against slump in Europe, even from the viewpoint of the Italian.

Given that top-quality fixed-rate bonds are a slump-hedge, why should anyone be interested in issuing them? Why should someone wish to sell income contingent on an economic slump? Two types of issuers should be distinguished: private and public.

For a top-rated corporation, the main alternative form of loan finance to fixed-rate bond issues is short-term borrowing from banks, probably on a roll-over basis, with the interest rates reviewed according to market conditions. The attractions of such finance are that the exposure of the equity-holder to inflation risk is not aggravated thereby and the benefit of low real interest rates during recession would be obtained.[2] Nominal interest rates tend to move with inflation expectations, and the equity-holder in a corporation financed in part by floating-rate debt (and not by fixed-rate debt) does not risk that a pronounced fall in inflation expectations and bond yields would leave the corporation with an enhanced real liability and so reduce the value of his equity. Further, during recession, the fall in enterprise profits would be spread, albeit unevenly, between the floating-rate lender and equity-holders, with the former suffering a reduction in the real rate of interest.

The issue of short-term debt (principally in the form of bank-borrowing), in contrast to the issue of long-term debt, does nothing to dilute specific (as opposed to general economic) risks of owning equity in a given corporation X. Should X's profit prospects deteriorate by substantially more than for those of the economy in aggregate, X would find itself forced to pay a higher margin above prime rate at the next roll-over date. For long-term debt, margins – whether explicit or implicit – are not renegotiable: if X's credit-rating were to decline from AAA to B over the lifetime of the bond, the bond-holder would suffer some windfall-loss, relieving the equity-holder of some loss.

In sum, the issue of short-term debt dilutes general economic risk (for example, exposure to movement of the inflation rate and level of economic activity) borne by the equity-owner, whilst the issue of long-term debt dilutes specific risks (a change in the corporation's performance relative to that of the whole economy) to which he is exposed. Thus the issue of long-term debt does allow important redistribution of risks specific to the enterprise, albeit involving the equity-holder in the acceptance of a higher level of general economic risk. The particular corporation may be aiming to sell its equities to a clientele seeking a high level of general risk together with a high expected yield. Equivalently, by issuing long-term fixed-rate debt, a corporation reduces the extent to which its shareholders need to diversify their portfolios of equities in order to shed specific risks, and transaction costs should thereby be reduced.

The role of long-term borrowing in reducing specific risk is highly relevant to the owner–manager of a firm, who wishes to maintain a controlling interest yet shed specific risk. The demise of long-term mortgage and corporate bond markets in high-inflation countries – for example, during 1970s in Britain – has forced him to absorb a higher share of the specific risk of his enterprise, and has hence been a deterrent to entrepreneurial activity.

Short-term borrowing does expose the borrower (and hence the equity-holder) to the bad general states of liquidity squeeze or banking crisis. At such times, short-term real interest rates, expecially on bank deposits and loans, rise to very high levels, as banks compete for reserves which are in acute shortage. The shortage may be created deliberately by the central bank – when it is trying to engineer a sharp slowdown in the rate of monetary growth – or it may result from the public rushing to convert deposits into base money during a banking panic. The equity-holder in a corporation with large short-term debts outstanding is doubly exposed to the risk of a liquidity shortage occurring. Not only would his overall level of liquidity fall, in common with that other market participants, so limiting his flexibility of action, but also the value of his equity-holding would be diminished by large real interest deductions made from trading profit.

The advent of floating-rate notes (FRNs) and of term-loans has broken the identity of long-term borrowing and long-term fixed-rate borrowing. A corporation which issues a 10-year FRN, pays a fixed margin, over 6-month London Interbank Offered Rate (LIBOR) for dollars, which cannot change to reflect a deterioration in credit rating. The FRN thus allows risk specific to the corporation to be diluted.

The extent of dilution cannot be known for certain, as it is a function of the level of inflation expected generally. For if nominal interest rates and expectations of inflation were to rise sharply, then the rate at which the real value of the principal is repaid would accelerate.[3] Hence the effective maturity of the FRN would be reduced, and a greater share of risk specific to the corporation would be thrown back onto the equity-owners to bear. An increase in nominal coupons (accelerating the rate of real capital repayment) forces the borrower to negotiate an increase in his nominal credit limits and the lender would be likely to insist on a margin being fixed which was appropriate to his then credit rating. Moreover, the borrower is likely to have paid an excessive margin on the FRN in the false belief that he was obtaining a fixed margin, irrespective of subsequent credit-rating changes, for a long effective maturity.

In principle, this uncertainty as to the division of specific risk between note-holder and equity-holder, due to inflation expectations changing, can be reduced by modifying the conventional form of FRN. For example, if the issuer of FRNs undertook to pay in cash, on each coupon date, only a fixed nominal coupon of say 5 per cent, and to make a new issue of notes in lieu of cash for any due interest in excess of the nominal coupon, then the margin and the maturity date on the new issue of notes would be the same as on the original. The effective maturity of this new type of FRN would be invariant with respect to the inflation rate.

Fixed-rate bonds are subject also to inflation-induced maturity risk, but this is small compared to the risk of fluctuation in their real capital values due to changes in inflation expectations. For example, if inflation and nominal interest rates were to rise, bond-holders in corporation X would suffer a capital loss and equity-holders would gain at their expense. Losses would exceed gains, as enterprise values are a casualty of inflation (see previous chapter). It would be small comfort to the bond-holders that the effective maturity of their bonds – and hence their exposure to the specific risk of X – would be reduced.[4]

The uncertainty as to how risks specific to corporation X will be divided between its equity and bond-holders is, of course, a cost of inflation. The transaction costs of corporate financing are also made highly uncertain. For an acceleration of inflation, causing an acceleration in the rate of real repayment of loan principal subject to a floating interest rate would often necessitate the raising of additional finance (in nominal terms) and the further incurrence of transaction costs. Drawing up a long-term financing programme becomes hazardous. Transaction costs uncertainty applies also to the investor in FRNs. If inflation and nominal coupons rise, then the investor would have to turn over the real capital value of his note portfolio at a faster rate; for the rate of repayment of real principal would increase, and when the repayments are re-invested in new notes, transaction costs would be incurred.

FRNs have a very mild inflation-hedge property. At times of high and variable inflation investors are likely to decrease their demand for fixed-rate paper and increase their demand for floating-rate paper. This would cause FRNs showing a fixed margin above LIBOR to rise in value, and for margins set on newly issued FRNs to be below previous levels. Thus from 1977 to 1980, as a growing number of investors came to believe that inflation would remain high and volatile for a long time ahead, margins above LIBOR set for prime borrowers fell to $\frac{1}{8}$ per cent from $\frac{1}{4}$ per cent, and FRNs were issued at par instead of typically 1–1$\frac{1}{2}$ points below par. 'Old' prime FRNs traded at a premium compared to the new FRNs with squeezed margins.

A corporation, by issuing long-term FRNs, reduces the specific risks that must be borne by its equity-holders without increasing their exposure to inflation risks. Considerations of effective maturity risk, and the possibility of liquidity crisis, would most likely continue to make corporations wish to secure some long-term fixed-rate finance.

A major source of slump-hedges in the form of fixed-rate bonds comes from government. In a recession or slump, the value of fixed-rate government debt would be likely to rise, as interest rates fall. The increase in capital value has its counterpart in a mark-up of the present value of future tax payments. But assuming that tax payments are spread more evenly among the population than are wealth-holdings, and are imperfectly discounted, then the existence of government debt provides a slump-hedge for the wealthy class in aggregate. The provision of slump-hedges can be viewed as a 'social service'; by supplying insurance cover against slump, the government increases the readiness of those with capital to invest in high-risk areas of the economy. The value of the insurance is considerably reduced, however, by the outbreak of inflation and the lack of indexation.

Hedges against Banking Crisis and Official Borrowing Abroad

A portfolio which consisted largely of bank deposits, especially in the Euro-markets, would be exposed dangerously to the risk of banking crisis. If massive loan defaults in the developing world or by Comecon borrowers were to trigger bank failures and a shrinking of liquidity, the investor could find that his wealth was sharply reduced. By investing in a spread of names beyond the banking industry, the investor's exposure to banking crisis is reduced. The principal debt-forms issued to investors by the non-bank sector are bonds and bills (in the USA, commercial paper). Greater diversification between debtors is feasible in the bond and FRN markets than directly in the bank deposit market.[5]

The FRN market, although it has flourished since it was revived in the mid-1970s, has remained largely confined to bank issuers. Thus the investor who has been attracted to FRNs by their feature of low risk yet higher income potential than that of very short-term instruments has had to limit his purchases so as not to reduce his income (and wealth), contingent on realities marked by banking crisis, to very low levels. Very few issues by prime non-bank borrowers were outstanding at end-1980.

The failure of a non-bank FRN market to grow must be ascribed to three factors.

First, considerations of bank crisis were not widespread in investor thinking. The FRNs issued by top non-bank names did not sell at a premium over top bank names of equal maturity.

Second, competition in international banking was intense in the late 1970s, and margins on loans to top non-bank borrowers were reduced to very fine levels, often below what could be obtained in the FRN market. Banks are at a disadvantage compared to non-banks in obtaining long-term finance (at a floating rate) from other banks: not only are they reluctant to disclose information, necessary to a loan agreement, to potential competitors, but the value of the interbank loan would be highly correlated with the general profitability of the banking system. For example, during a crisis in the banking industry (an illiquidity crisis), the bank which had lent long-term to other banks would suffer particularly badly. Thus long-term lending to banks is of higher risk from the viewpoint of banks than of non-banks, and they can issue FRNs to the non-bank public on keener terms than those on which they can arrange long-term interbank finance.

Third, the financing of real capital repayment (implied by high nominal coupons) on FRNs during their lifetime would be expensive. In principle, the borrower could make small additional issues of FRNs each year to finance the real element in the nominal coupon, but this would be expensive in terms of transaction costs.

Whereas the government, by issuing fixed-rate debt to domestic residents, provides them with a slump-hedge, the issue of fixed-rate debt externally can have reverse effects. If the government's paper in external markets is bought predominantly by non-residents, then the government would be saddling its citizens with obligations that become especially onerous at times of world slump. For example, if France finances a current account deficit by issuing large quantities of fixed-rate external debt, its citizens would become more exposed to the risk of world slump, when they would have to collectively meet fixed payments out of diminished income.

External debt is of greater risk when denominated in a foreign currency than when denominated in the national money, whether comparison is made for fixed or floating-rate bonds. For a real depreciation of country X's currency *x*, which would increase the burden of external debt servicing denominated in foreign currency, is associated often with bad realities for X-residents, where their income-levels would be especially low. Examples of such bad realities include a deterioration in the terms of trade due to a weakening of demand for a principal export industry, or a general fear of approaching hyperinflation.

Exposure to the risk of slump can be reduced by the issue of external debt in floating-rate rather than in fixed-rate form. For then in conditions of world slump, the debtor country would find that the real value of its interest obligations would fall. This advantage is outweighed from the viewpoint of many Finance Ministries by the maturity risk implicit in floating-rate finance. If, for example, dollar interest rates and the expected US inflation rate were to move up from 10 to 20 per cent, the Finance Ministry would find its cash outgoings on external interest account increased by 100 per cent (and by over 80 per cent in real terms). Equivalently, the Finance Ministry may be forced, by an acceleration of inflation, to bring forward, under the guise of increased nominal interest payments, redemptions of large chunks of debt in real terms. Finance Ministries, whose thinking is confined typically within the framework of annual cash budgets, are unlikely to welcome such volatility of redemption schedules expressed in real terms. Further, national prestige may be at stake if a less than prime credit rating had to be accepted on emergency borrowing undertaken to finance the increased nominal interest payments.

US Inflation-hedges in the International Bond Market

The investor with a long-term horizon, resident in a high-inflation country, will often find that bonds denominated in a low-inflation money are, despite their exchange risk, an attractive component for his portfolio; for over long periods of time, real exchange rate risk is likely to be small relative to inflation risk. Real exchange rate movements in excess of 25 per cent have been rare historically,[6] whereas cumulative inflation differences over several years between major monies have often been much larger.

Suppose a US investor believed that inflation in the USA could average, at an annual rate over the next 10 years, anywhere between 5 and 20 per cent, whilst inflation in Switzerland could average anywhere between 1 and 3 per cent over the same period, and that the maximum cumulative real exchange rate movement of the franc against the dollar was 30 per cent. He would then consider a 10-year fixed-rate Swiss franc bond to be of lower risk than a 10-year fixed-rate US dollar bond.[7] At times of accelerating US inflation, when the variability of US inflation increases relative to inflation rates in Switzerland or Germany, it should be expected that the US investor, and other investors whose spending is concentrated in the dollar area and for whom the dollar is thereby their 'natural' store of value, would switch to some extent from dollar bonds to Deutsche mark and Swiss franc bonds.[8]

Given the preponderant share of dollar-based investors in the world investment community, and the smaller size of the mark and franc bond markets than of the dollar bond markets, the price-effect of inflows into the former can be appreciable. Their resulting strong performance at times of worsening US inflation expectations (not matched by a similar deterioration of the inflation outlook in Switzerland and Germany) makes them a type of impure US inflation-hedge. They are not a hedge, however, against US inflation which has its source in world-wide developments (for example, an oil-price explosion), and which would thereby be accompanied by an upturn of inflation in the traditionally low-inflation countries.

This limited hedge-role of Swiss and German bond markets may be observed in recent history. In 1977–78, as the great end-decade US inflation was in its early stages of development, inflows into the Swiss and German bond markets drove yields there to steadily lower levels, with 10-year prime paper in the third quarter of 1978 touching $3\frac{7}{8}$ and 5 per cent respectively, compared to $7\frac{1}{2}$ and 9 per cent in the mid-1970s. Barely 1 year later on, in the wake of the second oil crisis, which exacerbated inflation in both Western Europe and the USA, bond yields on medium-term Deutsche mark and Swiss franc paper had reacted upwards to $9\frac{1}{2}$ and $6\frac{3}{4}$ per cent respectively, with heavy falls in bond prices being recorded.

Indexed Bonds as Hedges

Historically, indexed bonds have existed in various forms. Bonds indexed to a general price index have been found in Finland in the aftermath of World War II, in Israel intermittently through its post-World War II history, and in Britain since the mid-1970s.[9] Bonds indexed to special prices have included gold-indexed bonds issued during the US Civil War,[10] Pinay and Giscard gold bonds in France, bonds indexed to the price of electricity (issue of the Caisse Nationale de l'Energie in France), bonds indexed to the price of oil (Mexican bonds), and silver bonds (an issue of Sunshine Mining Corporation in 1980). In France, there is an example of a bond issued in the 1950s whose principal was indexed to the level of nominal GDP.

A bond indexed to the consumer price index (CPI) provides protection against much more than simply an inflation of monetary source. It provides protection also against many bad realities symptomised by inflation of non-monetary source[11] – for example, war, energy crisis, fall in productivity, deterioration in terms of trade. In each of these bad realities, the price level would come under upward pressure for an unchanged supply of nominal money, due to falling demand for real money balances.

This multi-faceted insurance quality of indexed bonds must have been a powerful deterrent to their issue. Although the borrower, by switching to indexed from non-indexed debt, avoids being exposed to fluctuations in the real cost of borrowing due to inflation volatility, he undertakes implicitly to deliver (to the lender) an increased amount of income contingent on many bad realities marked by inflation of non-monetary source. For nominal debt, even in fixed-rate form, does not promise an unchanged level of real income in the same bad realities: the real value of nominal assets (for example, bonds of which principal and interest are fixed in nominal terms) is lowered typically by real shocks which are non-monetary sources of inflation. Thus effective leverage obtained by the issue of indexed bonds is more powerful than that obtained by the issue of nominal debt.

In addition to simply promising income-protection in various bad realities (including those of high inflation), CPI-indexed bonds also possess hedge properties with respect to these.[12] If the generally acknowledged probabilities of a fall in productivity, of a rise in oil prices, or of some other non-monetary source of inflation, increased, changing portfolio demands would lead to a rise in the real price of CPI-indexed bonds.

When inflation (of monetary or non-monetary source) is very low and predictable, the real rate of return on nominal bonds is less variable than on indexed bonds: at best, the calculation of a CPI index provides a loose and unsteady approximation of 'true' inflation, due to lags in data collection, to infrequent adjustment of many series prices,[13] to the inclusion of non-consumer items such as house prices, and to quality changes through time. These problems with the CPI as a measure of inflation become less of a drawback to indexation in debt markets when inflation is high and variable; the fluctuating degree of error in the recording of inflation – the negative feature of index bonds – pales in comparison to the uncertainty of the real value of money – the negative feature of non-indexed bonds.

At times of high inflation, together with high inflation uncertainty, investors are likely to reduce their net demand for nominal debt securities and increase their demand for indexed debt. Borrowers, also, are likely to increase their supply of indexed debt, thereby reducing the volatility of the real value of their outstanding liabilities. However, government itself is a principal supplier of debt, and is typically inflexible in its choice of financing.[14] Tax and legislative impediments limit severely the issue of indexed debt by private borrowers. Hence the advent of high inflation and great inflation uncertainty is likely to increase investor demand for indexed debt by more than any increase in its supply (which is almost entirely in the form of government issues). The resulting increase in net demand for indexed debt securities and fall in net demand for non-indexed debt securities should cause the real price of the former to rise, and so they yield an income bonus contingent on the advent of high inflation. Hence indexed bonds are hedges against inflation.

The size of income bonus, contingent on a given increase in inflation and inflation uncertainty, promised by indexed bonds, is a decreasing function of the extent of indexation in the capital markets. The larger is the proportion of bonds outstanding that is indexed, the smaller is the potential proportionate increase in demand for them and hence the smaller is their potential rate of return. At high rates of inflation the degree of indexation should be larger than at low rates. Thus indexed bonds become less powerful as inflation-hedges at successively higher levels of inflation.

Evidence for CPI-indexed bonds being more than simply riskless securities, but rising in real value in bad states, can be found from the Israeli experience of indexation.[15] From December 1979 to February 1980 the indexed-bond market went through a period of weakness, due to the announcement of lower-than-expected cost of living indices. By summer 1980, when hopes of an inflation slowdown had been dashed, the real value of indexed bonds had risen again.

Indexed bonds are unlikely to be a hedge against suppressed inflation; at such times published CPI indices understate the true rate of inflation, and so the real income from CPI-indexed bonds falls. In Israel, in April 1980, the announcement of new controls on food price rises caused the indexed bond market to fall sharply. Consumer durables are likely to prove the most effective hedge against suppressed inflation – for suppressed inflation is symptomised by long delays in obtaining goods, and the value of having inventory to hand increases.

Bonds indexed to nominal GDP rather than to the CPI have fewer hedge qualities and more fairweather qualities. Their real value is augmented by economic growth, whilst it is reduced by a contraction of productivity – a non-monetary source of inflation. Such bonds should therefore be preferred to CPI-indexed bonds by most borrowers.

Tax considerations heighten the potential inflation-hedge qualities of the CPI-indexed bond; for if the indexed bond is taxed on an indexed basis, whilst other assets are taxed on a non-indexed basis, its tax treatment would become steadily more favourable (relative to other assets) as the rate of inflation increased. The increasing premium which investors would be prepared to pay for the CPI-indexed bond's tax advantages would be a source of income contingent on the advent of high rates of inflation and heightens its power as an inflation-hedge.

As a hedge asset, gold-indexed bonds (such as the Pinay or Giscard bonds in France) are inferior to metallic gold. In social breakdown marked by hyperinflation or in war, where gold would again become a medium of exchange – at least for transactions in the black market – there is a significant chance that index clauses in gold bond agreements would be abrogated. We should thus expect that in situations of crisis – where the occurrence of war or hyperinflation were of high likelihood – the value of gold-indexed bonds would fall in terms of gold bullion. Even so, their price, quoted in paper money, should follow that of bullion, albeit by less, and they should yield some income contingent on war or hyperinflation crisis.

In the world of the Gold Standard, which is commonly dated from 1890 to 1914, bonds denominated in currencies convertible into gold were in effect gold-indexed bonds. At times of war crisis, investors feared that the gold-link of currencies would be broken and their rush to hoard physical gold would lead to upward pressure on interest rates and a fall in bond prices.[16] Thus history demonstrates the proposition that the gold-indexed bonds are a worse hedge than gold itself.

In the years 1977–80 the Mexican Government issued a series of petro-bonds.[17] These bonds were effectively a type of convertible. They were issued in denominations of 1000 pesos each, and with 3 years' maturity. Net interest was paid, in pesos, at the rate of 10 per cent per annum. At maturity, the amount repaid was the greater of 1000 pesos or the then value of the oil-backing less the cumulative total of interest paid over the bond's life; the oil-backing has typically been fixed as the number of barrels of oil equal in value to 1000 pesos at the start of the loan.

A straight peso-bond issued in 1977, with a maturity of 3 years, and a coupon of 10 per cent, would have sold at around 77 per cent of par. Thus the investor was paying 230 pesos for the privilege of being able to buy oil, valued today at 1000 pesos, at 1300 pesos in 1983. The Mexican petro-bonds were thus equivalent to a combination of a straight peso-bond and of an option, priced at 230 pesos, to buy at the end of 3 years a fixed quantity of oil at a peso price 30 per cent above its present peso price. To value this last option, the investor must take a view on the peso–dollar exchange rate and the dollar price of a barrel of oil in 3 years' time.[18]

The oil-bond, and to a lesser extent, the peso-bond, provides the investor with a hedge against energy crisis. Both the oil-bond, and the peso itself, should rise in value at times of soaring oil prices.[19] Unlike for the example of gold-indexed bonds compared to gold bullion, there is no reason to expect oil-bonds to seriously underperform oil itself as an energy-hedge. Indeed, at a time of sharply rising oil prices, Mexico's credit rating would be enhanced, and the chance of a break of the conversion-pledge would fade.

The Mexican petro-bonds are one of the closest examples found in practice of a pure hedge against energy crisis.[20] The petro-bond's imperfections rest on the sensitivity of their value to movement of peso interest rates, unexpected behaviour of the peso, and changed assessment of the Mexican political risk.

The last example of an indexed bond discussed here is a silver convertible – an example of which was an issue by Sunshine Mining Company in 1980, with a 1995 maturity.[21] In April 1980, Sunshine was a B-rated company, and a conventional 15-year bond could not have been issued at par with a coupon below 16½ per cent. At that date (the date of issue), the price of silver was $16.00 per ounce, and each £1000 nominal bond was backed by 50 ounces of silver. The bond-holder who purchased at par was thus buying a long-term option to buy 50 ounces of silver in 1995 at a price of $1000, showing a 25 per cent premium over its spot value at issue date. The price of the option was the difference in price between an 8 per cent bond maturing in 1995 showing a yield to maturity of 16½ per cent (and so priced at 560 per 1000 nominal certificate) and par (1000), making $440.

The advantages to Sunshine of this type of issue were two-fold. First, cover was obtained for its shareholders against the risk of fluctuations in the price of silver. Second, the implicit credit-rating obtainable on the 15-year option should be superior to that on a 15-year fixed-rate bond; volatility of the silver price affects adversely the credit rating of a nominal bond but not of a silver-bond. At times when the option becomes valuable, the company's earnings are boosted also by the high silver price. The silver-bond should share with silver its various hedge properties. But these are obtainable in a purer form by purchasing the underlying metal as an investment.

At various times proposals have been mooted that would extend the use of commodity convertibles to the financing of non-oil developing countries. For example, a sugar-producing country should obtain a superior credit-rating on the issue of a sugar convertible bond to that on the issue of a straight dollar bond (the reasoning is similar to that in the Sunshine example above). It is difficult, however, to imagine a wide spectrum of investors who would be interested in including long-term sugar options in their portfolio. A sugar shortage is not a bad general state of the world against which investors are commonly trying to obtain insurance. Further, the state-variables highly relevant to the sugar price are not highly correlated in value to those of major state-variables such as belligerency or economic activity. Thus a sugar option could not produce an indirect hedge against any bad general state. The same disadvantage applies to many types of possible commodity bonds, with the evident exceptions of gold, silver, and oil – the three types of commodity bond found to exist in practice.

Notes and References

1. For example, a 10-year 10 per cent coupon bond denominated in a money (dollars) with 10 per cent inflation per annum has a shorter effective maturity than a 10-year 5 per cent coupon bond denominated in a money (francs) with 5 per cent inflation per annum. The rate of repayment of real capital is greater for the first bond than for the second.
2. In a world of zero transaction costs, the equity-owner would be able to 'undo' on personal account any financing transaction effected by the corporation, and how it chose to package outstanding securities would be irrelevant (see F. Modigliani and M. Miller. 'The Cost of Capital, Corporation Finance, and the Theory of Investment', *American Economic Review*, vol. 48, no, 3, (June 1958) pp. 261–97. Implicitly various imperfections are assumed here, for example transaction costs, that make the corporate financing decision relevant.
3. For example, if inflation and nominal interest rates are 10 per cent per

annum, then on a 10-year FRN the real value of the principal is reduced by 10 per cent per annum, the nominal interest being a guise for repayment of principal in real terms. If inflation and nominal interest rates rise to 20 per cent per annum, then the rate of real repayment would rise to 20 per cent per annum on a declining balance.

4. The rise in nominal interest rates and inflation expectations reduces the present value of far-distant interest and capital repayments more than that of near-term inflows, and hence the effective maturity is shortened.
5. A bond portfolio of $1 million can economically be divided into holdings of $50,000 all within one safe-keeping account at a bank. In contrast, 20 deposits of $50,000 each with different banks would entail significant administrative and set-up costs, and frequent errors.
6. For evidence on deviations from purchasing power parity, see H. Genberg, 'Purchasing Power Parity under Fixed and Flexible Exchange Rates', *Journal of International Economics,* vol. 8, no. 2 (May 1978) p. 247–76.
7. Comparison here should strictly be made between two 10-year pure discount bonds, otherwise effective maturities are different. See S. M. Schaeffer, 'The Problem with Redemption Yields', in J. Lorie and R. Brealey (eds) *Modern Investment Management* (Dryden Press, 1978).
8. Their most significant switch, however, is likely to be out of fixed-rate into floating-rate bonds and deposits rather than between different currency denominations of fixed-rate bonds.
9. In Britain, indexed bonds were issued only by government, and were deliberately restricted in their marketability. Indexed bonds sold to the personal sector were rationed on a per capita basis, and according to age; they could be traded in a secondary market.
10. See M. Friedman and A. Schwartz, *A Monetary History of the United States 1867–1960* (Princeton, 1963) pp. 25–9.
11. For the distinction between monetary and non-monetary sources of inflation see Chapter 1.
12. Note, if the indexed bond was of unchanged (real) value in all realities, it would be a riskless asset, not a hedge asset. To be a hedge asset, it must yield especially high income in a bad reality (relative to what it yields elsewhere).
13. For definition of series price, see Chapter 1.
14. For details, see Part 3.
15. See Bank Hapoalim, *Monthly Review,* June 1980.
16. See P. H. Lindert 'Key Currencies and Gold 1900–13', *Princeton Studies in International Finance,* 1969, for a description of how the Agadir crisis of 1911 led to a simultaneous rise of interest rates in European reserve centres.
17. For details, see Merril Lynch, *International Research*, vol. 2, (21 May 1980).
18. If a 3-year forward peso-dollar market existed, the rate could be used as the 'best guess' of the spot peso-dollar rate at conversion date: in practice long-term forward contracting is not possible.
19. Indeed, during 1979-80, although the peso retained a fixed parity against the dollar, this was despite an inflation rate in Mexico some 20 per cent above that in the USA. Thus Mexico's oil riches allowed the peso to

appreciate by some 20 per cent in real terms against the US dollar.

20. Another close example of a pure hedge against energy crisis is a long position in a gas-oil futures contract in London. This market was set up early in 1981.
21. See Drexel, Burnham, Lambert's prospectus for the issue of $25 million $8\frac{1}{2}$ per cent Silver Indexed bonds, due April 1995, for Sunshine Mining Company.

8 Hedge Monies

Several monies have important hedge characteristics, providing especially high returns in certain types of crisis. Well-known examples include the British pound in its role of an energy-hedge, the Swiss franc and US dollar as war-hedges, the Deutsche mark and Swiss franc as hedges against US hyperinflation. Other monies have important counter-hedge or fairweather characteristics. Examples include the Japanese yen, for which the energy market being in glut is a source of strength, and the Canadian dollar which thrives on economic boom in the US and in the world economy. These possible hedge and fairweather qualities of monies have implications for both their exchange rate behaviour and their international popularity – the subject of the present chapter.

Petro-monies

Petro-monies have been defined abstractly (see Chapter 2) as currencies which yield especially high returns in conditions of energy crisis. The purchase of petro-monies is not the only method of obtaining income contingent on energy crisis; others include the purchase of oil equities, Mexican petro-bonds, equities in Swiss banks, and gas-oil futures contracts. In addition, the investor may take a short position in an energy fairweather good, such as the Japanese yen, against neutral currencies.[1] If any of these hedges against energy crisis were pure, then there would not be any need for the investor to diversify his portfolio of energy-hedges. But in practice each is impure, and diversification reduces the variance of the additional income, contingent on the state-variable 'conditions in the energy market' taking a bad value, bought indirectly. Technically, the task of the hedger against energy crisis is to combine impure hedge assets so that their combined return when regressed on the energy state-variable shows the best possible fit – that is, the highest possible R^2 and a low standard error.

Currencies differ in the degree to which they are sensitive to the energy-state variable. One prime determinant is the extent to which their dependence on net energy imports (measured as a proportion of GNP) differs from that of the OECD on average. In the OECD area, there were, in 1980, five currencies issued by energy self-sufficient economies – the British pound, Canadian dollar, Dutch guilder, Norwegian kroner, and Australian dollar. Norway, in contrast to the other four energy self-sufficient OECD economies, was set to have a growing net energy surplus in the 1980s, whilst the Netherlands was set to have a growing deficit.[2] Britain and Canada were expected to remain broadly self-sufficient in energy. Although oil production from conventional sources in Canada was on the decline, this was expected to be replaced by oil from non-conventional sources, including the tar-sands and new offshore wells off the Labrador and Newfoundland coastline; in addition, gas exports were growing strongly. In Australia, declining oil production was expected generally to be offset by strongly rising coal and gas production. Out of the five economies, Britain had the best established trade links with OPEC – these dated back to her imperial history – and stood to gain most advantage on non-oil account from rising OPEC purchasing power in the wake of an energy crisis.

Among the oil-importing countries, Japan stands out as being particularly dependent on imported supplies, with energy imports in 1980 accounting for near 7 per cent of GDP compared to an average ratio of 5 per cent for the OECD area excluding the five self-sufficient members. Japan lacks domestic non-oil sources of energy – whether in the form of coal, hydroelectric power, or natural gas. Yet the amount by which Japan's dependence on imported energy diverges in an unfavourable direction from that of the OECD on average is less than the amount by which that of the five OECD self-sufficient members diverges in the opposite favourable direction. Thus the currencies of the latter group should prove to be more sensitive to the energy state-variable than is the Japanese yen (in the opposite direction).

OECD currencies differ in their 'natural' appeal to OPEC investors. Because of their old colonial links with France and Britain, and the possible existence of pro-Arab sympathies among the ruling elites in these countries, many Arab investors continue to be predisposed favourably towards investment in the British pound and in the French franc. Thus a rise in the oil price would not only strengthen Britain's current account relative to that of OECD countries on average but would also strengthen its capital account as OPEC investors put a proportion of their new wealth into the British pound; a similar advantage would not apply to the other four OECD economies self-sufficient in energy. The British pound, being sensitive to the energy state-variable on three counts – capital, current oil and current non-oil account – should be the least impure energy-hedge among petro-monies. This, together with the greater liquidity of the pound markets than of those denominated in other petro-monies, made the pound the most prominent petro-money in 1979-80 (see Table 8.1 for movement of the real effective exchange rate index of energy-monies in the OECD during 1979 to 1980); the atypical behaviour of the pound was due not just to its superior quality as an energy-hedge but also to Britain's fast transition to energy self-sufficiency in these years, to the very high level of interest rates in Britain, and to strategic considerations as East–West tensions increased.

TABLE 8.1 *Five energy monies in the OECD, 1979–80*

	Canadian $	*British £*	*Dutch Fl.*	*Norwegian Kr.*	*Australian $*
1977	99.8	101.7	104.0	99.8	92.0
1978	92.9	106.5	103.9	95.6	87.3
1979	92.9	118.9	100.5	90.5	86.1
1980					
March	92.2	132.9	98.6	93.1	87.5
June	91.9	137.3	97.0	91.7	86.0
September	91.6	142.3	97.6	92.6	88.3
December	89.6	146.7	95.3	93.3	91.2

SOURCE: Morgan Guaranty's *Real Effective Exchange Rates.*

In most areas of investment, a trade-off exists between the reduction of risk and the reduction of transaction costs. Thus consider two alternative methods of obtaining a hedge against energy crisis – buying pound investments or borrowing yen to invest in neutral monies.[3] Now, because movement of the state-variable 'energy market conditions' has a more diluted effect on the yen's value than on the pound's – the yen is less pure as an energy-fairweather good than the pound is pure as an energy-hedge – the investor must take a larger position in yen than in pounds to obtain the same amount of extra income contingent on the state of energy crisis. Equivalently, the investor must assume more risks specific to Japan when using the yen vehicle to obtain a given amount of energy crisis-contingent income than risk specific to Britain when using the pound to obtain the same amount of cover against energy crisis.

Yet in a world where transaction costs are significant, and important spreads exist between borrowing and lending rates of interest, the yen may prove a more popular vehicle than the pound for indirectly trading in income contingent on conditions in the energy market. For most potential sellers of income contingent on energy crisis are in the oil-exporting countries which are natural lenders, whilst most potential buyers are in the oil-importing countries which are natural borrowers. Thus both sellers and buyers of income contingent on energy crisis can save transaction costs by lending and borrowing yen respectively rather than by borrowing and lending pounds.

The British Pound – Evaluating a Petro-money

Most calculations of the pound's real effective exchange rate in the last quarter of 1980 showed it to have been some 40 per cent above its level in the 1971–73 period and even more above its level of the crisis year 1976. The power behind that remarkable upsurge came by four clearly identifiable channels from the world oil market.

First, between the mid-1970s and 1980, Britain was transformed into an energy self-sufficient economy. In the mid-1970s the cost of Britain's oil imports ran at around $2\frac{1}{2}$ per cent of GNP, the same as for other major OECD economies. By 1980 Britain was virtually self-sufficient in oil, while energy imports into most OECD nations had grown to around 5 per cent of GNP. To balance that relative improvement in Britain's current account strength, the pound would have had to appreciate to the point where it would generate an increase in Britain's non-oil deficit equivalent to 5 per cent of GNP (or 18 per cent of exports of goods and services). An econometric study by London Business School's Centre of Economic Forecasting[4] found that a 12 per cent real appreciation of Sterling would have been enough to generate that order of deterioration in the non-oil balance over a period of 2 years.

Second, market-participants expected the real price of oil to continue to rise, say by a normal amount of 5 per cent per annum, in the absence of a crisis erupting in the Middle East. If the oil price were to rise by this 5 per cent per year in real terms – the crisis-free scenario – a further enlargement of the non-oil deficit by $2\frac{1}{2}$ per cent of GNP would have to occur by 1990. If there were no other influence – such as especially low productivity growth[5] – tending to widen Britain's non-oil deficit, an extrapolation of the London Business School's relation between real exchange rates and current account changes suggests that the pound would have to appreciate by 0.6 per cent per year in real terms above its up-valued base rate necessary to accommodate the oil price rises of 1978–80. If we assumed that real interest rates in the UK were to average somewhat below those on other currencies during the 1980s (for reasons discussed in Chapter 3), then this normal expectation of future increases in the real price of oil would not imply a high rate of return on the pound.

Third, reserve-demand (to be distinguished from hedge-demand) for pounds increased from OPEC, given their swollen oil revenues. This should be a source of transitory upward pressure on the pound; for in the longer term the increased reserve demand should be satisfied from a deficit emerging in the aggregate of other balances in the UK's international payments. This emerging deficit would be encouraged by the influence of the real exchange rate appreciation – itself due in part to OPEC reserve demand – on the volume of British exports and imports. For example, it may be that a 10 per cent real appreciation of the pound in 1979–80, over and above the minimum level consistent with enlarging the non-oil deficit to the 5 per cent of GDP described above, followed by an expected real appreciation diminished by 1 percentage point per annum from what it would have been in the absence of the OPEC reserve factor, would have cooled OPEC's thirst for pounds and led to its being eventually satisfied through the current account. Further, if real oil prices were expected to rise, so would OPEC's demand for reserves including Sterling, curtailing subsequent downward correction in the pound's value.

Fourth, the emergence of Britain as a petro-power made the pound a vehicle for obtaining insurance against an energy-crisis. The hedge-investor, looking at the pound, would realise that in normal conditions (excluding an energy crisis) the pound would be likely to depreciate in real terms by around 0–1 per cent per annum on account of the inferior productivity growth in Britain to that in the average of OECD economies; other normal influences mentioned above on the real exchange rate from year to year are likely to be self-cancelling. Further, the hedge-investor would expect real interest rates (measured in domestic terms) on the pound to be below those on energy-neutral monies, for reasons of domestic equilibrium discussed in Chapter 3. Given those expectations, what premium would the hedge-investor pay for the pound over and above the real exchange rate that would be consistent today with eventual basic balance in Britain's international payments in the absence of hedge demand? More precisely, how much would he be willing to pay for pounds over and above the 12 per cent premium explained by the improvement in Britain's current account to date together with the 10 per cent premium (which diminishes in the long run) due to OPEC's reserve demand?

Using the illustrative arithmetic here, the investor at end-1980 must have been just satisfied at the margin in buying pounds at an 18 per cent premium over and above their equilibrium value in the absence of hedge considerations, whilst acknowledging moreover that their real (domestic) rate of return would be especially low. The investor's willingness to buy pounds, nevertheless, must have been based on the realisation that the pound would pay bonus income contingent on an energy crisis. The investor, in evaluating the effective cost of energy-risk insurance via the pound vehicle would have to estimate the probability of chaos in the oil market and its implication for oil prices. Then he would calculate the implied effect of a crisis-induced rise in the oil price on the minimum exchange rate of the pound consistent with basic balance of payments equilibrium in the absence of hedge demand.

Suppose that in any future year there were a 10 per cent chance of oil-market chaos so serious that the real price of oil would rise by 55 per cent (the normal 5 per cent yearly increase commonly assumed plus an additional 50 per cent) above its year-earlier level; thereafter, he would assume that the normal 5 per cent annual rate of increase would be resumed. In the early 1980s, an additional 50 per cent uplift would require a deterioration in Britain's non-oil trade equal to $2\frac{1}{2}$ per cent of GNP to balance the increased oil deficit of most OECD economies; this would require a 6 per cent additional real appreciation of the pound. In addition, a further 5 per cent real appreciation should be expected on account of greatly increased OPEC reserve demand for pounds.

Given these suggested probabilities, the mathematical expectation of the pound's bonus each year, contingent on an energy crisis, equals £0.01 per pound in the early 1980s, rising towards £0.015 per pound at the end of the decade. The investor cannot hope to obtain even-odds on insurance, simply because insurance against oil-market chaos is so highly desired and so scarce (oil crisis is a bad general state of the world). If the calculation were limited to a 10-year horizon and the hedge-investor were willing to pay for insurance at the margin an annual premium showing an 80–90 per cent mark-up over even–odds (i.e. the mathematical expectation of return), then he could be willing – even taking into account the low real rate of return on pounds under normal conditions – to pay the 18 per cent surcharge on the pound revealed earlier.

The currency forecaster is on especially treacherous ground when studying a hedge currency such as the pound. It is not enough to forecast reserve demands and current accounts, using some econometric relationship between exchange rates and trade flows. Hedge demand must in principle be forecast also. But this latter forecast depends on non-observable magnitudes such as the market's estimate of the probability of an energy crisis and what would occur there, on the assumed degree of market participants' risk-aversion, and on how much above even-odds they are prepared to pay for insurance. The currency forecaster must examine, further, the likely rate of supply of income, contingent on energy crisis, from other energy-hedges (for example, oil shares), and the elasticity of demand for income contingent on an energy crisis. When new supplies of such contingent income increase, through the new issue of oil-equities, petro-bonds, and pounds produced through the current account deficit of the UK (itself enlarged by the up-valuation of the hedge surcharge above), how far will the margin above actuarial odds, that investors are prepared to pay, fall? (Equivalently, what is the elasticity of demand for income contingent on energy crisis?)

Just as government action in the form of a windfall profits tax can reduce oil equities' income contingent on an energy crisis, so governments can severely reduce the hedge qualities of their own money. Thus, if the pound were fixed rigidly to another currency or currency-basket (for example, the SDR), it would yield no direct bonus in an energy crisis. The improvement in Britain's current account, relative to that of OECD countries on average, and reserve inflows from OPEC, would cause her monetary aggregates to grow at an increased rate relative to demand. The real exchange rate appreciation of the pound, made necessary for basic payments equilibrium by the improved relative current account and by increased reserve demand from OPEC, would be effected by the inflation-rate in Britain rising above that in the country (or group of countries) to whose money (monies) the pound was fixed as *numéraire.* The rate of inflation of traded goods' prices must be the same as in the *numéraire* country; hence the rate of inflation of non-traded goods' prices must rise relative to that of traded goods.

If the pound were to be fixed as above in the exchange market, then non-traded goods in the UK would be a type of impure hedge against energy crisis; at times of crisis their prices would rise relative to those of traded goods, and so they would score real capital gains from the viewpoint of investors in most parts of the globe. But non-traded goods markets suffer typically from illiquidity. Further, the prices of non-traded goods are subject to many highly particular state-variables of whose value the international investor cannot hope to be aware. In short, non-traded goods in the UK would be potentially much more impure as energy crisis-hedges under a fixed exchange-rate regime than are pounds under the floating exchange-rate regime.

Residents in a petro-economy are likely to display a restrained appetite for foreign currency investments, whether in the form of deposits or bonds. For any change in the composition of their portfolios away from being invested entirely in domestic money would reduce their endowment of income contingent on energy crisis. In that state of the world, foreign currencies would fall in value against the pound and in terms of real domestic purchasing-power within the UK (where the typical shopping basket contains a significant proportion of non-traded goods).[6] By contrast, investors in an economy which is particularly dependent on imported energy, for example Japan, are likely to show especial favour for foreign currency investments, as these add to their income endowment contingent on energy crisis relative to that contingent on most other states of the world. In energy crisis, the relative price of non-traded in terms of traded goods in Japan would fall. At a time of increasing risk of energy crisis, the British themselves are likely to be observed either scurrying into their domestic money and disposing of foreign currency holdings, or increasing their holdings of oil-equities, petro-bonds and gas-oil futures contracts whilst leaving the currency composition of their money and bond portfolios substantially unchanged.

The example of lack of enthusiasm on the part of British investors for foreign currency investments can be generalised. Where the national money is a hedge money, resident investors are likely to be predisposed against foreign currency placements. If the particular bad state of the world (against which the national money, say francs, was a hedge) were to occur, foreign monies' purchasing power would fall sharply in terms of non-traded goods in the country issuing francs, aggravating the poverty there of residents who had invested in foreign currency. In subsequent sections the Swiss franc will be shown to possess hedge-properties against war and banking crisis. This should predispose the Swiss against foreign currency investment, and when either type of crisis increases in likelihood, they should repatriate funds into francs. The Swiss who held a large portfolio of foreign currencies would be a double loser from the occurrence of war or banking crisis, suffering an exchange loss in addition to a direct loss of income. Repatriation of funds at times of crisis by residents in the country of issue of the hedge money accentuates the latter's hedge quality.

Currencies as Inflation-hedges

In the 1970s and into the early 1980s, Germany and Switzerland gained the firm reputation of being low-inflation countries, in contrast to the high-inflation countries of Britain, France and the USA. The Swiss franc and Deutsche mark thus became perceived as US inflation-hedges. At times of very high US inflation, not accompanied by high inflation in Germany and in Switzerland, international investors – and to a lesser extent US investors – would switch out of US dollars into Deutsche marks and Swiss francs, causing these to rise strongly in both real and nominal terms in the foreign exchange markets.

A high and volatile rate of inflation in the USA causes the dollar's real purchasing power both in terms of non-traded goods in the USA and in terms of internationally traded goods to become more variable. International investors (for example, OPEC) who are concerned to reduce the variance of the real value of their wealth in terms of internationally traded goods would tend to increase the share of the franc and the mark in their portfolios. Domestic US investors, who are concerned in particular with the variance of the real value of their portfolio in terms of US non-traded goods, may diminish somewhat the share of the dollar in their portfolios, but by less than the international investor. The purchasing power of the foreign currency in terms of US non-traded goods (but not in terms of traded goods which have a common world price) is likely to remain more volatile than that of the US dollar over short periods of time.[7]

Only in conditions of near or actual US hyperinflation would marks or francs have lower volatility than dollars in terms of US non-traded goods over short periods of time.

The concept of a currency as a hedge asset with respect to inflation, has applicability only to inflation in the US. Although residents of a smaller country, say France, may believe that an investment in Deutsche marks would provide bonus income (measured in terms of French non-traded goods) at times of high French inflation,[8] high inflation in France is not a bad general state. France is a small country in the world economy and there is no reason to expect that income contingent on high French inflation should be driven up to a significant premium above its actuarial value.

The Swiss franc's international value would rise by more than that of the Deutsche mark in a US inflation crisis where investors made large switches of funds from US dollars into Deutsche marks and Swiss francs. The much smaller size of the Swiss than of the German economy means that net capital inflows of similar size represent a considerably higher proportion of Swiss GNP than of German GNP and call for a larger exchange rate adjustment. Indeed it is a recognised feature in the exchange markets that the Swiss franc tends to swing with a larger amplitude against the dollar than does the Deutsche mark.[9] Hence the Swiss franc is potentially a purer hedge against US inflation than is the Deutsche mark.

The Swiss franc's superiority as a US inflation-hedge does not make it overall a more popular international money than the Deutsche mark. For the franc's hedge-property predisposes it to a greater degree of instability than is common for non-hedge currencies.[10] This instability tends to make the international investor weight the franc to a lesser degree than the mark in his low-risk international money portfolio – even when he believes the variability of inflation to be about equal in West Germany and Switzerland. Yet the franc should feature more than the mark in his hedge portfolio, serving to insure his international money portfolio against the risk of inflation in the USA rising to levels far above those presently expected.

Currencies as a Hedge against War

The designation of currencies as war-hedges depends on a summation of certain strategic and historical factors. For example, the Swiss franc is widely believed to yield income contingent on war; the belief is founded on Switzerland's neutrality, her success in preserving neutrality during World War II, and her presumed ability (in part due to the nature of Switzerland's terrain) to impose large losses on any aggressor (hence making such aggression unlikely).

Econometric evidence does suggest that the Swiss franc's hedge properties (on account not only of war, but also of US inflation, banking crisis and social revolution) are reflected in the real rate of return obtainable on franc investments. Aliber, for example, in a study of the deviations of interest rates from Fisher Open (the proposition that interest rate differentials between currencies are unbiased predictors of exchange rate change) found that franc interest rates tended to over-predict the appreciation of the franc. Equivalently, the expected real rate of return on the franc appeared to be particularly low, consistent with the proposition that investors pay a premium to obtain the income bonuses which the franc would yield contingent on certain bad realities.[11]

Other currencies which have the property of being a war-hedge owe it to the strategic position or power, rather than to the neutrality, of the issuing country. The US dollar is viewed widely as a hedge against East–West conflict due to the widely perceived greater security of the USA than of Europe against Russian invasion. Thus during the Afghanistan crisis of early 1980, and again during the Polish crisis of 1980–81, funds flowed from Continental European currencies into the US dollar. The strong correlation between the state-variables of conditions in the energy market and belligerency adds to the apparent correlation of dollar strength with the degree of crisis in international political relations. The greater abundance of domestic sources of energy in the USA than in Continental Europe would stand the USA in better stead should a conflict involve a cessation of oil supplies from the Middle East.

The US dollar's property as a war-hedge was not newly perceived in the 1980s. As war-clouds built up in Europe in the late 1930s, funds flowed from Europe to the USA at an increasing rate, and the gold reserves of the USA bulged.[12] In the event, US dollars did perform as a war-hedge, albeit imperfectly, from the viewpoint of most Europeans. During World War II and into the early 1950s, US assets held by non-residents in enemy countries (and in Switzerland) were frozen, and frozen deposits were traded at steep discounts to the official exchange rate for dollars in the Zurich market.[13]

The British pound has been perceived at times as having war-hedge properties. Britain's strategic position as an island is believed to make her less pregnable to an attack. Even in the present nuclear age, the island-base of the pound is appreciated by scared investors; some part of the pound's remarkable strength in 1980 was attributed to Continental investors seeking a hedge against a Russian advance westwards on the European Continent. Japan – the other major island economy in the OECD area – was similarly perceived in 1980 as being safer than Continental Europe against the risk of a Russian invasion, with yen investments proving especially popular to OPEC investors concerned with the risk of possible conflict in Europe. Another island economy, New Zealand, similarly comes into the focus of investors at times of war panic. However, the New Zealand dollar has been fixed traditionally to another currency or to a basket of currencies. It does not therefore respond in value to an increase in the likelihood of war occurring, and this limits severely its attraction as a war-hedge. International bonds issued by the New Zealand government are, however, up-rated in relative value at times of war panic. In 1980 for example, Euro-dollar bonds issued by the New Zealand Government obtained top credit ratings, despite a current account deficit for New Zealand running at $5\frac{1}{2}$ per cent of GDP.[14]

Island currencies in the OECD (in particular, the Japanese yen and British pound) draw their property of being hedge investments from economic as well as strategic considerations. An island does not have a frontier region where residents can profitably make large switches between domestic and foreign purchases in response to even minor exchange-rate change. A significant appreciation of the Dutch guilder (in response to increased energy risks) or the Swiss franc (in response to war risks) would precipitate a surge in over-the-border shopping.[15] In Switzerland, the important centres of population are all within low-cost reach of foreign centres. Further, tourism is more responsive to exchange-rate change in a small continental economy than in an island economy; only a few extra miles in the car can bring large price gains. For residents of an island, significant fixed costs – both in time and money – are involved in crossing a national frontier. The absolute response of tourism to exchange-rate change is greater for rich economies than for poor. Thus in the Netherlands, where real per capita income in 1980 was double the level in the UK, the response of tourism should be correspondingly greater to exchange rate change – given that tourist expenditure is an increasing function of income.

The low response of over-the-border shopping and tourism to exchange-rate change in an island economy increases the potential volatility of its currency. Whereas a sharp movement of a small continental currency would quickly generate current account flows which would tend to put it into reverse, a sharp change in an island currency's exchange rate influences the current account only over a longer period of time and has a more limited area of impact in the national economy. Thus an island base for a currency makes it particularly sensitive in the short run to the movement of state-variables which are very significant for the international payments of the issuing country; the impact of an important change in the value of a state-variable on the island currency's exchange rate would not be undermined by a swift reaction of trade-flows.

In between the extremes of the island currency and of the small continental currency there exists a range of currency types. For example, France is a much less open economy than the Netherlands or Switzerland, with its border regions representing a small share of the total economy. The US dollar, being the currency of a country whose border regions are small in economic size relative to the hinterland, has characteristics nearer to those of an island currency than to a small continental currency.

The principal fairweather currencies with respect to the state-variable of belligerency are the Austrian schilling and Deutsche mark. In any East–West conflict, West Germany and Austria would be the most exposed, being immediately next to the Iron Curtain. Further, the banking systems and official credit agencies in both countries have large loan exposures to Comecon countries, and in an East-West conflict, or in Cold War, Comecon borrowers could default on their loans. Not only would a default impact directly on the current account of West Germany and Austria, but the then perilous state of their banks could precipitate capital outflows into other currencies.

Currencies as Hedges against Social Revolution and Banking Crisis[16]

Switzerland occupies the top-rent position within the European continent. It is placed in the economic centre of gravity of Western Europe, with its average distance from economic centres in Benelux, France, Germany and Italy, being less than for anywhere else. Switzerland has capitalised on its geographic position in a number of ways, including the provision of banking services under its umbrella (not 100 per cent proof) of secrecy. The combination of a central position and natural beauty has made tourism a prominent industry in Switzerland; the industry stands to gain custom from rising energy prices, as this makes Europeans of nearby countries decide to take short-distance holidays to Switzerland instead of journeying to more distant parts.

At times of political crisis in any of the West European countries – all within easy reach of Switzerland for the purpose of depositing fugitive funds – the Swiss franc is likely to gain in value from capital inflows. Thus in early 1978, when a left-wing victory was feared in France, the Swiss franc was pushed up against other currencies. Similarly, at times of Italian political crisis, such as in 1976, the Swiss franc is pushed up by large new supplies of liras in Switzerland. In terms of the concepts developed in Chapter 2, the Swiss franc may be described as an impure hedge against political crisis in France or Italy. The Frenchman or Italian who hold Swiss francs realises that there is a high likelihood of obtaining bonus income in realities where political crisis erupts in their own countries – a reality where their natural endowment would be low. For the non-resident of France or Italy, the Swiss franc's hedge property against social or political crisis in these countries detracts from its other hedge properties, making it a less pure hedge against war, banking crisis, or high US inflation.

The possibility of an international banking crisis has increasingly haunted participants in international financial markets since the mid-1970s. The source of concern has been the growing loan exposure of the international banking system to the less developed countries and to the Comecon countries.[17] The first task of the defensive investor, when considering how to protect himself against an international banking crisis, must be to map out the possible nature of such a crisis.

Suppose that the perceived risk of loss on a bank's portfolio of loans to the non-oil LDCs was to suddenly increase sharply – due, perhaps, to a sharp increase in the price of energy, or to the shock-effect of one important country re-scheduling its debts. Take, first, a simplified example, where all loans were made with a 'floating' margin; the margin which the borrower paid over interbank interest rates would change according to market conditions. Then, if the risk of default by a borrower increased, the margin he would have to pay would rise, and probably by more than the increase in the (mathematical) expectation of loss per 100 dollars lent. A significant share of bank deposit business comes from investors who are unable to 'diversify away' specific risks (due to the small size of their total portfolio) and who would buy bank deposits only of very low risk. To preserve the low-risk feature of its deposits, the bank which experiences an increase in the risk of loss on its portfolio of loans to non-oil LDCs must increase its equity backing. If the supply of equity capital were less than perfectly elastic, the minimum acceptable expected return on any given risk-class of loan must rise, and margins would be pushed up on outstanding loans to non-oil LDCs both because of their increased risk and because of the increased cost of capital.

Now there may be no level of margin, given the increased probability of default, at which the bank would willingly lend the amount which is presently outstanding to a given non-oil LDC, Oceania. This would be so if Oceania's total borrowing outstanding already exceeds the shrunken limit of its re-payment capacity. This is illustrated in Figure 8.1. below.

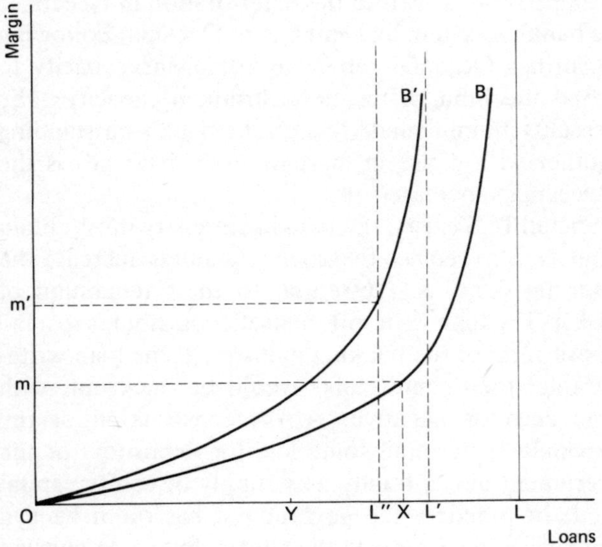

FIGURE 8.1 *Loans of the banking system to Oceania*

The downgrading of the market's estimate of the potential for Oceania to generate foreign exchange towards repayment of loans and their servicing leads to a shrinking of its borrowing capacity from L to L′: for banks would not willingly lend to Oceania if its total debt outstanding already exceeded the maximum present value of net foreign exchange inflows that could be generated under any feasible economic path that Oceania could be constrained to follow.

Now suppose that the banking system had loans outstanding of nominal value OY to Oceania. In practice, the position of Y should be compared not with L′ but with L″, (Oceania's effective loan capacity): banks could not charge huge margins on loans to reflect a high probability of some shortfall on repayment, without implicitly increasing the incentive for the borrower to default,[18] and the policing costs of the loan agreement would be very large. The shrinkage in Oceania's effective loan capacity to OL″ would increase the risk of default on her outstanding borrowing of OY. The supply curve of loans to Oceania would rotate upwards from OB to OB′. This upward rotation would be accentuated by any rise in the cost of equity capital to the banking industry, as greater equity backing was required for any given volume of loans outstanding.

Now suppose that when OB was the operative supply schedule for bank loans to Oceania (that is, before the deterioration in Oceania's credit rating), the banking system had lent OX to Oceania. Following the shock, which brings Oceania's effective borrowing capacity to OL″, X lies beyond the limit of the new shrunken capacity. The amount L″X represents an immediate loss on the bank's outstanding loans which, together with a rise in margins from m to m′, is the consequence of Oceania's increased risk.

If, indeed, a shortfall L″X exists, the banking industry must obtain more equity capital so as to replace that loan loss and to increase the equity backing for its deposits – essential to their remaining of unchanged low risk.[19] The loan write-off, in itself, contributes to a fall in the equity–deposit ratio of the banking industry. If the loan write-off were considerable, then some banks would be bankrupt, with their equity value zero or negative. Any reconstruction of the banking industry would then entail some loss for depositors or the extending of government aid; a totally new supply of equity capital would be required. In practice, the government has often been a principal source of new equity capital in the aftermath of a default-led crisis; in the bank crises of the early 1930s arising out of large loan losses to borrowers in Central Europe, many large French and Italian banks fell into public ownership, and have remained there since.

The above description of how a downgrading of a major borrower's perceived credit quality would affect the banking system highlights an important principle. A banking crisis can erupt without a single major borrower declaring a moratorium or defaulting on its payments; all that is required is a change in the perception of the value of the banking industry's loan portfolio. Further, an 'in-between' type of crisis is possible, short of widespread bankruptcy, where the banking system is successful in raising the large amount of new equity capital to replace that lost through loan write-offs and to increase equity backing for deposits. Both types of crisis can have their source in the capital market, where panic-stricken investors rush to sell their shares in the banking industry, believing that its loan assets have sunk in value. Depositors, alarmed at the fall in equity protection, would rush to convert their deposits into reserve money. Depositors may put a lower value on banks' loans portfolios than the equity holders, making it necessary for the banking system to raise a large amount of equity capital to preserve the perceived low-risk status of deposits. In turn, such large equity funding – given that the supply of equity capital were not perfectly elastic – would cause margins to rise further and so effective borrowing capacities would shrink further. Thus second-round losses would be inflicted on the value of bank loan portfolios.

In the period following an 'in-between' type of crisis, banks would be likely to re-balance their portfolios – emphasising low-risk loan assets (including marketable paper) at the expense of high-risk ones. Thus they would reduce their required equity–deposit ratio[20] back towards its previous norm. It is possible that margins for prime borrowers would fall below their previous level during this transitional period. Bank thirst for prime non-bank paper is a further factor making this a hedge against bank crisis (see Chapter 7). In the longer term, the slowed growth of the banking system – due to the raised cost of equity finance to the banking industry – would lead to a larger share of intermediation between borrowers and lenders being effected through non-bank channels. Top-rated borrowers, who have ready access to capital markets, would raise finance there to a greater extent than previously. Low-rated borrowers, who do not in general have access to non-bank markets, would find that their margins rose by more than those of top-rated borrowers – given the reluctance of banks to allow a deterioration to occur in the overall quality of their loan portfolio. Thus low-rated borrowing would diminish as a share of total uses of credit (bank and non-bank combined).

It has been assumed so far that margins are 'floating'. Suppose, instead, that they are fixed for a period of years. Then the downgrading of the payment-ability of the non-oil developing countries would lead to a loss being realized on banks' loan portfolios due to margins having been fixed below current market levels. This loss would be additional to those due to the shrinkage of borrowing capacity to less than the nominal amount of borrowing outstanding. The practice of fixed margins increases the risks of banking crisis, but it does not influence the above analysis in any other major respect.

Swiss banks stand out as having typically the highest equity–deposit ratios in the banking industry and the lowest loan exposure (proportional to their balance sheet) to the non-oil developing countries. In an international banking crisis, the demand for domestic deposits with Swiss banks would be likely to increase, and the franc would come under heavy upward pressure. This upward movement would be accentuated by present customers of Swiss banks, who have used their bank as a fiduciary agent for the placing of funds in the Euro-market, requesting that their fiduciary deposits be repatriated into domestic deposits. Thus there exists a large population who have the facility to quickly make the switch between the Euro-markets and the domestic franc market.

The dollar would be likely to be hard hit in an international banking crisis. Certain important official holders have a definite preference for offshore dollars compared to onshore dollars, due to the risk of assets in the US being frozen.[21] If offshore deposits in general became high-risk, these present holders would switch to domestic deposits in European centres rather than in the USA. As a large share of these offshore deposits are in dollars, the implied switch would push the US dollar downwards against the European currencies. Thus the dollar may be described as a fairweather good with respect to liquidity conditions offshore.

Currencies as Economic Activity-fairweather Goods

The basic balance of payments of each country is sensitive in different degrees to the level of economic activity in the world economy. For example, the Canadian current account deficit is likely to widen by a large margin at times of world slump and to narrow or move into surplus at times of world boom. This behaviour of Canada's current account is the basis of the Canadian dollar's property of being a fairweather good with respect to economic activity.

More generally, we may examine the likely response of a country's basic balance of payments to the level of economic activity by asking whether it has typically a surplus or deficit on each of the following sub-accounts, and by how much as a proportion of GNP: fuels, agricultural produce, raw materials, manufactured goods, travel, investment income, and transfers.

At times of economic boom the trade deficit of the OECD area, in aggregate, tends to increase. The OECD is a large net exporter of manufactured goods to OPEC and non-oil LDCs, and is a large net importer of primary commodities (excluding agricultural goods) and oil. In boom, the terms of trade move against the OECD, and the real incomes of the world outside the OECD increases. Those OECD countries which have normally a large deficit on primary commodity trade must increase substantially their net exports of manufactured goods at times of boom; those which are self-sufficient in primary commodities are spared such adjustment, and their currencies thus receive an upward boost.

A country which has a particularly high degree of specialisation in manufactured goods, and runs normally a large surplus in these, is cushioned in world economic boom against an enlargement of its deficit on primary commodities; for it gains then from the strong demand for manufactured exports. In contrast, an OECD country which is less specialised in manufactures, self-sufficient or an exporter of agricultural goods, and a primary commodity importer, would find that its trade balance was more adversely affected in world boom: agricultural exports, both in volume and value terms, are not significantly correlated with the world business cycle.

Goods and services traded between the OECD countries themselves are sensitive (in terms of demand) in different degrees to the level of economic activity in the world economy. For example, tourist expenditures are particularly sensitive to the business cycle; a country which has a large deficit on tourist account has its current account strengthened on this score during periods of low economic activity. A rentier nation – one which has large net receipts of investment income – is in a similar position to the exporter of manufactured goods with respect to the course of world economic activity. Interest and profits, and so the surplus on this account, rise at times of high activity, and fall at times of low activity.

In summary, an OECD currency which is a fairweather good with respect to world economic activity is likely to be issued by an economy whose trade has most of the following characteristics: a large surplus on investment income, self-sufficiency in primary commodities, a large net surplus on trade in manufactured goods, and a large surplus on tourism matched by deficit on other accounts (for example, on fixed transfers or on agricultural products). An OECD currency which is a hedge currency with respect to world economic activity is likely to be issued by an economy whose trade has the opposite characteristics to those just described.

In practice, most countries' trade has some characteristics drawn from both the hedge and the fairweather category (with respect to economic activity). Table 8.2 lists the characteristics for the USA, Germany and Japan. Both Japan and Germany have the fairweather characteristics of large surpluses on manufactures trade but have large deficits on raw material account. They are both about equally dependent on agricultural imports. Japan is the more dependent of the two on raw material imports, but Germany has a much larger tourist deficit. It is on fuel account – assuming that fuel prices are highly correlated with the world business cycle – that Japan is a greater loser than Germany during boom.

TABLE 8.2. *Current accounts of the USA, Germany, and Japan in 1980*

	USA	*Japan*	*Germany*
Merchandise trade	−41	−17.5	5.5
fuels	−85	−73.5	−36.1
agriculture	25	−13.7	−11.5
raw materials	–	−21.3	−9.5
manufactures	19	91.0	62.5
Invisibles	34	−13.5	−24.0
travel	−2	−5.7	−14.0
investment income	37	−4.8	2.2
on direct investment	36	1.5	2.2
other services	5	−3.0	−7.3
transfers	−6	−1.5	−11.8
military transfers	–	–	5.3
Current account	−7	−20.0	−13.4

SOURCE: IMF

The USA has a surplus in agricultural trade with only a small surplus in manufactures and this on balance should predispose the dollar to being a slump-hedge currency. However, the USA is also a large net recipient of interest and investment income, which tends to move positively with the business cycle. But a high proportion of investment income is typically reinvested abroad, and so the cash inflow shows a less pro-cyclical fluctuation than the reported surplus on this income account. Of the major currencies, the dollar may therefore be mildly boosted by a slowdown in world economic activity. The influence of the state-variable of economic activity on the US dollar is likely to often be dwarfed by other considerations.

Other Uses of Currency in Defensive Investment

In this chapter, currencies have so far been examined as hedges against bad general states of the world. In addition, currencies may be used as vehicles for trading income contingent on the value of distributive state-variables. In each currency area, producers of domestic non-tradable goods gain, whilst those of tradable goods lose, from a real appreciation of the domestic currency. By the domestic producers of tradable goods lending the national currency to the domestic producers of non-tradable goods, and borrowing from him foreign currency (these transactions are likely to be effected via the banking system) both reduce the exposure of their wealth to shifts in the real exchange rate. Thus the owner of an export business should borrow to some extent in foreign currency and have an especially large long net position in domestic currency – and conversely for the owner of a business specialising in non-traded goods.

Investment in foreign currency cannot provide perfect protection for an enterprise against fluctuation of the real exchange rate. The foreign currency may show a large depreciation against the domestic one, due to unexpectedly low inflation at home, whilst the real exchange value of the domestic money may actually have fallen. The domestic producer of tradables cannot be sure that by taking a short position in the foreign money against the domestic one he would obtain an income bonus in all realities where the relative price of non-tradables in terms of tradables rises.[22]

In principle, it should be possible to construct for each trading enterprise a basket of monies, whose individual representation in the basket is increased regularly in proportion to rises in the price level in the respective countries of issue, such that the enterprise's profits expressed in terms of one currency, say dollars, were influenced by exchange rate change only if the US purchasing power of the basket changed. More technically, the corporation's dollar profit function need include only one variable for exchange rates, the real value of the specific basket. Some currencies may receive a negative weighting in the basket.

Thus the *numéraire* basket for a trading enterprise specialising in the extraction of oil from the North Sea would contain a heavy weighting of US dollars, and a negative weighting of British pounds. For oil is itself a dollar commodity, and so a strong dollar is positive for profits; costs of extraction are sterling-related, and so a strong pound, *ceteris paribus,* is negative for profits.

The construction of basket-*numéraires* for each trading enterprise, and their variation between projects, has an important implication for investment. A project with a *numéraire* which has a heavy weighting of hedge currencies on which rates of return are comparatively low should be acceptable at a lower expected real rate of profit than one with a *numéraire* which has a heavy weighting of fairweather currencies on which rates of return are comparatively high.

The variation of basket-*numéraire* appropriate to alternative investment projects does not mean that these appeal to distinct clienteles differentiated by their natural base currency. A dollar-based investor, in appraising a project whose *numéraire* is composed largely of non-dollar currencies, can operate in forward exchange and credit markets to make the project more 'dollar-like' from his viewpoint. The rates at which he can sell hedge-monies forward are especially favourable, given their low expected yields, and so projects with a *numéraire* biased towards hedge currencies will still have a natural advantage. However, the potential to transform project *numéraires* by credit and forward market transformations is limited by inflation risk. Project *numéraires* are baskets of constant purchasing power amounts of each currency, whilst forward and credit market contracts are in nominal terms.

Notes and References

1. Neutral currencies are those which possess no hedge characteristics.
2. For the prospective time-path of the Netherlands' dependence on net energy imports see 'Moving into Energy Deficit', *Petroleum Economist* (March 1980) pp. 107–11.
3. Neutral monies are those which do not possess hedge characteristics.
4. See *Currency Outlook*, September 1980, published by the London

Business School.

5. See further discussion of differential productivity growth under the fourth factor below.
6. Energy crisis is a bad reality even from the viewpoint of British investors, despite Britain being self-sufficient in energy. Britain would suffer as a result of growth of demand in many export markets being reduced.
7. Even in terms of internationally traded goods, the dollar has an advantage compared to the franc or mark as a stable store of value, due to the large share of US purchasing power in world markets. The threshold of inflation in the USA that would trigger international investors to move out of the dollar as a store of value (for the purchase of internationally traded goods) is higher than the threshold in Germany that would trigger international investors to move out of the mark.
8. Then many French residents would switch a portion of their monetary portfolio from francs to marks, causing the franc's real exchange rate against the mark to fall.
9. There are exceptional periods. For example, during the Deutsche mark crisis of Autumn 1980, the franc moved with a smaller amplitude than the mark against the US dollar.
10. Consider a currency which promises a fixed return plus a bonus income, in proportion 'a' to the fixed return, whenever state-variable x takes its bad value x_0 (notation here is the same as in Chapter 2). The price of such a currency is $1 + as_{x0}$. A change in the price s_{x0} to $s_{x0} + ds_{x0}$ causes the currency's price to rise by the proportion:

$$\frac{1 + a(s_{x0} + ds_{x0})}{(1 + as_{x0})} - 1.$$

    The variance of this proportional change, per time-interval dt, is,

$$a \text{ var } \frac{(ds_{x0}/dt)}{1 + as_{x0}}$$

    Now, from the properties of hedge-investments, var (ds_{x0}) is greater than var (dS_x). Thus, for small changes, a 'standard' hedge-currency will be more volatile in price than a standard fairweather one.
11. See R.Z. Aliber, 'Attributes of National Monies and the Interdependence of National Monetary Policies' in his edited book *National Monetary Policies and the International Financial System* (University of Chicago, 1974).
12. For a history of international capital flows during the late 1930s, see Stanley Black, 'International Money Markets and Flexible Exchange Rates', *Princeton Essays in International Finance*, no. 32, 1973; for statistics on gold movements, see M. Friedman and A. Schwarz, *A Monetary History of the United States* (Princeton, 1963), pp. 473–7.
13. See L. B. Yaeger *International Monetary Relations* (Harper & Row, 1965) pp. 338–9 for details of transactions in Switzerland involving frozen dollar deposits.
14. See *OECD Economic Outlook for New Zealand*, 1980.
15. For an estimate of the degree of switching during 1978 – a year when the Swiss franc appreciated sharply – see *OECD Economic Outlook for Switzerland,* 1980.

16. Decisions where to shop and where to travel on holiday are more sensitive over short periods of time to exchange rate change than are commercial trading decisions – where contracts and delivery periods can be long term.
17. For a discussion of the possibility of crisis, see C. Kindleberger, *Manias, Panics, and Crashes* (Macmillan, 1978) Chapter 10.
18. The borrower would feel that, if he did not default, he would have paid an exorbitant cost to the lender.
19. New equity capital may be very expensive in these circumstances due to the market viewing the write-off as symptomatic of managerial incompetence in the banking industry. This may force a further up-turn in margins, causing L″ to shrink even further to the left, and so causing even larger write-offs. A change in management may be a way of lowering the cost of new equity.
20. Required to preserve the low-risk characteristics of their deposits.
21. For example, after the freezing of Iranian assets in the USA at end-1979, certain OPEC nations moved dollar holdings offshore. At any time, Comecon has held its dollar assets almost exclusively offshore, rather than in the USA.
22. The distinction being made here is similar to that of R. Z. Aliber in 'The Firm Under Pegged and Floating Exchange Rates' in J. Herin *et al.* (eds), *Flexible Exchange Rates and Stabilization Policy* (Macmillan, 1977). Aliber distinguishes here between 'price risk' (a shift in the ratio of the price of tradable to non-tradable goods) and 'exchange risk'.

9 Gold and Silver

Gold is the king of bad news goods. The principal source of the metal's value is the income which it would yield contingent on certain bad realities – war, energy catastrophe, hyperinflation, social revolution – each of which has small likelihood. Gold has further come to have a dominant influence on the movement of a wide range of bad news goods.

De-composing Gold

In a state of world war or hyperinflation, gold would become a fully fledged money providing all three services of money – medium of exchange, unit of account, and store of value. The monetary services that gold would yield contingent on these bad realities are one source of its value; the potential services are discounted by a rate which allows both for the small likelihood of the bad realities occurring and the high valuation of income there.

In conditions of high inflation or of widespread inconvertibility of paper monies, gold would be likely to assume at least one of the functions of money – namely as a relatively low-risk store of value. For example, suppose US rate of inflation were to become high and variable, so that an investor with a 5-year horizon believed that the average annual inflation rate would lie within a normal range of 5 to 30 per cent. Then the real value of an investment in gold at the end of the 5 years may be less uncertain than the real value of an investment in 6-month dollar deposits (rolled over on maturity) at the same horizon date. The rate of increase in above-ground gold supplies each year would be considerably less uncertain than that of the supply of dollar deposits worldwide. In conditions of great inflation-instability, this advantage of gold from the side of supply may outweigh its disadvantage from the side of demand. Demand (measured in units of constant purchasing-power) for gold would remain less stable than the demand for dollars with its large monetary component. In-between conditions may be found where a diversified portfolio of gold and dollar deposits has a lower variance of possible real values at the investor's horizon date than one containing exclusively either gold or dollars.

If inflation in the USA were to exceed the trigger-point at which gold comes to have a place as a store of value in low-risk portfolios it would be likely to soar in value due to the concentration of a new type of asset demand on the metal. Gold may also, under such conditions, come to have a limited use as *numéraire* in long-term capital markets, if borrowers and lenders believed that the real cost and rate of return respectively (expressed in units of constant purchasing power) was less uncertain when the contract was denominated in gold rather than in dollars. The soaring in gold's value that would occur in the transition from low to high US inflation would provide an income-bonus contingent on that reality. This bonus is distinct from that promised on transition to realities of hyperinflation or of social breakdown where gold would become a medium of exchange.

The threshold of inflation at which asset demand for gold as a component of the investor's low-risk portfolio becomes significant is lowered by tax considerations. Given the non-indexation of tax on nominal interest and expense, real rates of tax on interest (that is, the rate of tax expressed as a proportion of the real interest component of nominal interest) becomes exorbitant at times of high inflation (see Part 3). This creates an incentive for investors to switch into low-risk real assets, and into gold, as substitutes for nominal assets whose real income has become subject to a very high tax burden. Gold should gain in value from such tax-propelled asset switches. A further feature promoting gold's use as a store of value at times of heavy taxation on nominal assets (due to high inflation) is its anonymity – purchases and sales can be made anonymously and theoretical capital gains tax liabilities cannot be made effective thereon.

The risk of exchange restrictions is ever-present for paper monies. In a world where most of the major international monies were inconvertible, gold would be likely to assume both a medium of exchange and widespread *numéraire* use in the world economy.[1] The potential monetary services which gold would yield, to a large number of investors, contingent on inconvertibility of international paper monies, are another source of gold's value.

Gold's intrinsic beauty is essential to its being a potential store of value and medium of exchange, and hence to its having various hedge qualities. The existence of a consumption-type demand for gold, based on its ornamental (including jewellery) services, should set a base value for gold, even in the absence of investor demand, that was high relative to both volume and weight of the metal. High value per unit weight and volume is responsible for the low storage cost of gold investment. Further, this ornamental demand is widely spread throughout the population and can be summarised as a function of a few general state-variables – most importantly, the level of real income. The broad base of the ornamental demand for gold stands in contrast to the consumption demand for collectables – for example, very rare stamps and fine paintings – for which demand is a function of many highly particular state-variables and is more unstable than for gold. A simple and stable ornamental demand function for gold provides an anchor to its price which is essential to the growth of pure investment demand, whether as a store of value or as a hedge asset. If ornamental demand for gold were unstable, gold would be less reliable as a store of value.

The hedge qualities provided by gold have been sharply altered in scope by the dollar's break from gold – first for private investors in 1968, and then for official holders in 1971. In the days of the gold–dollar exchange system (1945–68), the gold price was fixed within narrow bands against the US dollar. So long as the system was maintained, gold could not yield bonus income contingent on the movement of any state-variables. The investor could expect bonus income from gold contingent only on realities where the gold–dollar standard had broken down – and that would be in already extreme circumstances.

In contrast, the investor today can expect contingent income from gold in less extreme circumstances than previously. A movement of the state-variable belligerency from a value representing full peace to one of cold war would today cause gold to yield large income, as the gold price rose due to the increased probability of those bad realities occurring where gold would yield monetary services. Thus gold is today a hedge both against cold war and full-scale war – not just against the latter as in the dollar–gold exchange system.

Similarly, when – like today – no paper money is convertible into gold (at a fixed rate of exchange), gold is a hedge against a range of inflation rates starting from a lower level than under the dollar–gold exchange system. There, US inflation could accelerate, as during the

Korean and Vietnam Wars, without gold providing any bonus income compared to US dollars; today, with gold floating, extra income would be provided. Additionally, the demise of the dollar's link to gold has increased the likelihood of high inflation rates occurring and so raised the price placed by the market on gold's income contingent on high inflation. Today, the immediate source of that contingent income is the ignition of 'low-risk store-of-value' demand for gold as the rate of inflation becomes sufficiently unpredictable; in the gold–dollar exchange system the source could only be the breakdown of the system.

In the gold–dollar exchange system, gold would not have been a hedge against energy-crisis. Indeed, if the present petro-monies had retained a dollar–peg, neither would they have performed a hedge role. Gold's bonus income contingent on an energy crisis has a principal source in OPEC's high marginal propensity to invest oil revenues in gold, so pushing the gold price upwards in terms of paper monies. But if the dollar had been pegged to gold, then OPEC's propensity to invest in gold would have been lower,[2] and any tightness in the physical gold market would have been relieved by the raising of interest rates in the USA, deflating aggregate demand there. In the deflation, the real value of metallic gold above ground would have risen. Gold would not have yielded superior income to dollar money itself.

Gold Jewellery and Coin

It has been seen how the ornamental attractions of gold are fundamental to its other properties. In terms of end-usage of newly mined gold, jewellery is still the most important category (see Table 9.1). Jewellery demand is itself positively related to aggregate income levels, being a luxury type of expenditure. The fall in jewellery demand that occurs during slump usually overrides the rise in investment demand for bullion due to the low opportunity cost of holding gold as the rate of return on alternative assets falls; gold is not a slump hedge.

TABLE 9.1 *Use of newly mined gold by the non-Communist private sector (metric tons)*

	1975	*1976*	*1977*	*1978*	*1979*
Total fabrication	*983*	*1384*	*1420*	*1596*	*1315*
Of which					
carat jewellery	523	935	1003	1007	737
electronics	67	76	77	86	94
dentistry	62	77	82	89	74
other industrial decorative uses	59	64	65	76	74
medals, medallions and fake coins	21	47	47	50	33
official coins	251	185	146	288	290
Net private bullion purchases (sales)	129	55	222	156	450
Total net private purchases	1112	1439	1642	1752	1765

SOURCE: Consolidated Gold Fields, *Gold,* 1980.

Underneath the title of so-called jewellery demand for gold can be discovered often an element of investment demand. Gold jewellery offers the same type of contingent incomes as gold bullion, given the close correlation of their prices; it also offers aesthetic pleasure to the consumer who beholds the ornamentation; gold jewellery is a joint product of pure gold plus labour and capital used in its fabrication. A large body of investors hold both gold jewellery and gold bullion in their portfolio. For them, the present value of the prospective non-pecuniary (ornamental) services attributable to their marginal holding of jewellery (over and above that attributable to its underlying gold bullion content) must equal the marginal cost of its fabrication. Conceptually, these investors have decided to 'jewellerise' a portion of their investment holdings of gold bullion, and do so up to the point at which the above marginal condition is satisfied. Their indirect demand for gold bullion through their demand for gold jewellery should be treated as wholly for pure investment purposes.

Many investors, however, hold gold jewellery and no gold bullion. For them, the marginal cost of fabricating gold bullion into gold jewellery must be less than (or equal to) the present value of the marginal non-pecuniary services of gold jewellery over and above those provided by its underlying gold content;[3] either they have a particularly great appetite for gold jewellery or they attach little importance to gold's non-ornamental services.

A clear pattern is observable of fabrication demand for gold, principally for the making of jewellery, to fall off at times of high gold prices.[4] This suggests that a large number of actual and potential holders of gold jewellery are in the second category above – investors who hold gold jewellery, but no gold bullion. Thus the 'consumption' motive appears to be of great importance in the gold market, and this is significant for gold's property as a hedge investment. The high elasticity of consumption (jewellery) demand with respect to price constrains the width of fluctuation of the gold price. In turn, the marked sensitivity of jewellery demand to the level of real incomes, and the importance of fabrication demand in the gold bullion market, give a fairweather characteristic to gold with respect to the level of economic activity.

Demand for modern gold coins (these are coins which are still in current production and sell at only a small, fairly steady margin over the value of their gold content) is based on pure investment considerations, with ornamental services not being obtained; modern coins are a very close investment substitute for gold bullion. Coins have the advantage compared to bullion of being officially stamped as being of true weight and content, and they are available in large quantities in very small sizes – making them readily usable as money in realities where gold were again to become a circulating medium of exchange. Gold bullion, even when stamped in small sizes by a well-known bank, is at some disadvantage as a circulating medium compared to widely held coins which have legal-tender status. Coins often have the advantage compared to bullion of receiving more favourable tax treatment.[5]

The market for new coins is not perfectly competitive. The coins struck by different national authorities are only imperfect substitutes for each other. The British investor has a distinct preference for sovereigns, the North American investor for Krugerrands, Eagles, Maple leafs, and Mexican coins, and the Swiss investor for Vrenelis. The producers of each type of coin do not operate according to some simple profit criterion, for example the maximisation of gross premiums collected (per period) over the gold contents of the coins.

Different supply policies and different popularity of respective coins leads to them typically having different agios (the technical term for a gold coin's premium over its gold content) as illustrated in Table 9.2.

TABLE 9.2 *Agio of gold coins on February 1980*

	Price	*Agio (%)*
Gold bullion (1 ounce)	$653	0
	Sfr.	
Vreneli	222½	11
Helvetia	235	18
New sovereign	263	4
Krugerrand	1088	2
Mexico	1324	3
½ Vreneli	250	21
Old sovereign	290	14
Eagle, Liberty	617½	19
½ Eagle, Liberty	569	120

SOURCE: Union Bank of Switzerland

The advantages of gold coins compared to gold bullion should normally be invariant with respect to the gold price.[6] Thus at times of strongly rising gold prices the agios on gold coins should tend to fall. Recent experience confirms this pattern. In the heady days of December 1979 and January 1980, when the gold price soared from under $500 to near $900 per ounce, the premium on new sovereigns narrowed from 12 per cent to near 2 per cent; the narrowing of premiums was considerably greater on old coins which typically have a larger agio than do new coins.[7] For example, the agio on a 20-franc Vreneli gold coin dropped from 51 per cent to 27 per cent between December 1978 and December 1979, and that on a 20-franc Helvetia from 147 per cent to 60 per cent.

Relevant to the determination of agios on new coins is not only the level of the gold price, but also the composition of demand for gold. Thus in late 1979 and during the first quarter of 1980, OPEC governments were a principal source of new demand for gold as they invested a portion of their swollen oil revenues in gold bullion. At the high prices for gold which resulted, other investors, who traditionally hold a larger proportion than OPEC of their gold in coins, withdrew from the market, depressing the demand for coins relative to demand for bullion.

The supply of gold coins, in contrast to the supply of new coins, is fixed. They yield the non-pecuniary satisfaction that can be derived by some from the possession of something old – analogous to the nostalgic enjoyment of popular music of a previous age. This nostalgic demand is probably highly sensitive to the level of incomes – being a luxury-type of expenditure; hence old gold coins are more exposed to the risk of slump than are new coins. Old coins' potential services as a medium of exchange in certain bad realities are less than those of new coins; being less widespread and in non-standard quality, they would make a poor circulating medium of exchange.[8] Further, given the likely instability of nostalgic demand, old gold coins are inferior to bullion or to jewellery as a potential low-risk store of value.

Gold Shares

Gold yet-to-be-mined, in addition to above-ground gold supplies, can form part of a defensive investment portfolio. Gold equities represent claims to the profits from the mining of gold in future periods. The price of gold equities is highly correlated with the price of the metal; a rise in the spot price of gold causes inventories held by the mining companies to rise in value, and increases the potential profits from mining in future years.

Indeed mining companies' equities are often highly levered on the gold price. The profits from mining may be approximated as the value of gold produced less costs of production; and these costs, though sensitive in some degree to the gold price, fluctuate by much less. Hence profits fluctuate to a greater extent than the gold price itself; the extra leverage is particularly great for mining companies with a large proportion of low-quality mines, for which the fixed costs of exploitation are high. In itself, this quality of high leverage should not cause gold shares to command a premium valuation over gold bullion, for the investor can alternatively lever his investment in gold bullion by borrowing against it (or equivalently, by buying gold futures).

The existence of a large market in gold equities reduces the potential volatility of the gold price itself. For when the risk increases of a bad reality where gold would yield contingent income (as a medium of exchange, store of value, or both), the supply of gold-related assets that can be bought by investors increases also; investors can buy new issues of gold equities made to finance the increased volume of gold that can now be mined profitably in future years.[9] During the gold bullion price boom of end-1979 and early 1980, exploration activity and extension development picked up strongly, as did new issues of gold-mining equities (largely in the form of rights issues).[10] In South Africa, new investment was aimed at extending the life of existing mines; in Australia, an exploration boom got under way; in the USA, prospecting companies turned to old ore-bodies hoping to re-work the tailings left behind in the Gold Rushes of the nineteenth century.

Yet gold-mining shares are a more impure hedge asset than gold itself. In certain very bad realities, where gold bullion's yield would be especially high, that of gold equities could be very low. For example, in conditions of world war, dividend from gold shares may be frozen or the mining companies may be nationalised, whilst gold bullion and coins may become a medium of exchange, at least in black markets. Whilst gold bullion is a hedge against the state-variable belligerency moving all the way to full-scale war, gold shares are a hedge against the same variable taking bad values only up to a point just short of its worst extreme. Thus during December 1979 and January 1980, when the gold price soared under the influence of the increased probability of East–West conflict in the wake of the Russian invasion of Afghanistan, gold shares rose by less in value than gold bullion, despite their naturally higher leverage. In contrast, during the period 1977 to mid-1979 when the gold price was rising under the influence of rising inflation (and inflation-panic) in the USA and then rising energy prices, the *Financial Times* gold share index rose by a similar proportion to the bullion price. High running dividend yields were also obtained.[11]

An overwhelming proportion of gold shares are South African, due to the concentration of new production in that country (see Table 9.3). The value of South African gold shares is especially sensitive to conditions in South Africa – more so than is the value of gold bullion: social pressures in the Republic may force employers to make a large increase in the wage of black mineworkers, which would have a much larger proportional effect on the earnings of gold companies than on the gold price itself. Cost of production is a very loose anchor to the movement of the gold price. A revolution in the Republic could reduce the value of gold shares to zero, whilst having only a moderate influence on the long-term movement of the gold price – assuming that a new Government would maintain production, albeit from nationalised mines, at the same rate.

TABLE 9.3 *New Gold supplies 1975–9 (metric tons)*

	1975	*1976*	*1977*	*1978*	*1979*
Net sales of Communist bloc	149	412	401	410	229
Net official sales	9	58	269	362	574
New production in non-Communist world	953	969	971	980	962
South Africa	713	713	699	706	703
Canada	51	52	54	54	49
USA	32	32	32	30	28
Other Africa	40	39	41	34	29
Latin America	41	55	55	62	68
Asia	26	26	29	32	31
Europe	11	11	13	12	10
Oceania	37	38	45	48	43

SOURCE: Consolidated Goldfields

There are a small number of Canadian and one principal US gold equity (Homestake Mining) in addition to the plethora of South African gold equities. Even these North American gold equities are indirectly sensitive in value to changing political conditions in South Africa. An increase in the probability of revolution in the Republic should lead to a rise in the bullion price and an even stronger rise in the price of North American (and Australian) gold shares; South African mining issues would probably fall in value.[12] If revolution were to occur in South Africa, gold production there could be halted or cut back for at least several months. During that period a squeeze may develop in the gold market, with the spot price of gold rising far above its long-term forward price.[13] Gold producers outside South Africa would be able to take advantage of the squeeze by accelerating production and reducing their inventories.[14] In addition, many investment institutions cannot, according to their statutes, invest in gold bullion, but they can invest in gold equities: if the South African mining sector were nationalized then the weight of such institutional demand would be concentrated on North American and Australian gold equities, causing them to rise strongly in price relative to gold bullion. In short, non-South African gold equities thrive on bad news (from the viewpoint of whites) from South Africa, and by considerably more than bullion itself.

The values of gold equities are sensitive to many particular state-variables which do not influence directly the price of gold bullion. In particular, rates of taxation on the profit or sales of gold mining corporations can change; there is always the possibility that a large rise in the gold price could lead to the introduction of a windfall profits tax. In addition, each mine is subject to highly specific risks - including its prospective level of reserves, and a change in the efficiency of its management. Major gold-mining corporations outside South Africa have usually diversified interests extending into areas such as lead, zinc, uranium, oil and gas. Such dilution lowers still further the purity of gold shares as hedge assets compared to an investment in gold bullion.

It is possible for market segmentation to exist between investors in gold equities and those in gold bullion. Then if investors in the gold-equity market believe that the bullion price has been driven up by short-term speculative factors which are likely to be reversed gold equities may trail behind the rise in the gold price. In these circumstances an arbitrage opportunity would exist for investors in gold bullion to switch into gold equities, and failure for this to occur would imply market segmentation (institutional-type restrictions on arbitrage). In practice, it is difficult to distinguish market segmentation and differing hedge qualities (in particular, the inability of gold equities to insure against world war) as explanations of gold equities following an atypical price path relative to that of gold bullion.

Silver

Like gold, silver is a potential medium of exchange in certain bad realities. In conditions of social breakdown or of hyperinflation, silver may circulate alongside gold, providing a medium of exchange for small transactions. Even the smallest gold coins would be much larger in value than many types of retail transactions. It is likely, though, that the realities in which silver would be transformed into a money alongside gold would be much worse than those where gold on its own would assume some monetary role. In a war economy, not beset by hyperinflation, gold would be likely to assume a monetary role as a medium of exchange for large transactions in the black market; but banknotes would be likely to remain as the medium of exchange for small transactions.

It is generally assumed that the very bad realities in which silver would be monetised are of lower probability than the bad realities where only gold would be monetised. Given that the market's estimate of the probability of very unlikely realities fluctuates (in percentage terms) by more than that of less abnormal realities – as hypothesized in Chapter 2 – the present value of the contingent monetary services of silver should be more volatile than those of gold.[15] Another factor making for greater instability of the silver price than of the gold price is the much smaller ratio for silver than for gold of outstanding inventories to potential changes in demand from investors seeking a low-risk store of value. For example, a rise in the US inflation rate to high and variable levels would prompt investors to include some silver and gold in their portfolios; but a given absolute increase in stock demand by investors would have a much larger effect on the silver price than on the gold price. In turn, the greater volatility of the silver price makes silver less popular than gold as a component of low-risk portfolios (for which the intention of the owner is to minimise the volatility of real returns considered from now until his horizon date).

Silver is more sensitive than gold to the level of economic activity, detracting from its quality as a hedge asset. A greater share of the end-uses of silver than of gold are industrial, especially when it is realised that fabrication demand for gold includes a large investment element. Further, the marked sensitivity of silver values to highly specific state-variables (described below) makes gold a less impure hedge asset than silver with respect to general state-variables. Given the smaller ratio of outstanding inventory to production for silver than for gold, current tactics of producers can have a greater potential impact on the silver price than on the gold price. Massive hoards of silver are held in India, and the extent to which export controls are enforced there has great relevance to the silver price. A large market-participant can more easily influence prices in the small silver market than in the large gold market. Photography is an important end-use of silver, and yet it is not assured in the long run; there is the ever-present risk of an alternative to silver being found in the photographic process and this adds to riskiness of silver's income contingent on bad realities.

Notes and References

1. See Brendan Brown, *Money, Hard and Soft* (Macmillan, 1978) Chapter 5, pp. 145–9, for a discussion of how, in a world of monetary nationalism, gold would be forced into the limelight as the principal international money.
2. The existence of a close substitute for gold – dollars – together with the more limited scope of gold's hedge functions would have reduced OPEC's demand for the metal.
3. Equality will hold only if the investor is poised to buy gold bullion were fabrication to become very slightly more expensive.
4. For comment on this, see Consolidated Gold Fields *Report on Gold,* 1980. Both in 1974 and in 1979/80 – years of very high gold prices, jewellery demand slumped.
5. For example in the UK coin sales, but not bullion, are free of value-added-tax; further, coins which are of legal tender in Britain (sovereigns) are not subject to capital gains tax.
6. It is conceivable that in a dangerous crisis, where a major country was on the brink of hyperinflation, and hence gold coin was on the brink of becoming a medium of exchange, the agio could widen sharply.
7. For evidence on coin-price movements, see Swiss Bank Corporation's *Price List* (foreign exchange, banknotes, gold) published monthly.
8. Coin dealers classify the state of preservation of old gold coins into seven grades – see, for example, Krause's *Standard Catalogue of World Coins* (London, annual).
9. This supply-elasticity of gold claims should not be confused with supply elasticity of contingent income itself (see Chapter 2).
10. See *The Economist*, 27 September 1980, pp. 89–90, 'Prospectors gamble that every cloud has a gold lining'.
11. Even in this earlier period, gold shares did not show their typical leverage with respect to the gold price: this was due to accumulating political worries concerning South Africa. For evidence on the historical relation of gold share prices to bullion's prices, see *Gold Review*, Messel & Co., January 1981.
12. This pattern of price movements was observable at the time of the sabotage of the Sasoil Plant in mid-1980, which incident sparked off new fears about political stability of the Republic.
13. In normal times, gold is an investment commodity for which there exists a large body of present non-commercial holders: many of these are willing, if the spot price were to rise above the forward price discounted by the cost of storing gold (including financing charges) to sell physical metal spot and buy it forward, so preventing a squeeze from developing on physical supplies. However, when newly mined supplies are cut drastically, such one-way arbitrage could prove insufficient to relieve the squeeze.
14. In North America, alluvium mining techniques are used for extraction of gold, and this allows supply to be adjusted as suggested. In South Africa, deep shafts are predominant, and producers respond to a rise in gold's price by mining inferior ores and hopefully extending thereby the life of the mine. Unlike in North America, the South African mines cannot

expand overall production over the short or medium term.

15. The reasoning here is the same as in the demonstration that in a two-period world, hedge investments are likely to be particularly volatile in price (see Chapter 2).

10 Collectables

'Collectables' is used here as a generic term to include stamps, rare books, fine paintings, oriental rugs, and antiques of various types. Collectables all have certain features in common. First, their running cash yield to the private holder (in contrast to their yield to the museum) is zero or negative (when allowance is made for costs of storage). Second, taste for them is acquired or cultivated – it does not exist 'naturally'. Third, there is a large amount of non-standardisation, even for narrowly defined categories of collectable. Fourth, their rate of physical depreciation is extremely low, with their lifetime extending sometimes into centuries. Fifth, they are luxury items with demand for them being a strongly rising function of income levels.

The fifth feature above ensures that collectables are fairweather goods with respect to the level of economic activity and with respect to economic growth. They possess further fairweather characteristics; they are likely casualties of social revolution or of any major redistribution of income from profits to labour. The principal types of hedge properties which certain types of collectables are found to possess in practice are with respect to war, high inflation in a major part of the OECD area, energy crisis, and a fading of investment opportunity.

Collectables as Inflation-hedges

A rise in the inflation rate and inflation risk would be likely to raise demand for collectables. Investors would respond to the increased volatility of real returns on traditionally low-risk nominal deposits and bonds by decreasing their demand for them and increasing their demand for low-risk real assets. Consumer durables, including housing, have been discussed already in this context; but they had the disadvantages of high storage costs and a significant rate of physical depreciation (including obsolescence). Thus some collectables, with their low rate of depreciation, are attractive as an alternative to monetary assets at times of high and uncertain inflation, despite their values being more volatile than those of consumer durables.

Not all collectables are likely to appeal to the investor as an alternative to money under inflationary conditions. He would favour those for which the demand is comparatively stable. A collectable for which there are many close substitutes – for example, a Penny Black stamp of which there are several thousand in existence – is more attractive as a store of value than a one-off rare stamp whose price is highly sensitive to the tastes of perhaps two or three investors.[1] A fine modern Qum rug in silk, of which there are many thousand in existence, is similarly preferable as a low-risk store of value to a rare eighteenth-century rug made in Persia in Polonais style; the demand for the former is widespread and is a fairly stable function of well-known macroeconomic variables, whilst the price of the latter is highly dependent on the present endowments and tastes of a few key collectors.

The same principle concerning the suitability of collectables as a money-alternative at a time of highly uncertain inflation may be extended to works of art. Paintings of a prolific and popular artist are more suitable than one of six specimens of Leonardo da Vinci or a rare masterpiece of El Greco. The existence of many close substitutes for a given collectable should reduce the extent to which its value is sensitive to a few highly particular state-variables and hence its price volatility should be reduced. When considering the works of a prolific painter, those for which close substitutes exist should be especially suitable as money-alternatives. The market-price of one of Cezanne's many paintings of Mont Ste. Victoire should be less sensitive to the movement of highly particular state-variables than that of a unique portrait by the same artist.

The importance of the existence of close substitutes to a collectable in determining its potential as a money-alternative may be illustrated also in the rare-book market. There are 2000 first editions of Adam Smith's *Wealth of Nations*, of which 12 to 15 come to the market each year. Hence the *Wealth of Nations* is more suitable as a money-alternative than one of the 200 first editions of Marx's *Das Kapital* of which one comes to the market only at 2- or 3-yearly intervals. The price realised at these infrequent auctions is heavily dependent on the tastes and budgets of a few collectors at that time.

Collectables share with consumer durables the property of a significant proportion of their potential return being in the form of non-pecuniary services to the owner. Only in direst inflationary conditions and when access to precious-metal markets is restricted, are automobiles, for example, likely to be bought as a money-alternative by non-drivers.[2] Similarly, a 'philistine' would be unlikely to regard a collectable as an attractive money-alternative (but exceptions exist, as discussed below), even though the collectable be a comparatively low-risk real asset, because its yield excluding non-pecuniary returns would probably appear to be very low.

Consider the marginal investor in different categories of collectable. The investor in a collectable well-suited as a money-alternative, and which has thereby many close substitutes, should find that the proportion of its income yield which is non-pecuniary in form is especially low. The price of a collectable is determined at the margin of the class of close substitutes to which it belongs by the investor who (out of the successful bidders) would be willing to pay least for its non-pecuniary services. The larger is the class, the less important should be non-pecuniary services to the marginal holder.

The assumption of a hedge characteristic by the given collectable lowers still further the relative contribution of non-pecuniary returns to its value. Investors perceiving that some collectables are money-substitutes in uncertain inflationary conditions, realise that they are inflation hedges, albeit impure; in the transition to high and unstable inflation rates, increased demand from collector investors wishing to include them in their low-risk portfolio would cause their price to appreciate. This capital gain is, in effect, an income-bonus contingent on realities of high inflation. A high valuation put on such contingent income from a hedge collectable reduces the proportion of its yield (to the marginal investor) which is non-pecuniary in form, as explained below.

If the risk of high inflation were to increase, the value put on collectables' income contingent on inflation would increase; the expected non-pecuniary yield (as a proportion of market value) from the collectable would be depressed also by the immediate increase in demand for it as a money substitute. The raised valuation of the collectable may 'price out' of the market the collector of modest means whose low wealth leads him to seek less inflation-contingent income and to have a smaller appetite for money substitutes than a wealthier, less enthusiastic collector. Indeed, it is possible that, as the valuation given to inflation-contingent income increases, enough collectors would be 'priced out' of the market to bring to the margin a layer of investors who derive no convenience yield from the collectable. The collectable could then be described as having become a pure investment good, suitable for inclusion in large portfolios of owners with no interest in the collectable *per se*.

There is some evidence that this type of metamorphosis of a collectable into a pure investment good has occurred for classic stamps in recent years. In the period 1975–80, high-quality stamps enjoyed spectacular price gains. Very few rare stamps did not appreciate by at least ten-fold during those 5 years.[3] Many small collectors were priced out of the market by large investors seeking inflation-hedges and realising that rare stamps fell into this category of asset. By the late 1970s, Britain's Stanley Gibbons was creating for investors portfolios that consisted of two to ten well-balanced items. Such portfolios usually included a single rare classic stamp issued before 1900, and other issues between 1900 and 1930. The average value of these portfolios was around $10,000. Stamps also came to be included to a very limited degree in the portfolios of pension funds.

A classic stamp of which there are several thousand in existence has a greater potential to be transformed into a hedge asset suitable for purchase by the non-collector than do extremely rare collectables for which there are no close substitutes. Even a first edition of Adam Smith's *Wealth of Nations* is in too short supply for the enthusiastic collector to be priced out at the margin by the hedge investor who is not a collector.

Interest in collecting can be stimulated by inflation, pushing up the threshold rate at which a collectable becomes a pure investment good. High inflation, accompanied by non-indexed tax, penalises the saver with an acquired taste for collectables to a lesser extent than the saver whose enjoyments are derived entirely from services that must be bought with cash at the point of enjoyment. The former is likely to keep a smaller proportion of his savings in conventional form, and must undertake less portfolio adjustment – switching from money into low-risk real assets – with the advent of high and uncertain inflation. The saver, who has hitherto not been a collector, can reduce the burden of inflation by turning himself into a collector, acquiring the knowledge and taste necessary to the enjoyment of the non-pecuniary and non-taxed services of a range of collectables. This increase in potential demand from collectors on the advent of high inflation is an extra source of income contingent on inflation from collectables.

Tastes for different types of collectables differ across national frontiers. The French are especially keen collectors of Persian rugs, the British of old English furniture and Commonwealth stamps, the Americans and Japanese of impressionist paintings and the Americans of old American stamps. Thus Commonwealth stamps and old English furniture are hedges against inflation in the UK in particular;[4] impressionist paintings are hedges against US inflation in particular. Inflation in each country makes collector-investors turn to distinct collectables as money substitutes.

Collectables may be more hazardous as hedges against hyperinflation than against high inflation. Hyperinflation is likely to be accompanied by social breakdown and a sharp fall in aggregate real incomes. Even so, the distribution of income under conditions of hyperinflation may become much more unequal, with huge fortunes being made simultaneously with growing misery of wage earners. These huge fortunes can be the source of demand for collectables. In the German hyperinflation of 1923,[5] Bresciani-Turroni noted the lavish expenditure of the new rich on collectables of the top quality. However, he noted also, as a typical symptom of the poverty of the old rentier classes, the great number of little shops which sold furniture, objets d'art, jewellery and carpets, belonging to the many families, who, once well-to-do, were now living on the proceeds of the sale of their personal property. The example of the German hyperinflation calls into question the potential of moderate to low-quality collectables, likely to be held widely by the rentier class, to perform a hedge function.

Other Hedge Properties of Collectables

Collectables are bearer assets whose value does not depend on a set of legal obligations. The owner of a rare stamp or fine painting does not, in contrast to the owner of a bearer security, face the risk of capital loss due to the imposition of exchange controls, default, or arbitrary government action (including taxation). Collectables, unlike bearer bonds and securities, but like gold, can be owned clandestinely; in contrast, securities must be serviced – they must be produced to a paying agent in order to obtain cash against coupons. Under present arrangements, bearer securities can be serviced clandestinely, through a financial centre whose banking secrecy is assured. But these institutional arrangements are subject to change, especially in very bad states of the world such as war.

In Table 10.1 stamps are illustrated as the collectable with the strongest hedge potential against war. In war, a rare stamp is enhanced as a store of value and also performs a limited medium of exchange function. The rare stamp's property of having the highest ratio of value to space and weight of any collectable, yet (like the Penny Black) being one of many thousand similar specimens, makes it both a very convenient way in which to hold clandestine wealth, and suitable as a medium of exchange for large transactions that must be hidden from the authorities. In particular, stamps are the most efficient vehicle for smuggling wealth across frontiers; the investor in stamps increases his chances of being able, on the onset of a war or domestic revolution, to start a new life in another country. These contingent-services of rare stamps are one component of their present value. But as for gold, a prerequisite of stamps' potential to yield these services is their highly valued non-pecuniary services to the collector; their high valuation is responsible for the important property of a high ratio of value to weight and volume.

TABLE 10.1 *Collectables as hedges*

	Hedges against			
	War	*High inflation*	*Energy crisis*	*Shrinking of investment opportunity*
Stamps	×	×		
Paintings		×		×
Rare books		×		×
Oriental rugs		×	×	×

Oriental rugs are harder to conceal than stamps and are unlikely ever to perform the function of medium of exchange. They should, however, act as inflation-hedges. In addition, modern Persian carpets should act as an energy-hedge; for a sharp rise in energy prices would be likely to raise living standards in Iran, and make labour in the carpet industry more expensive. Wealthy Arabs represent a large market for the Iranian carpets. Their demand for these should rise strongly as their wealth increases in the aftermath of a large rise in the oil price.

All collectables should gain in value from a shrinking of investment opportunities; for a falling rate of return on physical investment in industry and commerce should make it more attractive to simply hoard goods to be consumed in the future than to invest in commercial and industrial capital. Risk of obsolescence and depreciation is a disincentive to the hoarding of consumer durables, but not to investment in collectables. The attractions of investing to provide a stream of certain non-pecuniary services from a collectable increase as the marginal rate of return on commercial and industrial capital falls. In the longer run, however, if the diminishing of investment opportunity is associated with a slowing of economic growth, then the value of collectables may fall below their previously projected path.

Notes and References

1. For an analogy of the present discussion in the real estate market, see Chapter 1.
2. This type of investment was reported in Greece during 1979 and 1980, as inflation soared to 25 per cent per annum.
3. See *Stamp Price Movements, 1960–80* (Maxwell Stamp Associates, 1980).
4. For evidence on the responsiveness of each category of stamp to inflation in different countries, see *Stamp Price Movements* (Note 3).
5. See Bresciani-Turroni, *Economics of Inflation* (Keeley, 1968) p. 378.

Part III

Indexing the Taxation of Saving

11 Indexing the Taxation of Saving

At various stages in this book it has been illustrated how inflation uncertainty, which rises with the level of inflation itself, can seriously distort the direction of investment flows. Non-indexation of the taxation of savings causes monetary assets to be taxed at increasingly onerous rates as inflation rises, seriously aggravating these distortions. In the USA and Britain, governments have failed to index the taxation of saving despite inflation rates that have run well into double digits. Non-indexation has been a disincentive to the assumption of business risk. The wealth and power of tax-exempt institutions – pension funds and insurance companies – have been increased. Such distortions and redistributions were not planned. No politician in the mid-1960s drew up a war-plan, whereby an escalation of inflation was to stunt private savings and risk investment and to increase the power of the investment institutions. Yet no government has attempted seriously to attack the source of these developments.

Macroeconomic Benefits of Tax-Indexation

Escalation of inflation, together with a non-indexed tax structure, causes income from debt securities (including bank deposits) to be especially penalised, whilst leverage is heavily subsidised. For example, with an inflation rate of, say, 16 per cent per annum, and an interest rate of 17 per cent per annum the investor subject to a tax-rate of 30 per cent on marginal nominal earnings would pay tax on real net interest earnings at the rate of 510 per cent (his post-tax nominal return is 11.9 per cent per annum, making a net real return of −4.1 per cent per annum). If his net taxable interest earnings are negative – equivalently, if tax-deductible interest on his outstanding borrowing exceeds interest income received – he would receive a subsidy at the rate of 510 per cent on his cost of borrowing. It can be shown that such a high tax rate on interest income and subsidy on borrowing costs hinders investment in high-risk projects and encourages investment in solid low-risk areas. As innovations essential to productivity growth are generally the result of high-risk investment, this distortion of investment flows has a negative impact on economic growth.

To demonstrate the above proposition, let us compare World A, with a high tax rate on interest income and an equally high subsidy rate on net interest paid, with World B, where these tax and subsidy rates are low. It is assumed at first that only corporations can claim tax relief on net interest payments. Thus individuals in order to lever their portfolio (that is, increase the ratio of debt outstanding as a proportion of their wealth) generally buy equities in corporations which are highly levered, rather than borrowing directly themselves. Further, corporation tax is assumed to be fully offsettable against personal tax. Both assumptions fit closely the UK fiscal system in 1980; assumptions closer to the US situation are examined subsequently.

In both World A and B, an individual's portfolio can be described as a combination of (1) government bonds; (2) shares in private enterprises' trading assets; (3) consumer durables (including housing); (4) interpersonal debt securities, which include both consumer loans and lending to corporations, whether in direct form or indirectly via the banks. An investor who purchases debt securities issued by a corporation is in reality lending to other investors to purchase a share in its underlying trading assets; the investor in equities of a highly levered corporation is effectively borrowing from holders of its debt securities to buy a share in its trading assets.[1]

Consider a state of equilibrium in World B. Then, suddenly, tax conditions are changed (due most likely to a jump in the rate of inflation) and tax payers find themselves in World A. Investors would then, at unchanged real yield differentials between securities, wish to reduce their net holdings of bonds (or increase their leverage) and increase their holding of enterprises' trading assets and consumer durables. Yet this increased demand would not be dispersed evenly; it would be concentrated on low-risk areas (for example, prime real estate let to first-class tenants' residential property), whilst demand for high-risk enterprises' assets would fall.[2] The swingeing tax imposed on the lowest-risk type of security (bills and bonds) would cause investors to want to switch to securities in the nearest risk-category that is exempt from the new tax; further, their appetite for high-risk enterprises' assets would fall as the offsetting of risk by holding bonds or bills would be penalised.

In the short run, equilibrium in the assets markets would be restored by the real yield on debt securities (the real interest rate) rising, the yield on low-risk enterprises' assets falling (their price rising) and the yield on high-risk enterprises' assets rising (their price falling). The price of consumer durables, including housing, which are low-risk assets, would tend to rise. The expected rate of return on the market portfolio (a portfolio consisting of all real assets in the same proportion to each other as their outstanding stock) would decrease, as the increased proportion of low-risk assets on which the expected yield is lower than on high-risk assets would drag down the average return.

In the medium term, the changed yield differentials necessary to stock equilibrium would have three principal influences on savings and investment flows. First, the rate of productive saving and industrial investment would fall as stocks of consumer durables and housing were being built-up. Second, the rate of investment in low-risk enterprises would increase. Third, the rate of investment in high-risk enterprises would decrease.

In the UK, a transition was made from World B to World A over the 1970s as the acceleration of inflation caused tax on interest to be levied at an increasingly high rate. Over the same period, the average rate of return on trading assets in UK commercial and industrial enterprises tended downwards.[3] There are many explanations for this fall. One factor, suggested by the argument here, is the diversion of investment from high-risk, high-return trading assets to low-risk, low-return ones.

In the US fiscal system, unlike in the UK one, interest expense on personal borrowing is in general tax-deductible. In the transition from World B to World A, there would be scope for the individual without financial savings, whose only assets were his human capital and some durables (including perhaps his home), to borrow at the heavily subsidised rates to buy consumer goods, especially durables. Thus, in the USA, the transition to high inflation would be marked by a greater rise in the real interest rate, a greater rise in consumer spending, and a greater reduction of commercial and industrial investment, than would be transition under the British-type assumptions.

The macroeconomic disadvantages of the high tax on debt-securities are not confined to the distortion of investment flows. Many people see considerable political advantages in restoring the power of decision to the small saver who, due to the penal treatment of debt securities (which form an especially large proportion of small portfolios), has channelled funds increasingly through the tax-exempt institutions. Dangers of oligopoly and collusion in financial markets have been increased thereby.

Indexation of tax would lift the special burden on savings held in liquid form – deposits, bills and bonds – which results from their having typically high nominal but low real yields. Increased rewards for private saving in liquid form would pave the way for greater financial independence throughout society.

Administrative Feasibility

Given the macroeconomic benefits of eliminating the special burden of non-indexed taxation on interest income and the large subsidy given on interest payments at times of high inflation, let us consider the administrative feasibility of tax reform in this direction. The essence of reform must be changing the base of tax from nominal to real interest income (and payments) and specifying tax rates as a proportion thereof. Such indexation would eliminate the danger of unintended increases in the tax burden on interest occurring with their untoward macroeconomic implications. Comprehensive indexation of savings tax would extend also to capital gains, with tax rates being expressed as a proportion of real gains.

The practical difficulty encountered by schemes to index the taxation of savings is that neither the inflation rate nor the level of interest rates is knowable with certainty at the start of the fiscal year. Hence it is impossible to specify nominal tax rates (i.e. tax rates expressed as a proportion of nominal income) at the start of the year, if real tax rates (i.e. tax rates as a proportion of real income) are to be fixed. Resolution of this difficulty is possible by the fiscal authority specifying real tax rates at the beginning of the year, to be converted into nominal tax rates at the end of the year. A sample table for converting real into nominal tax rates is presented in Table 11.1.

TABLE 11.1 *Converting real into nominal tax rates*

	Real tax rate								
	75%			*50%*			*25%*		
Inflation rate	*real interest rate*								
	2%	*1%*	*0%*	*2%*	*1%*	*0%*	*2%*	*1%*	*0%*
20	6.82	3.57	0.0	4.55	2.38	0.0	2.27	1.19	0.0
15	8.92	4.68	0.0	5.88	3.13	0.0	2.94	1.56	0.0
10	12.50	6.80	0.0	8.33	4.55	0.0	4.17	2.27	0.0
5	21.42	12.50	0.0	14.29	8.33	0.0	7.14	4.17	0.0

Note: Each row shows the rates of tax on nominal interest which correspond to the rate of tax on real interest and the level of real interest rate under each column heading.

For each pair of real interest rate and inflation rate, the nominal tax rate corresponding to a given real tax rate can be read from the table. It can be seen there, for example, that with a real interest rate of 1 per cent per annum, and inflation rate of 20 per cent per annum, real tax rates of 75, 50, and 25 per cent correspond to nominal tax rates of 3.57, 2.38, and 1.19 per cent respectively.

In the special case where the real rate of interest is zero, all tax rates on real interest income would convert into a zero tax rate on nominal income irrespective of the rate of inflation. During the 1970s, in Britain, the real rate of interest (using MLR as yardstick) was, indeed, often zero or negative. In principle, full indexation would imply that investors obtained tax credits when the real rate of interest became negative. In practice, tax rates would have a lower limit of zero.

In its conversion of real into nominal tax rates, effected at the end of the year, the fiscal authority must use a yardstick for calculating the average real interest – an obvious candidate in Britain is MLR; in the USA a possible candidate is an annual average of the 90-days Treasury Bill rate. To take the average interest yield on savings as equal to MLR is an approximation only, but is essential to a simple method of converting real into nominal tax rates. Any injustice resulting for the small saver, who earns less than MLR on his deposits, may be rectified by exempting a first slice of interest income from tax.

Many bonds have current yields different from MLR. On those with low current yields, a capital gain should be expected: indeed, for a rational investor, expected capital gain plus current income yield should equal at least the expected average MLR for each period.

Capital gains (or losses) realised on such assets should be consolidated with their interest income and together be subject to the indexed income tax described. Losses and gains realised on foreign monies would be treated in similar fashion.

If, instead, gains on assets, whose direct yield was subject to the indexed income tax, were taxed separately as capital gains, double compensation would be awarded for inflation. The tax rates on interest income are themselves calculated to allow for erosion of the real value of nominal principle: an application here of an indexed gains tax would allow a deduction for this erosion a second time. The consolidation of interest and capital gains (losses) on foreign monies and on domestic or foreign bonds would mean that short-term large speculative profits or losses would be taxed or obtain tax-credits at much lower rates than at present.

The indexed income tax on interest could be made progressive, with the marginal rate of tax on real interest income being a rising function of amount earned. Thus, real interest income below £500 may be taxed at 0 per cent, £500–2000 at 25 per cent, £2000–4000 at 50 per cent and above £4000 at 75 per cent. Translation of these real income slices into nominal income slices would have to await the end of the fiscal year. If inflation of 10 per cent is realised and MLR averages 11 per cent, then real interest would be translated into nominal interest income by multiplying by the factor 11. £30,000 of nominal interest income would be taxed as £5500 at 0 per cent, £5500–22,000 at 2.27 per cent, £22,000–30,000 at 4.55 per cent, making a total tax bill of £738.55.

Consolidation of the indexed tax on interest with tax on labour income is possible. For example, each of the above real income slices may be lowered by £100 for each £1000 of labour income received. A tax payer whose labour income totalled £10,000 would find his real interest income split into bands of £0–100 at 25 per cent, £1000–3000 at 50 per cent, and above £3000 at 75 per cent.

Interest paid by borrowers represents in large part simply inflation compensation to the lender. Comprehensive indexation of the taxation of interest would require that, in inflationary conditions, the present practice of offsetting nominal interest against taxable income should be markedly curtailed. Only the real element in nominal interest payment should be deductible from gross profits to calculate taxable profit.

There are two possible methods of indexing tax deductions for interest paid. First, where a corporate borrower produces inflation-adjusted accounts, taxation on real rather than nominal profit would allow implicitly for the discrepancy between nominal and real interest. Second, nominal interest may be disallowed completely as a deduction against nominal income, and a tax credit calculated separately on real interest payments which may be offset against other tax liabilities. Loan expenses, whether in the form of margin over base rate or bond issuance costs, would remain offsettable against mainstream income, the tax credit being calculated on net real interest (i.e. gross real interest minus margin and issuance costs).

Using the second method, a corporation which had paid £12,000 gross nominal interest including margin costs of £2000 would – if 50 per cent of real net interest costs were allowed as a tax credit and MLR and inflation during the year were 15 and 16 per cent respectively – be allowed to claim a tax credit equal to 3.13 per cent (see Table 11.1 for conversion) of net nominal interest, making £313. The further £2000 would be deductible from gross earnings in arriving at taxable profit.

So long as inflation-adjusted accounts are not regarded as a suitable basis for corporation tax, the second method of assessment would be applied generally, including the household sector in respect of mortgage borrowing. Administrative simplicity and political necessity may well require that a high flat-rate credit, say 75 per cent, be allowed on the real content of nominal mortgage interest payments. MLR (or the average US Treasury Bill Rate) would again be used as yardstick for converting tax-credit rates expressed as a proportion of real interest (real tax-credit rates) into tax-credit rates expressed as a proportion of nominal interest (nominal tax-credit rates). With inflation at 15 per cent, average MLR and mortage rates at 16 per cent a £50,000 mortgage would produce a tax-credit of £374.50 (a 75 per cent real tax credit converts into a 4.68 per cent nominal tax-credit at the levels of inflation and real interest specified). That tax credit of £374.50 would be offset against total tax due on income.

The shift of tax advantage away from the mortgagee, implied by the above calculation, is startling, yet no more so than the shift which would be brought about by success in reducing substantially the rate of inflation. If inflation were brought back to zero and nominal (and real) interest rates brought back to 1 per cent the mortgagee would suffer a loss of tax-advantage to almost the same extent as from the simulation of zero inflation for tax calculation – the purpose of tax indexation. One important characteristic of the mortgage which would be different under conditions of simulated than of authentic zero inflation would be the effective maturity of the mortgage. A 20-year mortgage at an interest rate of 1 per cent with zero inflation has a much longer effective maturity than a 20-year mortgage at an interest rate of 16 per cent with inflation at 15 per cent. On the latter, high nominal interest is effectively a guise for early repayment of capital in real terms; high nominal interest compensates the lender for the combustion of the real value of loan principal by inflation. A cashflow crisis among mortgagees has been avoided so far by the growth in tax relief which has offset to some extent the accelerated repayment of real capital brought about by rising inflation and nominal interest rates. It is probable that tax indexation would hasten the lengthening of the effective maturity of mortgages which would be effected by contracts providing for 'top-ups' of the nominal ceiling each year to allow a lower rate of real capital repayments.

Revenue Costs of Indexation

Tax indexation would reduce the subsidy obtained by private-sector borrowers and would reduce the tax paid on real interest receipts by investors. But a simple move to indexation would reduce the government's net revenue. A significant volume of debts outstanding are issued by the public sector on which investors would obtain large tax reductions, and for which there would be no counterpart saving in borrowing subsidies. One method of correcting for this shortfall would be imposition of a special tax on banks to cream off the inflation revenue they derive from non-payment of interest on sight-deposits at times of high inflation and high nominal interest rates. In addition, some of the revenue shortfall may be re-couped by curtailing some of the tax advantages presently enjoyed by institutional savers.

To illustrate the budget arithmetic of indexation a plan can be drawn to show how indexation could be introduced in the UK without expanding the budget deficit. The calculations are shown in Table 11.2. The table is constructed on the following assumptions:

1. The rate of inflation is 15 per cent and MLR is 16 per cent in the year for which comparison is made between indexed and non-indexed tax structure.
2. A flat rate tax on real interest income of 50 per cent is assumed,

and the rate of tax credit on net real interest paid by industrial and commercial corporations is also set at 50 per cent. A flat-rate tax credit, of 75 per cent on mortgage real interest (for mortgages up to a maximum of £50,000), is assumed.

3. Tax-exemption of institutional saving is abolished. Their real interest earnings are taxed at a flat rate of 50 per cent whilst nominal yields on real assets (properties and equities) are taxed at a flat rate of 30 per cent. The justification for this different treatment of current income from real assets is that in the long term their capital values should be expected to keep up with inflation. For individuals also, nominal income yield would remain the basis of taxation for real assets. The ending of tax exemption for institutions should be easiest to effect when simultaneously the introduction of indexation lightens substantially the burden of tax on the private saver. The need for a non-taxed institutional outlet should then be seen widely redundant.
4. Although banks are large net recipients of interest, this should not be treated for tax as investment income according to Table 11.1. Their net receipt of interest is due to charges for current account services being derived principally in the form of non-payment of interest. Net interest income is, in reality, mainly fee income.
5. Taxation of capital gains is indexed with only real gains being taxable and at a rate of 30 per cent. Present exemption of houses and gilt-edged stock from gains tax is cancelled, although roll-over relief may be extended to principal residences (for gilt-edged stocks would be combined with interest income for the purpose of tax, described earlier).

The calculation in Table 11.2 shows that at the sample tax rates used, indexation would be effectively self-financing. Households with mortgage debt outstanding unmatched by interest-bearing savings, and investors with a large share of their wealth in low-risk real assets (such as prime real estate, residential property or shares in low-risk enterprises trading assets) would lose; households with net holdings of interest-bearing assets and a large share of their wealth in high-risk real assets (such as shares in high-risk enterprises' trading assets) would gain.

TABLE 11.2 *Effect of indexation of tax revenues in the UK (£ million)*

	Losses	*Gains*
Taxation of capital gains[4]	170	
Mortgage relief[5]		1499
Loan relief for business		
(1) Commercial and industrial[6]		1292
(2) Financial[7]	25	
Removal of tax exemption for institutions[8]		681
Taxation of liquid assets held by household sector[9]	3323	
	3518	3472

SOURCE: *UK Financial Statistics* (CSO, 1980).

It would be misleading to consider the £1292 million extra tax paid by the corporate sector, due to the curtailment of interest deduction against tax, as creating a cash shortage there. So long as the move to indexation does not diminish the community's propensity to save, and does not increase either the public sector's borrowing requirement or the attractions of overseas relative to domestic investment, the corporate sector should be able to readily[10] replace a diminished source of finance from retained earnings with external finance in the form of equity and bond issues, or bank borrowing; further the rate of interest should fall as described earlier. It has been shown already that indexation should reduce the hoarding of consumer durables and increase the propensity to save in productive forms; calculation in Table 11.2 shows that the public sector's borrowing requirement should be almost unchanged; indexation should diminish the incentive for individuals to switch out of domestic deposits with their high nominal interest returns, into lower inflation monies abroad.

Indexation in Capital Market

Even in a world of zero taxation the transition from a state of low inflation to one of high and variable inflation would be marked by a distortion of saving flows towards the accumulation of low-risk assets.[11] However, beyond a certain threshold of inflation uncertainty the indexing of loan contracts would begin to be observed, and this would set a limit to the distortions. The imposition of positive non-indexed tax rates would raise the threshold of inflation at which the practice of indexation would take off and would thus increase the potential distortionary effects of high inflation on savings flows.

Consider, under a non-indexed tax regime, the issue of an indexed 1-year bond which promises a real return of r per cent per annum; $1 invested today would produce a nominal sum at maturity of

$$\$\,(1+r)\,\frac{p_{t+1}}{p_t}$$

where p_t, p_{t+1} are the price indices at time t (now) and at $t+1$ (1 year from now). The post-tax real return on the bond, assuming a marginal tax-rate of q on nominal income (including capital gain), is:

$$(1-q)r - q\,\frac{(p_{t+1}-p_t)}{p_t}.$$

This expression shows that the post-tax real return, unlike the pre-tax real return, is a function of inflation: a non-indexed tax regime prevents borrowers and lenders from excluding inflation risk by agreeing to an indexed contract.

Inflation risk, measured post-tax, pertaining to the indexed contract, is less than that pertaining to the non-indexed contract but not by as much as when measured pre-tax. The post-tax real return on a 1-year non-indexed (nominal) bond yielding a nominal R per cent per annum is:

$$(1-q)R - \frac{(p_{t+1}-p_t)}{p_t}$$

which is more sensitive to changes in the price level than the expression above for a post-nominal tax return on an indexed bond. The limiting by the non-indexed tax regime of indexation's power to reduce inflation risk means that inflation uncertainty must reach a greater height before the natural disadvantages of indexed contracts are overcome.[12]

A scheme to index the taxation of savings, such as that discussed in the early part of the present chapter, should promote the spread of indexed contracts at a lower threshold of inflation than at present. Indexed bonds would be treated as real assets, with only the coupon –

and not the growth in the nominal principal to keep pace with inflation – being taxable.

Even without introducing a full scheme to index the taxation of savings, the government could remove the special disincentives to the spread of indexation as a means of reducing inflation risk by putting indexed securities outside the reach of the nominal-based tax regime. Instead, only their coupon would be subject to tax, or allowable as a tax credit (from the viewpoint of the borrower).

A dual tax system – with one regime applying to nominal contracts and another to indexed contracts – would present large tax-arbitrage opportunities which could substantially reduce government revenue. The introduction of a dual system would have to be accompanied by a set of rules which severely limited the scope for arbitrage. Tax arbitrage would take the form of high marginal-rate taxpayers borrowing on a non-indexed basis – so obtaining a large tax subsidy – to invest in indexed notes and bonds, on which the burden of tax would be small. Lower marginal-rate taxpayers would borrow by issuing indexed paper and invest in non-indexed paper; although the latter would be taxed more heavily than the former, the real yield differential would reflect the tax advantages to be derived by high marginal-rate taxpayers, making it profitable for the lightly taxed investor to operate in the opposite direction.

The direction in which any individual taxpayer, with marginal tax rate of q_m, arbitrages, would depend on whether:

$$r \text{ is less than or is more than} \qquad R - \frac{E(p_{t+1} - p_t)/p_t}{1 - q_m}$$

where r is the interest rate on a 1-year indexed bond, R is the interest rate on a 1-year nominal bond, and $E(p_{t+1} - p_t)/p_t$ is the expected rate of inflation over the next year. If r were less than the expression on the right, then arbitrage would be profitable in the direction of borrowing at the indexed rate and buying non-indexed paper; if r were greater than the expression on the right, then arbitrage in the reverse direction would be profitable. Arbitrage would not be riskless, for the rate of inflation is uncertain, and risk-aversion would set a limit to the arbitrage process. The more strongly graded are marginal tax rates for wealthy investors, the more scope there would be for tax arbitrage; the existence of tax-exempt institutions furthers arbitrage possibilities.

The fiscal authority could set limits to tax arbitrage in various ways.

One sample set of rules would include strict absolute limits (possibly equal to zero) on the deduction of interest payable under contracts against taxable personal income; the corporate sector would continue to obtain tax relief on net interest paid whether under nominal or indexed contracts – but only at the standard rate of income tax, not at the higher corporate rate of tax. Thus if the corporate tax rate were 50 per cent and the standard personal tax rate were 30 per cent then only 60 per cent of net nominal or indexed nominal interest payments would be deductible against corporate income for the purpose of taxation.

Under the above set of rules, if the public sector itself continued to issue only nominal debts, then the following equality would hold:

$$r = R - \frac{E(p_{t+1} - p_t)/p_t}{1 - q_s}$$

where q_s is the standard tax rate. The equality must hold if the corporate sector is to be indifferent between the issue of indexed and non-indexed paper. Given the equivalence, investors paying tax at the standard rate should be indifferent (ignoring risk) between investing in indexed and non-indexed paper: investors subject to a marginal tax rate in excess of the standard rate would derive tax advantage from investment in indexed form. The tax saving which they would derive from the introduction of the dual system would have to be balanced by tax increases elsewhere if fiscal neutrality were to be ensured. Revenue losses to the fiscal authority could be curtailed by restricting the scope of dualism principally to the personal sector. Net income received by a corporation on indexed securities, including inflation compensation payments, would be subject to tax under the nominal regime. Thus banks, the principal type of corporation to have a long net position in debt securities, would not gain relief from the introduction of dualism.

If the public sector itself became an issuer of indexed paper, the government's revenue loss from a dual system could increase. That would occur if supplies of indexed public debt became so plentiful that r rose above:

$$R - \frac{E(p_{t+1} - p_t)/p_t}{1 - q_s}$$

so crowding out the corporate sector from making indexed issues, and increasing their total net supply.

In a dual system, indexed notes, especially of long maturity, would be powerful inflation-hedges. For when inflation expectations rose, the differential between r and R,

$$\frac{E(p_{t+1} - p_t)/p_t}{1 - q_s}$$

would rise by a greater amount. Hence indexed bonds outstanding, would score a real capital gain. This inflation-hedge property of indexed notes could make them popular investments even for individuals whose marginal tax rate q_m, was such that r was less than:

$$R - \frac{E(p_{t+1} - p_t)/p_t}{1 - q_m}$$

The transition to a dual system, financed by a tax on banks and the withdrawal of certain tax exemptions from institutions, would be marked by some fall in nominal interest rates; for the availability of indexed securities to investors paying the standard rate of tax or more would reduce their exposure to inflation risk on bond-holdings and increase their demand for bonds (now indexed) and high-risk physical investments at the expense of low-risk physical investments. In the new stock equilibrium, nominal interest rates must have fallen somewhat, yields on low-risk physical assets have risen and those on high-risk physical assets must have fallen, so that low marginal-rate taxpayers (including investment institutions) would have been tempted to change their portfolio weightings in the opposite direction to that of high marginal-rate taxpayers.

Conclusions

High and variable inflation rates have had great significance for the distribution of investment flows both in the USA and Britain. Industrial and commercial investment in risky, yet progressive, areas of the economy have suffered at the expense of hoarding of consumer durables (including housing) and collectables. Awareness of the ill-effects of inflation led governments at the turn of the decade to move to a policy of deflation, accepting that sacrifice of economic output was a cost worth paying for the benefits of a lower and more predictable inflation rate. Yet this policy of deflation had certain heavy real costs – loss of output at a macro level corresponded to hardship at a micro-level. The question which received surprisingly little consideration was whether costs of a high and variable inflation rate could not be reduced by the programmed *simulation of*, rather than *achievement of*, low inflation. Two methods of simulating low inflation have been considered in Part 3 of this book. One involved the wholesale conversion of taxation of savings to an indexed basis. The other, possibly simpler to administer, involved the introduction of a dual system – with indexed contracts being taxed on an indexed basis and nominal contracts on a nominal basis.

Both methods of simulating low inflation would doubtless bring some of the advantages of a low-inflation environment, without incurring the costs of actually realising a low inflation rate. Surely such relatively painless devices deserve serious attention as an alternative to the hugely expensive war against inflation.

Notes and References

1. This similarity of obtaining leverage by borrowing directly or by buying shares in a levered corporation is discussed by M. Modigliani and M. Miller in their classic article 'The Cost of Capital, Corporation, Finance, and the Theory of Investment', *American Economic Review*, vol. 48, no. 3 (June 1958) pp. 261–97.
2. Risk of security is measured as its addition, at the margin, to the total risk of a well-diversified portfolio.
3. See *Bank of England Quarterly Bulletin*, June 1980, for details about recent trends in profitability.
4. It is assumed that revenue from capital gains tax would be cut in half, if full indexation applied.
5. Mortgages outstanding are estimated at £37 billion, and a 30 per cent average tax credit on nominal interest tax credit rate of 4.68 per cent.
6. Sterling borrowed by industrial and commercial corporations exceeds their holding of interest-bearing liquid assets by £17.2 billion. A 50 per cent tax credit on nominal net interest paid is compared with a post-indexation tax-credit rate of 3.13 per cent on nominal net interest (equal to 50 per cent of real net interest paid).
7. It is assumed that indexation of taxation is applied to banks and building societies according to the method stated in the text. Other financial institutions are estimated to have net interest receipts of approximately £100 million.
8. Institutions include long-term funds of insurance companies and superannuation funds. They hold £19.9 billion tax of interest-bearing deposits and securities. A 50 per cent tax on real interest (i.e. a 3.13 per cent tax on nominal interest) would produce revenue of £141 million. A 30 per cent tax applied to nominal income from real assets, totalling around £36 billion, would produce £540 million revenue.

9. Total interest bearing deposits and gilt-edged securities held by the personal sector are estimated at £77.31 billion and a 30 per cent average tax rate on nominal interest is compared with a post-indexation rate of 3.13 per cent.
10. That is at an average cost of capital certainly not above its previous level.
11. See Chapter 5, in the discussion of real estate as an inflation hedge.
12. See Chapter 7, for a discussion of the natural disadvantages of indexed contracts, and the threshold rate of inflation at which these take off.

Index